What people are saying about ...

A Million Ways to Die

"Many of us live today in a constant state of overdrive—what experts call 'hurrysickness'—cramming each moment so full of events that we have no time to think deeply about life or death. Rick James invites us to slow down and consider how a rich and purposeful life can flow out of a serious reflection on death. *A Million Ways to Die* is engaging, counterintuitive, and above all, life-affirming."

Tim Muehlhoff, PhD, coauthor of
*The God Conversation: Using Stories and
Illustrations to Explain Your Faith*

"This book will bring you to life by putting you to death. It's one of the most thought-provoking books I've read in a long, long time."

Mark Batterson, lead pastor of National
Community Church, Washington,
D.C., and author of *In a Pit with a Lion
on a Snowy Day* and *Wild Goose Chase:
Reclaim the Adventure of Pursuing God*

"A book on death? Sounds deadly! But Rick James shows how death is really a key to life. Only through death is life realized. Here is a book whose teaching we must live by. Well done, Rick!"

James W. Sire, author of *The Universe Next Door*,
and former chief editor of InterVarsity Press

"Everyone wants to find true life, but few are willing to sacrifice themselves to find it. This central calling of Jesus as amplified by Rick James, especially in a culture of feel-good Christianity, is a breath of fresh air. I pray that this message, counter to both our culture and human nature, settles in the hearts of Christ followers young and old."

Aaron Stern, college pastor of theMILL at
New Life Church, Colorado Springs, CO

"When Christians think about the cross, they often think of Christ's atoning work at Calvary. But there is another aspect of the cross that seems to be almost forgotten by the Christian faith. It's the cross-bearing and death to self that Jesus so often talked about. It is only by dying that we learn to live. *A Million Ways to Die* reintroduces us to this neglected but needed dimension of the cross in simple and clear language. Read this book, then go back and reread what the New Testament has to say about the cross in the believer's life."

Frank Viola, author of *The Jesus Manifesto,*
From Eternity to Here, and *Reimagining*
Church, www.FrankViola.com

"Rick James opens our eyes to the critical importance of embracing the concept of death as an opportunity for spiritual growth. Focused on the example of Jesus, James helps us discover the necessary steps involved to experience the abundant life offered in the gospels. This is a message every follower of Christ needs to read."

Dillon Burroughs, coauthor of the best-
selling *What Can Be Found in LOST?*

"Who would have thought that death is the pathway to life? It is so counterintuitive. We spend our lives running from the inevitable. Yet in *A Million Ways to Die,* Rick James outlines the ultimate paradox for us humans. Rick uses wit, metaphor, and story to masterfully illuminate the biblical teaching on death. *A Million Ways to Die* is not a feel-good self-help story. It is not about the picture on the front cover of the American family living the American dream without a single blemish. This is a call to the cross … with Jesus. To death … with Jesus, and ultimately to resurrection … with Jesus. Life is full of paradoxes. We must take the pain and suffering seriously as Christians. The way to understand all the 'little deaths' we die is to link them back to the greatest sacrifice in the history of mankind. God, as man, came to die on our behalf. His death and resurrection show us the way, through so many little deaths, to life, abundant here and eternal with Him. The American dream gives way to the dream of the Father in heaven: a movement of Christ-followers dying in order to learn how to live. This is a must-read for all who name Jesus as Lord. May *A Million Ways to Die* teach us all the more excellent way and show us therein joy beyond a million deaths."

D. Jim O'Neill, PhD, executive vice president
of Tennessee Temple University and dean of
Temple Baptist Seminary, Chattanooga, TN,
and former president of CrossWorld mission

A MILLION WAYS TO DIE

THE ONLY WAY TO LIVE

RICK JAMES

David C Cook®
transforming lives together

A MILLION WAYS TO DIE
Published by David C Cook
4050 Lee Vance View
Colorado Springs, CO 80918 U.S.A.

David C Cook Distribution Canada
55 Woodslee Avenue, Paris, Ontario, Canada N3L 3E5

David C Cook U.K., Kingsway Communications
Eastbourne, East Sussex BN23 6NT, England

David C Cook and the graphic circle C logo
are registered trademarks of Cook Communications Ministries.

The website addresses recommended throughout this book are offered as a
resource to you. These websites are not intended in any way to be or imply an
endorsement on the part of David C Cook, nor do we vouch for their content.

All Scripture quotations, unless otherwise noted, are taken from the *Holy
Bible, New International Version*®. *NIV*®. Copyright 1973, 1978, 1984 by
International Bible Society. Used by permission of Zondervan. All rights
reserved. Scripture quotations marked ESV are taken from *The Holy Bible,
English Standard Version.* Copyright © 2000, 2001 by Crossway Bibles a
division of Good News Publishers. Used by permission. All rights reserved.

LCCN 2010932712
ISBN: 978-1434-7020-43
eISBN 978-1-4347-0272-2

Published in association with the literary agency Creative Trust,
Inc., 5141 Virginia Way, Suite 320, Brentwood, TN 37027.

The Team: Alex Field, Erin Prater, Karen Athen
Cover Design: Amy Kiechelin
Cover Photo: iStock.com

Printed in the United States of America
First Edition 2010

1 2 3 4 5 6 7 8 9 10

073110

To Katherine, My Own

"Those who are wise will shine like the brightness of the heavens, and those who lead many to righteousness, like the stars for ever and ever." (Dan. 12:3)

CONTENTS

Section Five - Ode To Courage

Section Six - Humbled and Mortified

Section Seven - The Passion of Love

Epilogue - REQUIEM   319

Endnotes   333

ACKNOWLEDGMENTS

While no one likes reading a long e-mail, mine contained somewhere north of one hundred thousand words: "Book attached; read over and tell me what you think." And yet several dear friends printed it out, read it word by word, and provided me with the benefit of their wisdom. I am most grateful for the friendship and assistance of Joe Torres, Neil Downey, Byron Straughn, Tim Henderson, Tom Hudzina, and Brett Payne. I also want to thank Keith Davy and Peter Nelson for their friendship and for the models of true spiritual wisdom and godliness they've been.

I also want to acknowledge Kathryn Helmers of Creative Trust. I would, quite literally, be lost without her. No one would have seen or read this book if not for Kathryn. My manuscript and I arrived orphaned at her doorstep. She took us in, believed in me and in the book, helped shape its content, and then represented it like it was her own.

I would also like to thank Alex Field for his excellence, expertise, and stamina in taming this beast. Alex takes thoughts and makes them better, clearer, smarter, and faster (usually in half the amount of words); his own words are always kind, gracious, and encouraging. I appreciate you and your work on this, Alex.

Along these same lines I'd like to thank Erin Prater for her editorial work on this manuscript and for keeping this a book and not a twelve-volume set. Thanks, Erin.

Last, and first, I want to thank my wife, Katie, for the Million Ways she has shaped this book and its author. No Katie, no book. And while this goes without saying, I cannot go without saying it— thank you, my dear, precious Savior.

CHAPTER ONE

BETTER OFF DEAD

As the story goes, in 1972, a young Egyptian businessman lost his wristwatch, valued at roughly $11,000. That's some wristwatch. It's amazing that anyone who found it in the rough-and-tumble city of Cairo would have attempted to return it, and it's shocking who did.

The city of Cairo has its own unique version of poverty called the Garbage City: a city in the sense that an ant farm is a city. The population of this slum lies somewhere between fifteen and thirty thousand people, though no one really knows for sure. Its name comes from the fact that it is both a garbage dump and home for the city's garbage workers. Each morning at dawn some seven thousand garbage collectors on horse carts leave for Cairo, where they collect the many tons of garbage left behind by the city's seventeen million waste-producing citizens. After their day's work they return to the Garbage City, bringing the trash back to their homes, sorting out what's useful, and living in and among what isn't. In Muslim countries there are certain religious restrictions on sifting through refuse, so the inhabitants of the Garbage City are either nonreligious or of some kind of Christian heritage, typically Coptic. These are the poorest of the poor—outcasts among outcasts.

As you can imagine, it would be unthinkable to have such a valuable timepiece returned by a member of Garbage City. Yet when the wealthy businessman lost his watch, an old garbageman dressed in rags returned it, saying, "My Christ told me to be honest until death."

Because of this act of obedience-faith-death-insanity, the Egyptian businessman later told a reporter, "I didn't know Christ at the time, but I told [the garbageman] that I saw Christ in him. I told [him], 'Because of what you have done and your great example, I will worship the Christ you are worshiping.'"

The man, true to his word, studied the Bible and grew in his faith. Soon he and his wife began ministering to Egypt's physically and spiritually poor, leading thousands to Christ. In 1978, he was ordained by the Coptic Orthodox Church and is now known as Father Sama'an. Father Sama'an leads the largest church of believers in the entire Middle East; each week some ten thousand believers meet together in a large cave outside the Garbage City.

For this garbageman, returning the watch was not martyrdom, but it certainly was a kind of death. I'm sure everything in him wanted to keep that watch—everything except his heart, which wanted to keep Christ.[1]

In John 12:24 Jesus states that "unless a kernel of wheat falls to the ground and dies, it remains only a single seed. But if it dies, it produces many seeds." Beginning with his own death, what Jesus is describing here is *the secret ingredient of kingdom growth*. Death. Death is the fertilizer, the turf builder. The kingdom sprouts out of our daily choices to "die to ourselves." You plant an $11,000 Rolex in the dirt and out of it grows the largest church in the Middle East. Our willingness to die to ourselves and carry our crosses every day indicates the mechanism of personal transformation and evangelistic growth.

This is not mysticism, poetics, or philosophical abstraction. This is reality. It's as daily and as tangible as doing the dishes for someone when you don't feel like doing the dishes for someone. Every act of dying, done in faith, generates life in some way whether we see it, recognize it, or simply take it by faith. And how do we spot the many possible ways that life might emerge through our little deaths? We can find these opportunities in just about anything our flesh tries to resist.

A COSMIC RESTRUCTURING

In 1962, Thomas Kuhn wrote a book titled *The Structure of Scientific Revolutions*. In it Kuhn describes a fundamental change in basic assumptions, something so significant that it creates a whole new *paradigm*. Most people don't remember the book, but for the last fifty years we have been haunted by the phrase Kuhn coined, the ubiquitous "paradigm shift."

Since then, anything and everything has become a "paradigm shift." The Gillette Trac II razor was a new paradigm that "revolutionized" shaving; the Clapper changed our paradigm for turning off lights; the Chia Pet changed our gardening paradigm.

Many, many, paradigms; lots and lots of shifting.

Virginia Woolf famously wrote, "On or about December 1910, human character changed."[2] She was heralding a paradigm shift, but as the phrase "paradigm shift" had yet to be invented, she simply uttered the aforementioned phrase.

Woolf referred to the advent of postmodernism, modern claims to the title notwithstanding. Why 1910? In 1910 Einstein debuted his theories of relativity; Nietzsche expounded his philosophy of perspectivism; Picasso painted the multi-perspective cubist master-piece *Les Demoiselles d'Avignon;* and writers like Joyce, Stein, Proust, and Woolf began shattering the objective narrative of literature. Relativism and subjectivism were blooming everywhere.

This truly was a paradigm shift, challenging commonly held notions of objective truth and reality. We certainly don't view the world the same as those who lived before the turn of the twentieth century or, for that matter, give our children names like Rutledge or dress them like Howard Taft.

There have been many paradigm shifts, real, claimed, and imagined. Even now we are attempting to wrap our minds around globalization, learning to see the flatness of the earth. But no idea, concept, philosophy, or paradigm can deliver on Woolf's claim. Human nature didn't change on, about, or anywhere near 1910—only our thoughts about it did. Our paradigm shifted. Reality didn't budge. What Jesus brought to this world was not simply a new para-digm. Rather, circa 33 AD the very nature of life and death changed, not simply our thoughts about it.

Of course there are a million new paradigms, perspectives, and thoughts that flow from this fact, but this is not a new way of seeing reality. This *is* a new reality, a total cosmic restructuring.

THE WILD WEST

Here in America we see the new life of the gospel more clearly than most—at least we seem to see more of it. It's difficult to drive down the freeway or turn on the radio or TV without seeing or hearing an offer for this new and everlasting life. Most American non-believers know at least someone who's experienced this new life and are, therefore, privy to a personal demonstration. Not so elsewhere.

We are also witnesses of the societal implications of this new life. We can see where politics, human rights, freedoms, social conscience, education, and medicine have been touched by the Christian view of life. Christians might assume there are social implications to the gospel, but if they were to live in a Muslim country, they certainly wouldn't observe any.

Yet as much as our philosophy on life has been enriched by a Christian worldview, our understanding and apprehension of death has diminished. We live in one of the few places in the world where Christians aren't persecuted (generally speaking), and martyrdom is as likely as contracting malaria or Ebola. Add to this the unprecedented historical anomaly that since the beginning of recorded time, no people—except this current generation—have ever lived with a mind-set that ninety years of age is the horizon of human life. Not even remotely. Through wealth, medicine, technology, food, and cosmetics, we think of and relate to death in the abstract, as something requiring *life* insurance. This perspective is alien to Scripture, and it's alien to the majority of humanity.

And yet the symbol of our faith is a man nailed to a cross. It could have been something happier, like the yellow Walmart smiley face, but it's not. More than lepers and mustard seeds, death is the dominant New Testament metaphor for the Christian life. We were dead in our transgressions, and death was at work in us, but then Jesus died for us; now we are dead to sin but alive to God, and we must die daily (though we will never die); and yet we look forward to the resurrection of the dead, and on and on, as if Sylvia Plath had some hand in the writing.

And all this is just on the level of illustrations and metaphors. If we were to look at the New Testament from a historical or narrative perspective, it's immediately striking that all the main characters die. We get to know Paul a bit through his letters, but even as he writes, he's in prison awaiting execution. It seems like we're just starting to connect with Peter when he's crucified, and by the end of Christianity's opening season, John's the only one remaining of the original cast.

What happens in the New Testament?

Everyone dies.

To those of us living in a civilized superpower, all this talk about death is strangely foreign—something primitive, something out of *National Geographic* like foot binding, neck stretching, or packing a gourd into the lower lip like a pinch of Skoal.

My daughter is doing missions work in East Asia this summer, and the cultural difference that has struck her the most is the mentality that one simply leaves something—a rat, a cow, a person, whatever—where it dies. It's like in the rural South, where folks leave their car or tractor to rust in the spot it stopped working. I'm not saying this is a healthy view of death or that throwing a body into the Ganges River is more biblical than hosting an extravagant celebration-of-life ceremony. My point is that death is much more integrated into the fabric of *life* in almost every other place on the planet—and everyplace else in Scripture.

While we may not need to be tutored on the abundant life of the gospel, we need to be reacquainted with its more than *abundant death*. But don't let this scare you; death isn't quite the same since

Christ consumed it. It's been tamed and domesticated—it's the bee without the sting. We no longer serve it—it serves us.

REBRANDING

When I think of Bayer aspirin, I think of families, happy babies, the smell of Vicks VapoRub, staying home from school, and watching *I Love Lucy* reruns. This is quite remarkable considering the fact that the seemingly benign corporation was, at one time, part of the German pharmaceutical company I. G. Farben. Farben was disbanded in 1952 for its close association with the Nazi Party and active participation in war crimes. Farben had manufactured the gas for Nazi gas chambers and was the chief supplier of the toxic gas Zyklon B. Today, Bayer is obviously a different company, a company that seeks to save lives, not exterminate them. But can you imagine the task set before the PR and marketing departments to re-brand and reshape our perceptions of this company? To help us see it as a source of life and not death?

This, I'm afraid, is what we're up against here. Death has earned quite a bad name for itself—and, I might add, it's well deserved. What Madison Avenue delivery could possibly change our perspective and make us *want* to die? Could we say that it's been reformulated; that it's not the cold, tasteless, soggy mush we remember; that it's new and improved; that it's a heart-healthy, cholesterol-friendly, high-fiber, reduced-fat version of death; that it comes with an extra scoop of raisins in every box?

As you can tell, re-branding death is beyond my powers of persuasion. But it is not beyond the power of Scripture, which makes an outrageous marketing claim: that just as green is the new black, and small is the new big, *death is the new life*. And this, as you'll see, is not just a catchy jingle.

DEATH: NOW THE LEADING CAUSE OF LIFE

Hebrews tells us that Jesus suffered death so that by the grace of God He might "*taste* death for everyone." The writer of Hebrews defaults to what appears to be Scripture's metaphor of choice when speaking of death and resurrection—*digestion*. I will try to follow suit in reviewing the events of Jesus' resurrection.

There are food chains everywhere in nature: The grasshopper eats the grass; the rat eats the grasshopper; the snake eats the rat; and the hawk eats the snake. What's true of all food chains is that hawks and people and lions don't really occupy the top rung. Death is, in fact, at the top of the food chain; death devours everything but is devoured by nothing.

The resurrection changed this. When Jesus rose from the dead, death was "swallowed up in victory" and "swallowed up by life."

Throughout His ministry, Jesus warned of and predicted the dramatic change coming to the natural order: "As Jonah was three days and three nights in the belly of a huge fish, so the Son of Man will be three days and three nights in the heart of the earth" (Matt. 12:40). Jonah, if you remember, was swallowed *but not digested*.

As Jesus was placed inside the open mouth of the tomb, He entered through the jaws of death. Picture "the cords of the grave coiled around [him]" (Ps. 18:5), wrangling him down like a tongue. "The grave enlarges its appetite and opens its mouth" (Isa. 5:14). Death ingests Him, sliding lower and lower to the "lowest pit, in the darkest depths," to the very bowels of death.

But the Holy One cannot be digested, for "his body will not see decay" (Ps. 16:10). Regurgitation is the only option for that which is inedible. The Son is spit out just as the whale "vomited" Jonah back to the living. The stone rolls back, the mouth of the grave opens, and death forfeits its meal. Death cannot eat life. The empty tomb is death with its teeth kicked out.

In communion, our symbolic celebration of this victory, we swallow Christ (His body and blood), just as His life swallows us. We drink His blood, represented by wine, a fermented drink that was extracted from death and decomposition.

When Scripture declares that death has been swallowed by life, it is declaring a massive reversal of the natural order. Apart from Christ we deteriorate, body and soul. Death picks away at us little by little until the day its appetite swells to consume us whole.

As believers we experience the reverse: "For we who are alive are always being given over to death for Jesus' sake, so that his life may be revealed in our mortal body" (2 Cor. 4:11). The Christian life is a progressive march, not to death but to resurrection, where Christ slowly transforms us until the day His resurrection consumes us whole. Christ's resurrection power animates the life of the believer so that our trials and sufferings are continuously being consumed, metabolized, and transformed into new life. Resurrection—not death—is the reigning power within us so that "though outwardly we are wasting away … inwardly we are being renewed day by day" (2 Cor. 4:16). The hands of time are moving backward, and the sands in the hourglass pouring upward.

If all this sounds too flowery and poetic, here it is a bit more bluntly: The indwelling of God's Spirit turned our life into a piñata.

Now, the more you beat the thing, the more Christ's life showers out. "I have been crucified with Christ and I no longer live, but Christ lives in me" (Gal. 2:20). If life is on the inside, there's everything to be gained by having our lives turned inside out.

DEATH: NOW AVAILABLE IN FUN SIZE

With the best of intentions, preachers and teachers continue to attempt to inspire us to see the importance and relevance of death to the Christian life. We've heard countless stories of persecuted brothers and sisters around the world as well as tales of missionary heroics and sacrifice.

I can recall a sermon I gave once, a sermon laced with quotes from the journal of David Brainerd. Brainerd was a missionary to the Delaware Indians during the eighteenth century. He lived in the wilderness and slept on the ground, all the while dying of tuberculosis. Brainerd was Superman. Brainerd would preach, cough up his lungs, pass out, and then get up and preach another sermon. I tried to cast vision for a cross-bearing commitment to Christ, but it didn't work. "Remember David Brainerd" had the relevance of "Remember the Alamo" and the triviality of "Remember the Titans." Those listening to my message shared as much in common with the lifestyle of David Brainerd as they did with the lifestyle of Madonna.

It felt like I was a parent telling his child to eat all the food on his plate because there are children starving in other parts of the world. Has this ever prompted a single child to mop up the remains of his dinner? It seems like this argument should work, but the gap is so big and the cultural distance so far that it cannot be mentally crossed. Now, if you could scrape your plate into a box and next-day ship it to the starving children, well that would be different, wouldn't it? That would bridge the gap.

I think this is why our stories of martyrs and missionaries sometimes fail to motivate. What we are doing, in effect, is inflating the concept of death, sacrifice, and martyrdom, making them as big, as bold, and as graphic as possible in hopes of shocking people awake. But see, *it does the opposite.* The more horrible the stories, the more gruesome the deaths, the more courageous the martyrs, the more sacrificial the evangelists—the less like us these martyrs seem. We end up creating more distance between us and them, between us and death.

In focusing on these concepts as macro-events, as monumental moments of extinction, termination, and glory, we wrongly elevate these people as a superior class of Christians.

The creation of a Christian upper class automatically places us in a lower bracket, and we assume the discipleship requirements of such a bracket to be far less. With the lowering of expectations comes the lowering of ambition. Who can compete with a super martyr? They're the pros, and we can only hope to caddy for them. This makes what should be the normative life of cross-bearing seem unattainable, something for an elite class of ancient Christians, super leaders, and third-world believers.

The Scriptures do not attempt to inflate the concept of death. Rather, they seek to show its relevance to our daily lives and spiritual growth. The Scriptures challenge our cramped and claustrophobic view of the grave and lead us to see death as a process, inviting us to embrace it in its many varieties: death to self, death to the world, death to our pride, and so on. The Scriptures democratize death, requiring everyone to carry a cross and be a martyr. The Bible focuses on the concept, the practice, and the process—the small *d* of death—far more than on the capitol *D* of Death—*death as termination.*

The small *d* of death is critical to every Christian. While we may never die in our attempts to witness, our reputation might. Everyone has an ego, and the death of pride is a martyrdom to be shared by every Christian. Everyone can experience the death of a dream, a job, a hope, a relationship, an ego, or a reputation. We must all die to ourselves. There is no need to push or shove or wait in line; we will all get a chance to die.

This expanded meaning of death is clearly what's meant by the Scripture's rather elastic use of the concept, as we are admonished to "take up our cross," "die to sin," "die to the world," and so many other deaths beyond the funeral variety. The death envisioned is not a single tombstone, it's Arlington cemetery—row upon row of graves. To see the smaller, daily opportunities to die is as important as seeing the daily tokens of God's love and faithfulness that He bestows on us.

DEATH: OPPORTUNITY OF A LIFETIME

While neither God nor Scripture ignores or downplays the pain of our suffering and trials, they are unwavering in presenting it to us as an opportunity to be embraced, not a threat from which to hide. A thoughtful examination of a passage in 2 Corinthians explains why: "We always carry around in our body the death of Jesus, so that the life of Jesus may also be revealed in our body. For we who are alive are always being given over to death for Jesus' sake, so that his life may be revealed in our mortal body. So then, death is at work in us, but life is at work in you" (2 Cor. 4:10–12).

Let me rephrase this passage with explanation, expansion, and commentary so you can see the concepts in another way:

> *I endure many hardships. But I think of my trials like "little deaths" because I see how God resurrects, or brings life out of, them. You, Corinthians, are the ones who benefit from this, so I don't mind if God uses my life and faith as an engine to convert those deaths into life. In fact, once you realize that trials are fuel, or firewood, to be burned and transformed into life, you no longer run from them; you embrace them. This is why I rejoice in the severity of my trials, persevere in them, and embrace them by faith. I never think, "Oh, no ... another trial." I actually think, "Bring it on; it's just more logs for the fire."*

It is no doubt human nature to avoid pain; *it's definitely my nature.* I dare you to spring out of bed every morning like it were Christmas Day, anticipating what new deaths lie ahead and how God will transform them into life. It's not a normal way of looking at life, but then again neither is returning from a torture session "rejoicing because they had been counted worthy of suffering disgrace for the Name" (Acts 5:41).

If Mr. Thomas Kuhn were still alive, I believe he would call this a paradigm shift, a fundamentally different way of viewing life. In fact, when a perspective is so mind-altering and counterintuitive, we do not call it insight, but insanity. It's not just a different way of thinking, it's *too different*—odd different. Apart from faith, James' sentiment, "Consider it pure joy, my brothers, whenever you face trials of many kinds" (James 1:2), would have to be seen as gibberish, as would the affections expressed by Dietrich Bonhoeffer when he said, "Can you sense that I have now a terrible longing for my own suffering?"

However, when you begin to view death as an opportunity for more and greater life, here and now, as well as in the age to come, it changes everything. It reorients us entirely.

In the past year I've had the opportunity to share the gospel with something like ten thousand college students, with several hundred of those coming to Christ. This outreach to universities was launched from a book I wrote titled *Jesus Without Religion*. I can't prove this, but I don't think the fruitfulness of the book is necessarily tied to the book itself.

The book took me six months to write, and the very day after completing, it my computer crashed. As it turned out, the "heads" on the hard drive were cracked, and nothing was salvageable. This, at least, is what the repairman told me; I know nothing of the heads, hands, or feet of a hard drive, nothing of basic hard drive anatomy at all. This would have been the perfect time to pull out the backup copy that I'd saved—if there had been a backup copy. But I had nothing; the book was gone, dead and buried, its remains sprinkled throughout the cyber universe—from pixels it came and to pixels it returned.

Yet this perspective of death presented in Scripture ultimately led me to a sense of anticipation. Here, in the teaching of Jesus and the disciples, death (the death of a hope, dream, goal, or six months worth of work) doesn't mean dead—it means the opportunity for resurrection.

To give thanks and praise in such circumstances is one way in which death is transformed into life. The blackened logs of death consumed by faith's flame are transformed into wisps of praise drifting upward. Death is a consumable fuel for life, and any experience of death can yield spiritual life *if it is embraced by faith*. Giving thanks and praise is simply one method of transference.

I do not remember if I gave thanks. I might have sworn. But after regaining my spiritual equilibrium, I did start on page one, with word one, and with considerable anticipation that God would use the resurrected rewrite like Lazarus, drawing many to Himself.

I can't prove the connection in this particular case, but I know it's there. I know it's God's resurrection power working through a corpse. (Though in my enthusiasm for the metaphor, I have just called my book a corpse, which can't be good for future sales).

It certainly makes sense to me why an unbeliever would run from death. But for a believer, to run from death is, in reality, *to run from life*. This is why we embrace death and consider it pure joy in whatever form we encounter it. Death is no longer a dead end or detour to life; it's a fuel stop. Death, like gasoline, is combusted and converted into mileage, enabling us to get to our destination—the light and life of the great city glowing over the horizon.

DEATH OF A SALESMAN

I have briefly touched on some of the claims made in Scripture, why death is no longer death but "new and improved." We, of course, will be exploring all this in finer detail, but in these last few pages you should have grasped this message: In picking up our crosses and following Jesus, we walk a path *of* death, not a path *to* death. The path itself is one of death, but it leads to life—a life we care about and want. Not death.

Death has exactly zero intrinsic value. It's just that death is the only road that happens to be headed to resurrection, transformation, and transfiguration. By definition, resurrection can only be experienced by something dead, and *this* is what inflates the value of death. "Death has been swallowed up in victory" (1 Cor. 15:54), "swallowed up by life" (2 Cor. 5:4). Death is just something for eternal life to consume, digest, and metabolize into life.

When the apostle Paul states that "we always carry around in our body the death of Jesus, so that the life of Jesus may also be revealed in our body" (2 Cor. 4:10), what he is saying is simply this: During the Christian walk we live out the resurrected life of Christ, and we come to experience and participate in His resurrection power through a continual lifestyle of death. This simple. This painful. This glorious.

Nearly twenty-five years ago I left Manhattan. I handed in my resignation at the advertising agency where I worked, and my wife and I went into ministry. It's quite possible that I was a little hasty in leaving my job, for in our attempts to raise financial support, we found ourselves unable to pay our bills. This included our rent.

I frantically looked to grab a job—anything as long as it was immediately available. Unfortunately, only the local cemetery met the criteria for "immediately available." The Gates of Heaven cemetery was hiring, paid well, and boasted of being the eternal resting place of Babe Ruth. How could I not take the job? Among other macabre tasks, my responsibilities included planting geraniums in front of tombstones. Smaller tombstones receive five geraniums, larger stones receive seven (just in case you ever find yourself out of work).

The train I rode into Manhattan passed right through the Gates of Heaven cemetery. So each day I had the privilege of standing in the cemetery in my filthy overalls, with geraniums in my hands, watching my old life clack by. It was the metaphor of all metaphors for the life of a disciple. I might as well have found a job that paid me to carry a cross.

But instead of embarrassment, I experienced a profound sense of joy, an unexpected jolt of life. And it was through this discovery that I began to see death as the New Testament described it: as a vehicle for life, a bizarre form of blessing, something to be embraced and experienced daily. I saw those beautiful geraniums. I didn't see the tombstones so much as I saw the flowers in front of them. This was a garden within a cemetery. *Life emerging from death.* I have continued to ponder these things for the last quarter of a century, and what follows is the ordering of those thoughts.

And the proper order is to begin with the words of Jesus, His inaugural address to all would-be followers: "If anyone would come after me, he must deny himself and take up his cross and follow me" (Mark 8:34).

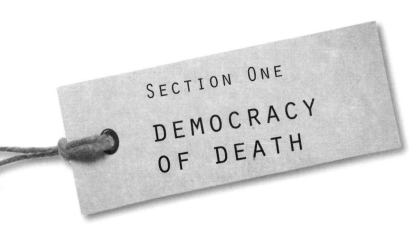

SECTION ONE

DEMOCRACY
OF DEATH

CHAPTER TWO

EVERYBODY DIES

With the exception of the Constitution, it's difficult to imagine a more complex and compressed piece of communication than a president's inaugural address. I can still picture Bill Clinton, suppressed thumb and pointed knuckle, directing the nation and controlling perception like he was holding a Wii controller. (Whatever opinion one may have of him, he is a master of communication.)

On the surface these speeches are visionary and inspirational, flowery flights of prose that, in order to evade all obstacles on the political landscape, never fly below forty thousand feet. On paper, however, an inaugural address might resemble a Wikipedia page, the entire document filled with links colored Web-browser blue, a double-click on any word opening up windows of meaning and scroll bars of references, implications, and entailments. Something to the effect of:

Our country needs to stay strong (I'll be writing a blank check to the Pentagon), boldly looking to the future (NASA gets to do more rock collecting on Mars), while growing the economy (we have no plan for the national debt). We must also stop the flow of drugs into this country (black ops are underway in Columbia— consider yourself informed!) and work together (you continue paying taxes, we'll continue spending them) to stay the course (please keep us in office for the next four years). And may God bless America (I'm desperate for the evangelical vote).

This, of course, is grossly exaggerated, but you see the point: The surface of an inaugural address is the language of metaphor and vision, while the subtext of the speech is, in fact, the speech.

In this sense, Mark 8's "carry the cross" discourse is rather similar and could be viewed as Jesus' "inaugural address" to potential followers. His words are visionary, mapping out the path to the future. They describe how the new administration will operate for the first one hundred days in office—and beyond. But if you fail to listen carefully, you will miss a million implications, and "bearing one's cross" will remain ethereal, meaning anything and therefore nothing, an adage with the practical import of "every cloud has a silver lining."

So let's listen carefully to the words of this inaugural address, Jesus' declaration of death's democracy. Listen for the subtext, the implications, the entailments. This is the cornerstone of what it means to follow Jesus: If it's askew, the building will shape up as straight and plum as the Guggenheim.

Here is the content of the message:

They came to Bethsaida, and some people brought a blind man and begged Jesus to touch him. He took the blind man by the hand and led him outside the village. When he had spit on the man's eyes and put his hands on him, Jesus asked, "Do you see anything?" He looked up and said, "I see people; they look like trees walking around." Once more Jesus put his hands on the man's eyes. Then his eyes were opened, his sight was restored, and he saw everything clearly. Jesus sent him home, saying, "Don't go into the village."

Jesus and his disciples went on to the villages around Caesarea Philippi. On the way he asked them, "Who do people say I am?" They replied, "Some say John the Baptist; others say Elijah; and still others, one of the prophets." "But what about you?" he asked. "Who do you say I am?" Peter answered, "You are the Christ." Jesus warned them not to tell anyone about him.

He then began to teach them that the Son of Man must suffer many things and be rejected by the elders, chief priests and teachers of the law, and that he must be killed and after three days rise again. He spoke plainly about this, and Peter took him aside and began to rebuke him. But when Jesus turned and looked at his disciples, he rebuked Peter. "Get behind me, Satan!" he said. "You do not have in mind the things of God, but the things of men." Then he called the crowd to him along with his disciples and said: "If anyone would

come after me, he must deny himself and take up his
cross and follow me. For whoever wants to save his life
will lose it, but whoever loses his life for me and for the
gospel will save it. What good is it for a man to gain the
whole world, yet forfeit his soul? Or what can a man
give in exchange for his soul? (Mark 8:22–37)

You'll notice first that in Mark's gospel, Jesus' healing of a blind man precedes both the interchange with His disciples and the "carry the cross" discourse. Mark has placed the story here for a reason, and the reason is that the blind man symbolizes the disciples in their perception of Jesus.

VISUAL AGNOSIA

In the book *The Man Who Mistook His Wife for a Hat*, the renowned neuroscientist Oliver Sacks recounts the stories of some of his more memorable patients: those experiencing rather unique symptoms of neurological disorder. The title of the book comes from one of Sack's patients, whom he identifies by the alias of Dr. P.

Sacks describes him as follows:

Dr. P. was a musician of distinction, well-known ... as
a teacher. Sometimes a student would present himself,
and Dr. P. would not recognize him; or, specifically,
would not recognize his face. The moment the student
spoke, he would be recognized by his voice. Such inci-
dents multiplied, causing embarrassment, perplexity,
fear—and, sometimes, comedy. For not only did Dr. P.

*increasingly fail to see faces, but he saw faces where
there were no faces to see: genially, Magoo-like, when
in the street, he might pat the heads of water-hydrants
and parking-meters, taking them to be the heads of
children; he would amiably address carved knobs on the
furniture, and be astounded when they did not reply.[1]*

At one point Sacks hands Dr. P. a red rose and asks him to describe what he sees. What Dr. P. sees is something "six inches in length; a convoluted red form with a linear green attachment."[2] Dr. P. had a condition known as *visual agnosia,* and it has amazing similarities to the blind man in Mark's gospel.

Visual agnosia affects a person this way: When you look at an object, the visual input provided by your eye enters the brain, and the information is instantly parceled out for processing along two separate pathways. One of those pathways is a shortcut directly to the prefrontal cortex; what arrives along that particular pathway is an undeveloped image. What it looks like to your brain is similar to a movie streaming over dial-up: a lot of unintelligible blobs of color—raw, unprocessed, visual data. If you were looking at a group of people, it might appear—*hmm, how would I describe it?*—well, like a lot of trees walking around (Mark 8:24).

The visual information traveling along the second, slower pathway arrives about fifty milliseconds later—which is an eternity in mental processing. But there's a reason it's late. The information detoured through the visual cortex, where it was analyzed before it joins up with the other parcel of information in the prefrontal cortex. So we actually *see* the object twice. The first look provides crude macro-data (which comes over the first pathway), while the second look (from the second pathway) provides visual evaluation and interpretation. First we see, and then our brain tells us what we saw. Perception is always a double take.

A person with *visual agnosia* simply doesn't receive that second parcel of information—they don't get the interpretation of what they are seeing. In fact if you want to know what it looks like to see the world in this condition, look at a painting by Cézanne. In *Proust Was a Neuroscientist,* author Jonah Lehrer suggests that Cezanne painted without imprinting his colors and shapes with a cognitive interpretation. He attempted to show only raw visual data—exactly, says Lehrer, like someone with *visual agnosia.*[3]

If the blind man in Mark's gospel does have this condition, he can see at the neurological level, but he lacks the ability to interpret what he's seeing. Could there, I wonder, be a better metaphor for the disciples at this point in Jesus ministry? They see Jesus, *but not fully.* They cannot yet make sense of Him or His meaning, His significance, His mission, His identity. They lack the interpretation.

With His second touch, Jesus imparts visual clarity to the blind man, and we rightly anticipate that something quite similar is about to happen to the disciples—that their perception of Jesus is about to become clear.

JESUS COMES INTO FOCUS
Jesus is the Christ

> *Jesus and his disciples went on to the villages around*
> *Caesarea Philippi. On the way he asked them, "Who*

*do people say I am?" They replied, "Some say John the
Baptist; others say Elijah; and still others, one of the
prophets." "But what about you?" he asked. "Who do
you say I am?" Peter answered, "You are the Christ."
Jesus warned them not to tell anyone about him. (Mark
8:27–30)*

When you focus the lens of a manual camera, you turn it this way, then that way, then this way, then that way, achieving focus through adjustment. Clarity and focus in this passage are gained when Jesus makes three distinct adjustments to the perception of the disciples, three turns of the lens.

Having just healed the blind man, the gist of Jesus' question to the disciples is this: "When people see me, what are they seeing?" The honest and embarrassing answer given by the disciples essentially is, "The people aren't seeing you at all." When the crowds gather to Jesus, they think they're seeing John the Baptist or Elijah. Very poor perception indeed.

Jesus' follow-up question is more personal: "How about you? What do you see?" Peter, in one of those Helen Keller moments of insight, answers, "I see the Christ."

To the knowing reader, Jesus' true identity has been about as disguised as Clark Kent, who is Superman ingeniously cloaked by … reading glasses. But for the disciples this is the moment of discovery, the turning point.

In the parallel account found in Matthew's gospel, Jesus excitedly declares, "Blessed are you, Simon son of Jonah, for this was not revealed to you by man, but by my Father in heaven" (Matt. 16:17).

The theological implications of this statement are not insignificant. Jesus is declaring that all of humanity has *spiritual agnosia*. Anyone can pick up a Bible, string Christmas lights, or tattoo a cross on his bicep; anyone can see Jesus. But only God can provide the missing interpretation of who He truly is—*the Christ*. This is the miracle of salvation: One moment you see Jesus, and the next moment you *see* Jesus.

The Christ Must Die

And so the lens turned 180 degrees, and the disciples grasped His true identity. But the image is still blurry. Unless they understand the cross, Jesus' redemptive mission and sacrifice for sin, they have not truly understood Him. To see Jesus but not the cross is to not *see* Jesus. So Jesus explains:

> He then began to teach them that the Son of Man must suffer many things and be rejected by the elders, chief priests and teachers of the law, and that he must be killed and after three days rise again. He spoke plainly about this, and Peter took him aside and began to rebuke him. But when Jesus turned and looked at his disciples, he rebuked Peter. "Get behind me, Satan!" he said. "You do not have in mind the things of God, but the things of men."
> (Mark 8:31–33)

For Jesus to have spoken of suffering and death before this point in His ministry would have only convinced His disciples that He was merely a prophet, for such treatment of God's messengers was standard etiquette in Israel. Only now that they understand His true identity can Jesus begin to explain the cross.

What's confusing is this: The Old Testament contains two very distinct and divergent portraits of the Messiah. One description is that of a powerful and majestic king; the other is of a humble, broken servant suffering for the sins of His people. It will probably help you to see both inferences to these portraits of the Messiah from the Scripture.

Two Portraits of the Messiah

> I saw in the night visions,
> and behold, with the clouds of heaven
> there came one like a son of man,
> and he came to the Ancient of Days
> and was presented before him.
> And to him was given dominion
> and glory and a kingdom,
> that all peoples, nations, and languages
> should serve him;
> his dominion is an everlasting dominion,
> which shall not pass away,
> and his kingdom one
> that shall not be destroyed.
> (Dan. 7:13–14 ESV)

In this first portrait of the Messiah, we see a depiction of a glorious king. In the second portrait, the Messiah is described as the suffering servant.

> *Surely he has borne our griefs*
> *and carried our sorrows;*
> *yet we esteemed him stricken,*
> *smitten by God, and afflicted.*
> *But he was wounded for our transgressions;*
> *he was crushed for our iniquities;*
> *upon him was the chastisement that brought us peace,*
> *and with his stripes we are healed.*
> *All we like sheep have gone astray;*
> *we have turned—every one—to his own way;*
> *and the LORD has laid on him*
> *the iniquity of us all.*
> *(Isa. 53:4–6 ESV)*

These two messianic images overlap and crisscross throughout the Old Testament like a shoelace, and Jesus must demonstrate how they tie together.

If we read Mark's gospel through to its end, the full answer Jesus provides is something to the effect of, "I am the messianic King, but the kingdom will be ushered in, not through power and glory, but through My suffering, rejection, and death. It is when the Son of Man returns that He will come in power and glory." Two portraits, two comings—the same Messiah.

This is just the first pass. Jesus will revisit this topic, and events will clarify its meaning. What is critical for us to see is that an accurate perception of Jesus involves an accurate perception of His death on the cross.

This Must Be a Mistake

> *He spoke plainly about this, and Peter took him aside and began to rebuke him. But when Jesus turned and looked at his disciples, he rebuked Peter. "Get behind me, Satan!" he said. "You do not have in mind the things of God, but the things of men." (Mark 8:32–33)*

If our goal was brevity, we might summarize this exchange as follows: Peter finds preposterous the idea that Jesus needs to suffer and die, while Jesus finds demonic Peter's idea about avoiding death.

Peter is incapable of seeing how Jesus could be the Messiah and yet still need to suffer. That's pretty understandable, isn't it? What is more difficult to understand is why Jesus does not simply correct him, but rebukes him and accuses him of being a mouthpiece for Satan.

It seems harsh and over the top—unless, of course, it's true, and at that moment Satan used Peter to speak those words. Then it's not an insult, but an observed fact: "Peter, Satan is speaking through you. Stop speaking."

You, Too, Must Die

> *Then he called the crowd to him along with his disciples and said: "If anyone would come after me, he must*

deny himself and take up his cross and follow me. For
whoever wants to save his life will lose it, but whoever
loses his life for me and for the gospel will save it. What
good is it for a man to gain the whole world, yet forfeit
his soul? Or what can a man give in exchange for his
soul?" (Mark 8:34–37)

At this point the disciples are no doubt ashen, horrified, and in
utter shock. Unfortunately, what they've just heard is *the good news.*
The bad news—at least as initially registered—is that they, too, will
have to die. Everybody gets a cross. Every friend and follower of
Jesus gets to experience similar rejection, every leader gets to wash
the feet of others, and everybody gets to give their lives away—it's the
democratization of the cross. Following Jesus means *cross-bearing.*

Jesus, quite unapologetically, tells His followers, "Not only will
I face rejection, suffering, and death, but so will you." The glory of
the kingdom will be ushered in through the suffering of the Messiah
... *and* His disciples. This is one heck of an ampersand. They, too,
will have to straddle two worlds, two identities: children of the Most
High God, and orphans, rejects, and miscreants of the world. The
glory of God will be revealed in their lives, not through strength,
power, or position, but through humility, sacrifice, and servitude.
This is the third and final focus of the lens, and the image is now
clear. But it's not a pretty picture.

As it would have been natural for the twelve disciples to think the
cross was only for Jesus, it's natural for us to the think the cross-bearing
Jesus spoke of was only for the twelve disciples. But there's no *I* in
team, and there's no "other guy" in discipleship. "That guy" with the

speck in his eye, "that guy" carrying the cross—*we* are "that guy."

Perception is not just seeing an object but seeing it in relationship to ourselves. I don't accurately perceive a chair until I gather that I'm supposed to sit in it. And that's why it's essential that Jesus explains our cross even as He reveals His own.

THE WAY OF THE CROSS

It could be said that the cross is simply an important tenet of what it means to be a follower of Christ. However, in light of the structure of his gospel, it seems Mark is trying to tell us that cross-bearing is not just *central* to discipleship, it *is* discipleship. Giving our life away in order to find it in Christ defines precisely what it means to follow Christ.

This section of the gospel (from Mark 8:27 to Mark 11:1) has long been referred to as the "The Way" section of Mark, named for the oft-repeated phrase "on the way." "If I send them home hungry, they will collapse on the way" (Mark 8:3); "On the way he asked them, 'Who do people say I am?'" (Mark 8:27); "On the way they had argued about who was the greatest" (Mark 9:34).

Mark is not at a loss for transitional phrases. "On the way" picks up phraseology of the Exodus: "See, I am sending an angel ahead of you to guard you along *the way*," where the Israelites journeyed from slavery in Egypt to the Promised Land (Ex. 23:20). Indeed, Mark wants us to have the Exodus account squarely in mind so we can fully grasp what's being communicated, which is essentially this: Jesus is leading His people (the new Israel) on a new exodus: an exodus out of slavery to sin and idolatry. Just as Moses ascended Mt. Sinai to receive the Law, Jesus ascends the Mount of Transfiguration.

There, God the Father, rather than dispensing new tablets of stone, declares the words of Jesus to be the new Law or Torah: "This is my beloved Son, listen to him." As gospel scholar Rikki Watts summarizes, "Jesus' teaching in general, and his word of cross-bearing discipleship in particular, are the essence of [this new] Torah. The new Exodus is the new Way and it is *the way* of the suffering Messiah, *the way* of the cross, which leads to the (Promised Land) Kingdom of God."[4]

This is a lot to digest, but it's an important concept. In context, Mark is saying that the new Exodus Jesus leads us on, the path of and to His Kingdom, is one long trip to the cross. Following Jesus means tracing His steps "on the way" to the cross.

While our cross does not involve dying for the sins of the world, this is where the difference ends. In most every other way, what's true of Jesus' cross is also true of ours. Let's look at how they overlap.

CHAPTER THREE

OUR CROSS, HIS CROSS

Margie had thought much about the fact that—surely— once the suicidal process was in play, regret would bubble up with a whine to steal her control. Because of her foreknowledge of this reality, she made every effort to put herself in an unredeemable situation. No turning back. She was impressed by Virginia Woolf's resolve and courage, although baffled that she would not have reached into her pockets as the cold current engulfed her, twining her hair and turning her with the judgments of the river, and taken the rocks out. The instinctive desire to live, it seemed to Margie, would aggressively take hold as the reality of the situation became fearful. Margie knew herself to be fundamentally a fearful person, and for this reason made every effort to tie the knots tight, use the heaviest rock possible, use the dark as cover. There would be no last minute rescues or acquiescing to regret.

I've lifted this passage from the unpublished manuscript of a friend of mine. The main character, Margie, is trying to kill herself, and as it turns out, the lake that she had hoped would drown her isn't nearly deep enough. Experiencing second thoughts, she ends up tiptoeing atop the large rock she's tied herself to and screaming to her neighbors for help.

There is something tragic and sad and funny and humiliating in an aborted attempt to end one's life. And yet on a spiritual level, we've all experienced it. At some point we have all renounced our lives, denied ourselves, vowed to live for Christ alone, and have gotten a little ways into the journey before doubling back.

This is reality, and it's important to keep reality in mind as we look at the idea of cross-bearing because all of us will stumble, trip, kick, drag, hide, or try to use a dolly to hoist that cross at some point.

In the inaugural words of Jesus' "carry the cross" discourse, the would-be disciple is introduced to the idea that following Jesus means following him to the cross. It is here that we are first introduced to the idea that death will play a significant part in what it means to walk with Jesus. It is here that we learn that the cross is the template, symbol, and executive summary of the Christian life.

The dynamic of death and resurrection will conceptually unfold and expand throughout the New Testament, but several principles are already in view—the principles that are true of His cross and ours.

As I've already mentioned, we do not share Christ's death and atonement for sin. *Our* cross consists of dying to self and finding our life in Christ—and finding life in Jesus is only true of our cross, not of His. These are important distinctions.

With that said, Jesus' words tell us that we are all to carry a cross *just like* He did. So we must look at the points of concurrence and overlap. Our comprehension of the cross is informed by its relationship and proximity to Jesus' cross.

So we are going to try to wrap our minds around the cross and what it means to carry it by considering the cross of Jesus. We must begin by asking this question: What was true of His cross and therefore true of ours? Though the "carry the cross" discourse is simply Jesus' introduction to the cross, several principles already emerge regarding what it will mean for the Son of Man to "suffer and die," and these principles are precisely what it will mean for us. The principles are:

- We live though we die.
- We die that others may live.
- We are tempted to live when we need to die.
- We die when we ought to live.

WE LIVE THOUGH WE DIE

> *He then began to teach them that the Son of Man must suffer many things and be rejected by the elders, chief priests and teachers of the law, and that he must be killed and after three days rise again. (Mark 8:31)*

In describing His mission, Jesus has taken the two opposing messianic portraits found in the Old Testament (suffering servant versus reigning king) and explained to His disciples that he would embody both roles at the same time. He is the messianic king, but His kingdom would unfurl through rejection, suffering, and death.

This, of course, is a paradox. For Jesus to embrace the cross is for Him to embrace the mystery of these dual identities. And so the symbol of our new *life* is an implement of *death*. Our king sits enthroned upon an electric chair (so to speak). His coronation was the crucifixion. He was sworn in by the testimony of false witnesses, robed, and crowned; his title, "King of the Jews," was written on a criminal's placard—oh, the many ironies created by paradox.

Well, that's fine for Jesus. He's already a crowded elevator full of paradoxes—both God and man, eternal and temporal, Lion and Lamb. What's one more? But it's not that simple. This particular paradox—that as His disciples, we would live though we die—has two enormous implications for us.

The first is this: If the King Himself is a paradox, so is His kingdom. King Jesus reigns, and His kingdom is over all the earth, but only kinda-sorta. Evil is given free reign ... *to accomplish God's purposes;* God pours out His judgment on the wicked ... by leaving them alone (Rom. 1); we are ruled by Christ when our flesh isn't controlling us; Satan has already been defeated but attacks us nonetheless; and the Holy Spirit dwells within us along with pride, vanity, selfishness, and other unsavory qualities.

Welcome to Crazy World. The common theological term for Crazy World is "the Kingdom already, but not yet." This phrase is commonly employed to describe the partially realized, partially inaugurated, messianic kingdom. This is, indeed, a peculiar terrarium we find ourselves in.

Which brings us to *us:* the citizens of this paradoxical kingdom and its paradoxical king. In His discipleship discourse, when Jesus informs us that we too must "take up the cross," He is telling us that we will need to embrace these paradoxes. While we will be "sons of the kingdom" (Matt. 13:38), we will also be "the scum of the earth, the refuse of the world" (1 Cor. 4:11–13). Like Jesus, the kingdom of God will manifest in our lives, not through majesty, strength, and honor but through weakness, humility, rejection, and death. *So we will live though we die.* Therefore, like Jesus, our dual identities as residents of the kingdom and outcasts of the world will define our Christian lives and the crosses we will bear as well.

Dynamic Tensions

There are some important implications of living out this particular paradox, and we'll look at those. But here we just want to understand it at its most practical level. How does one live out such a paradoxical idea without going stark-raving mad? The answer lies in *dynamic tensions.*

Let's be clear: No one can simultaneously live out two separate, distinct identities. Even if you had multiple personalities, you still could only look out on the world from one pane of glass at a time. This is the nature of a singular consciousness—very weird, but very true. As Christians, we believe that Jesus had two natures—*but that's Jesus.* As for us, we are incapable of envisioning such a state any more than our finite minds can envision eternity, a fourth dimension, or a new color.

Since we can't be two people at once, we live out these polarities in tension. Life as a Christ follower is a life of dynamic tension. As we mature, we grow in our ability to keep the paradoxes of the Christian life in balance, and we grow in our capacity to handle more and more of these tensions.

If, for example, I become too focused on the kingdom to come, I find myself growing overly apocalyptic, monitoring the news for potential antichrists. If, however, I focus too much on the kingdom of God in the world, I become utopian, trying to turn the world into the kingdom (which is impossible). These dual realities (the future kingdom and the kingdom here and now) must be kept balanced and in tension each with the other. I must walk between, not on, either path.

Or what about the tension between God's sovereignty and human responsibility? If I believe the salvation of my neighbor rests wholly upon my words and witness, I might knock on their door every hour. If I believe it rests wholly on God's sovereignty, I might never knock at all. However one works it out theologically, on a practical level the line between God's sovereignty and human responsibility must be kept taut. Tension after tension, always trying to find the sweet spot: This is the life of a Christ follower.

A benefit of this, and possibly the point, is a very pretty soul. One of the things that makes your face so beautiful is that you have two eyes, ears, nostrils, and eyebrows—juxtaposed, balanced, symmetrical, and held in dynamic tension. This is the beauty of symmetry. Through all of these tensions, God is stringing together within us a mature, well-ordered, and beautiful soul.

Our temptation, however, is to *avoid the tension*. It's just easier to say God never heals, or He always heals, rather than wrestle with the balance. It's easier to immerse myself in the world or hibernate from it rather than struggle to "be in the world and not of it." Embracing the cross means embracing the tensions brought on by our dual citizenship.

WE DIE THAT OTHERS MAY LIVE

When Jesus bends to the ground to pick up the cross, He could look at any one of us and ask, "Did you drop this?" What is fundamental about Jesus' cross is that it did not and does not belong to Him. It belongs to us.

The cross is an other-centered missionary enterprise. Jesus didn't just die; He died for *us:* "For even the Son of Man did not come to be served, but to serve, and to give his life as a ransom for many" (Mark 10:45). An implication of bearing our cross is embracing Jesus' redemptive mission—and doing so at any cost to ourselves.

For evangelical believers this has long been assumed. *Of course we believe in missions and evangelism. Who do you think invented the Bible tract?* But heritage and culture can be nothing more than the baggage we carry *instead of* the cross. As long as our hearts remain weak and deceitful (which is most of the time), we will always desire to distance ourselves from the scandal of the cross, and our evangelical convictions will only ensure that such efforts are justified, unconscious, and disguised from everyone (including ourselves). You cannot be too suspicious of the heart's promiscuity; it will always find ways to cheat on the cross's redemptive burden.

For several years following Hurricane Katrina, Campus Crusade for Christ, the ministry I work with, sent students to New Orleans for spring break. Thousands of students came to help with the rebuilding and, in the process, engage in spiritual outreach wherever God opened doors. The compassion displayed by these Christian college students was so overwhelming it gained national media attention, drawing CNN's Anderson Cooper to New Orleans for a live, two-hour special.

Cooper interviewed many of the students, asking why they were there and what motivated them to spend their spring break mopping up New Orleans. The show was live, so students were able to answer and explain with unedited and uninterrupted freedom. I mention this because over the course of two hours, not one student mentioned God, Jesus Christ, or prayer. Heck, by the end of two hours I would have taken a "we are all God's children"—something, *anything*. Such testimony didn't have to be contrived, just honest; almost without exception, God *was* the reason they were there.

I share this not to point fingers—I'm sure I would have found myself slack-jawed in the presence of Anderson Cooper as well—but to make a point. The redemptive and saving truth of the cross can be a source of embarrassment to Christians. A demonstration of Christ's love was clearly not lacking in New Orleans, and given Cooper's questions, it was certainly not socially inappropriate to confess a Christian motivation. Yet all of the students reflexively distanced themselves from the message of redemption or even the mention of their Redeemer.

Why? We *know* why; we've all sensed that invisible social barrier and with it the fear of rejection, loss of reputation, or being labeled a fanatic. This redemptive stench is integral to the death of the cross, and unless we reorient our thinking, we will instinctively put distance between it and us, not wanting to appear the source of the fragrance.

WE ARE TEMPTED TO LIVE WHEN WE NEED TO DIE

He spoke plainly about this, and Peter took him
aside and began to rebuke him. But when Jesus

> *turned and looked at his disciples, he rebuked Peter.*
> *"Get behind me, Satan!" he said. "You do not have*
> *in mind the things of God, but the things of men."*
> *(Mark 8:32–33)*

Through the words of Peter, Jesus is tempted by the thought of bypassing the cross. That's as refreshing as cold water, but as sobering as having it poured down your back. If it was a temptation for Jesus to discard the cross, how much more so is it tempting for us?

Most of us desire to see the kingdom of God proclaimed in and through us, but the temptation remains to broadcast it from a tower of strength and prominence. We want to be Mother Teresa, to love and serve Christ … and become famous for it.

As embarrassing as this may be, perhaps it would be of encouragement—or entertainment at least—for me to share my favorite Christian fantasy that recurs every football season. After I finish watching a game and turn off the TV, I imagine myself making some spectacular play or miraculous catch—some feat only Peyton Manning or the Lord Himself could perform. But, as I said, this is a Christian fantasy, and so I begin to imagine what I would say when interviewed for my heroics. I mentally craft the perfect sound bite that conveys strength, confidence, and a clear gospel message. Funny, for some reason I'm taller and twenty pounds lighter. Anyway, as a believer, my fantasy (or "temptation," rather) is to proclaim and advance God's kingdom, but to do so through success, talent, intelligence, strength, confidence, and—if it's not too much to ask—the appearance of Tom Brady.

This is also, roughly speaking, the fantasy of the disciples, a fantasy Jesus deflates. I think this entailment of the cross is more visible if we personalize the descriptors like we're playing Mad Libs:

I want to see God's kingdom proclaimed in and through my life—not through weakness, rejection, or humiliation, but through being seen as someone with no major problems, who is the _____ (job title) at _____ (name of church or workplace); through having my kids be smarter students and better athletes at _____ (name of a school); by being recognized as the leader and organizer of _____ (some activity or group); by being admired by _____ (someone influential); by maintaining a strong Christian witness to our neighbors and friends by _____, _____, and _____ (things you do to project success, strength, and competence); and by maintaining my image through hiding _____ (an area of sin, embarrassment, weakness, or shame). And if I filled this out honestly I would die of embarrassment if it were discovered and read by _____, _____, or _____ (people I respect, love, and admire).

Concealed in the language of a "powerful Christian witness," and with good evangelistic intentions, such thinking can easily pass through the baggage scan of self-reflection without setting off any alarms. The temptation is much harder to detect when it's concealed under a Christian mask.

In some ways we are blessed to be believers living in the West. But in this region of the world, our culture presents an enormous hindrance that negatively influences our understanding of cross-bearing discipleship. In America we are a parent of a democracy, which beckons us to a political path, to power and control. We live in a media-rich culture, carrying with it the allure of celebrity and fame. We are a wealthy culture, often yielding to the temptation to see wealth as a token of God's blessing. We are an educated and success-driven culture, filled with people who might aspire to greater degrees of intelligence rather than greater wisdom.

A secular news show recently interviewed Rick Warren live from South America. Although a prominent pastor, he was in an obscure South American country attending a conference dealing with AIDS. While our culture applauds such social conscience, it rarely applauds Warren because he's not shy in promoting the gospel of Jesus Christ. Though wealthy from book sales, Warren lives on a tithe and gives 90 percent of his income away because he can afford to do so. He had on a nice suit and spoke with self-depreciating humor. Here was a distinctly American, cross-bearing disciple. Somehow Warren has been able to embrace the cross despite our culture's best efforts to stone him with money, success, and fame. This makes me hopeful that we can do the same.

WE DIE WHEN WE OUGHT TO LIVE

Let's start with this snippet from the trial of Jesus recorded in Mark's gospel:

Again the high priest asked him, "Are you the Christ,
the Son of the Blessed One?" "I am," said Jesus.... The
high priest tore his clothes. "Why do we need any more
witnesses?" (Mark 14:61–63)

The answer to the high priest's question, "Why do we need any more witnesses?" is "we don't." Such a claim by Jesus automatically carried a death sentence.

The only reason that "many testified falsely against him" (Mark 14:56) was that a significant component of Christ's suffering—His cross—was injustice and false accusation.

Another aspect of His suffering was betrayal. Jesus had no shortage of enemies; anyone could have turned Him in. But it was Judas, a friend, one of the trusted twelve who twisted the knife in Jesus' back.

The hallmarks of Christ's suffering were betrayal, false accusations, slander, and the unjust nature of His death. Jesus could have died for our sins through any number of other God-orchestrated narratives, ones that didn't involve being given up by a friend or false witness and perjury. But this was the carefully selected template of death He chose, so when Jesus declares that we, too, must carry a cross, He means *this* template. He means that a part of being a disciple is to endure slander, betrayal, false accusations, humiliation, embarrassment, and unjust suffering.

I'm not sure we always see this. In fact, I'm sure we don't. When I was a campus minister at Rutgers University in northern New Jersey, there was a very strong and very vocal gay and lesbian community. At the time they boasted the only openly gay dormitory in all of academia, and nothing would have made them happier than to see all the campus ministries pull up their tent pegs and take their work elsewhere—not because we condemned or attacked them, but because they were intelligent. They knew that behind the care or compassion of our ministries breathed an ideology that believed homosexuality to be immoral. All of the good intentions in the world cannot remove that unassailable fact. If I were them, I wouldn't have wanted us around either.

Believe me when I tell you that we did everything in our power to reach out to them in love. We invited them to socials and events, and some of our students even accompanied their gay friends to gay and lesbian gatherings. Whatever was in our power to do, we tried to do.

So it came as a horrible shock when one morning I opened up the campus newspaper and read how Rick James (that's me), the director of the campus' ministry, railed against homosexuals in a talk given the previous evening. It wouldn't have been shocking to see a sermon taken out of context by the radical paper. It's just that I hadn't even given one. There was actually a photo of another man with my name and the name of our ministry in the caption.

As I read through the slander and false accusations, I could see our ministry efforts and reputation going down the sewer.

I was outraged. I couldn't wait to sit down and craft a response. I wanted to hold court, extract my pound of flesh, demand satisfaction, have someone's head on a platter. Where was the retraction, reparation, redress. *Where was the remorse?* An older, more mature believer who was also in the ministry suggested I get a folder, create a file, stick the article in it, file it away, and never look at it again.

He himself had created such a folder, and it had grown beefy over the years with requests for his letter of resignation, slanderous attacks, gossip, character assault, name-calling, and the like. Often raggedly written, he actually took the time to correct the spelling and grammar mistakes before filing each letter, article, and the like for time and memoriam. He embraced the reputation-killing aspects of the sufferings of Christ.

Some college campuses can seem like police states that withhold rights and privileges from dissenters. But my time ministering at Rutgers made me aware of how much my Christianity is affected by my American "right to bear arms and hold public assembly" worldview—and how much that worldview leads me to reject this fundamental prerequisite of Christ's suffering.

How much we've been affected by our cultural worldview is proportional to the degree of outrage we experience when our character, rights, and reputation are assaulted. But the problem is not what we do with the outrage, *it's that we experience it at all*. Christians *ought* to experience unjust suffering, and therefore this outrage (this feeling of un-oughtness) has no place in the Christian life.

I used to get e-mails from a conservative political group that kept me posted on what company was trying to rip Christ from Christmas, prayer from schools, God from the constitution, children from their parents, or Judeo-Christian values from the country. Of course they were entirely right. What was bizarre is that they seemed surprised by these attempts, and what was wrong is that they were trying to cultivate my outrage.

In a democracy we all have a voice, and it's our duty to exercise it. It's admirable when Christians spur us on to take this responsibility seriously, but plucking at the cords of outrage is an illegitimate means to a godly end—it's like trying to instill jealousy in order to heighten affection in a relationship.

Upon realizing this, I halted the e-mail alerts. It's certainly possible you could receive such e-mails without the resulting outrage, in which case you should probably stay informed. I just know how they affected me, making me want to assert my rights, flex my muscle, and retaliate. I'm an American Christian, and they were an appeal to the American in me, not so much the Christian. They made me perceive injustice as an alien intruder in my life when it is our promised companion.

I think we experience more of this type of suffering than we realize. I know so many Christians who, without reason, have been hated, shunned, and ridiculed without reason by neighbors, bosses, coworkers, even family members. I've known believers who have been misunderstood, betrayed, and had evil motives ascribed to them. I just don't think it registers as one of the unjust implications of cross-bearing discipleship. Tragic, because the fact that this kind of suffering is part of bearing our cross is our only comfort in it.

But while we may experience more unjust suffering than we realize, we don't suffer nearly as much as believers at other times and in other places. You could say it's because of God's incalculable grace. And that it may be. But you could also say it's God's discipline. There are worse things than being turned over to unjust suffering, such as being privileged and pampered. Zeal is baked in the furnace of unjust suffering. I'm not sure what bakes in the oven of prosperity—perhaps canoles or butter cookies or something.

Now one could say, with just a slight air of belligerence, "What, are we doormats?" to which I think I would say, "Yes, that's exactly what we are," and add that the church has always flourished when we've allowed unbelievers to wipe their feet on us. It's only in America where believers stand on their rights, retaliate against injustice, act out politically, and refuse to be trampled like doormats.

Where has that gotten us, exactly?

There is a time and place to engage in image management, something the apostle Paul demonstrates in his letter to the Corinthians.

> *We are not trying to commend ourselves to you again,*
> *but are giving you an opportunity to take pride in us,*
> *so that you can answer those who take pride in what is*
> *seen rather than in what is in the heart. If we are out of*
> *our mind, it is for the sake of God; if we are in our right*
> *mind, it is for you. (2 Cor. 5:12–13)*

The time to defend ourselves is when it would be hurtful, destructive, or a stumbling block to others to believe something false about us, impacting the way they see Christ. Beyond this one exception, unjust suffering is to be embraced as a part of our cross, for it was certainly a part of Christ's.

I SHOULD PROBABLY MENTION ...

While there are certainly other implications of cross-bearing discipleship, these are the predominant principles that are true of Jesus' cross and therefore true of our cross. Whatever else cross-bearing discipleship might involve, it will require no less of us than this.

But now would be a really good time to mention that we are not really interested in death at all. Death, and dying to ourselves, is of little or no intrinsic value. What we value is *life*, and what we desire is *Christ*. What we long to experience is the resurrected life of our Lord lived out in and through our lives. Death just happens to be the only road that leads to resurrection. The path of discipleship does not lead to death. It is the path *of* death that leads to life, and without this understanding, all our talk of death will simply lead us to empty religiosity and ascetic Phariseeism.

And so it is to this point that we now turn.

CHAPTER FOUR

OUR LIFE, HIS LIFE

In his book *Something Like an Autobiography*, the legendary Japanese film director Akira Kurosawa wrote about the day Japan surrendered at the close of World War II. The entire country anxiously awaited word from the emperor, wondering if he would order them to surrender or command them to forfeit their lives in what was termed the "Honorable Death of the Hundred Million," Japan's self-annihilation strategy:

> *On August 15, 1945, I was summoned to the studio along with everyone else to listen to the momentous proclamation on the radio: the Emperor himself was to speak over the airwaves. I will never forget the scenes I saw as I walked the streets that day. On the way from Soshigaya to the studios in Kinuta the shopping street looked fully prepared for the Honorable Death of the Hundred Million. The atmosphere was tense, panicked. There were even shop owners who had taken their Japanese sword from their sheaths and sat staring at the blade. However, when I walked the same route back to my home after listening to the imperial proclamation,*

> *the scene was entirely different. The people on the*
> *shopping street were bustling with cheerful faces as if*
> *preparing for a festival.*[5]

When worldly leaders face certain death, defeat, and humiliation, it is not uncommon for them to rally their loyal remnant to a final, glorious but suicidal surge of devotion. And yet having announced His imminent rejection, Jesus gathers His followers and instructs them to do the opposite—He tells them how to save their lives from certain ruin.

If we think that our dying and carrying the cross is a truly selfless act, we would misunderstand the words of Jesus and our human nature. Let's reread the last section of the discourse again:

> *For whoever wants to save his life will lose it, but who-*
> *ever loses his life for me and for the gospel will save it.*
> *What good is it for a man to gain the whole world, yet*
> *forfeit his soul? Or what can a man give in exchange for*
> *his soul? If anyone is ashamed of me and my words in*
> *this adulterous and sinful generation, the Son of Man*
> *will be ashamed of him when he comes in his Father's*
> *glory with the holy angels. (Mark 8:35–38)*

You'll notice that Jesus does not simply tell His disciples to be willing to lose their lives. Rather He explains to them how to get life, and the way to get life is to lose it for Jesus' sake.

The "carry the cross" discourse is the furthest thing from a communist manifesto. We are not called to give our life for the greater good, but for our own good. It would be difficult to imagine a piece of written or spoken communication more saturated with cost/benefit ratios: Lose your life in order to gain it; ponder the market value of eternal life; consider what you stand to lose for *not* making such an investment—it reads like *The Wall Street Journal.*

Such personal benefit in no way spoils the sacrifice, certainly not in the eyes of Jesus. As C. S. Lewis explains:

> *The negative ideal of Unselfishness carries with it the suggestion not primarily of securing good things for others, but of going without them ourselves, as if our abstinence and not their happiness was the important point. I do not think this is the Christian virtue of Love. The New Testament has lots to say about self-denial, but not about self-denial as an end in itself. We are told to deny ourselves and to take up our crosses in order that we may follow Christ; and nearly every description of what we shall ultimately find if we do so contains an appeal to desire.*

> *If there lurks in most modern minds the notion that to desire our own good and earnestly to hope for the enjoyment of it is a bad thing, I submit that this notion has crept in from Kant and the Stoics and is no part of the Christian faith. Indeed, if we consider the unblushing promises of reward and the staggering nature of the rewards promised in the Gospels, it would seem that [God] finds our desires not too strong, but too weak.*

> *We are half-hearted creatures, fooling about with*
> *drink and sex and ambition when infinite joy is offered*
> *us, like an ignorant child who wants to go on making*
> *mud pies in a slum because he cannot imagine what is*
> *meant by the offer of a holiday at the sea. We are far too*
> *easily pleased.*[6]

Following the logic of Lewis, the reason we are often unwilling to die is not because we value our lives or personal well-being too much, *but too little.*

THE PROCESS OF RESURRECTION

It will do us no good to see death in all of its smaller forms (death of hopes, dreams, trials, and the like) if we continue to view our resurrection as only a singular, future event. When Paul states that "life is at work in us," he is saying that God is continuously in the process of taking death, in whatever form it may occur in our lives, and transforming it into life. If the Christian life is a string of little deaths—and I contend that it is—it's more importantly a string of little resurrections.

This is the process that drives, energizes, and animates the Christian life. When we die to self and embrace our trials, unjust sufferings, and humiliations, we do so with anticipation (and hope) of how God is going to resurrect and transform it into life.

Let me be clear: I'm not saying that God's resurrection power is always discernible. I'm not saying that we can always see how and where God brings new life out of our circumstances. I'm not saying it's always immediate, or always happens on this side of heaven. But as we walk by faith with eyes of hope and expectation, we can see a whole lot more than we think we can. And where we can't see His hand and must walk blindly, we persevere through our circumstances by faith, knowing that God's resurrection power is always at work within us.

As death comes in a variety of forms, so does resurrection. We need to learn to recognize its familiar patterns so we can perceive God's orchestrating hand in our circumstances and perceive the way by which He is bringing life out of death.

We only hear the rhythm and melody of music by stepping back from the swarming notes, by perceiving their broader patterns and relationships. This is how we hear music and why we hear it flow together rather than as staccato notes. As we step back from Scripture, and step back from our circumstances, we begin to perceive some common patterns, music of resurrection and the different melodies created when God brings life out of death. Here are the major movements.

Rescue

> We do not want you to be uninformed, brothers, about the hardships we suffered in the province of Asia. We were under great pressure, far beyond our ability to endure, so that we despaired even of life. Indeed, in our hearts we felt the sentence of death. But this happened that we might not rely on ourselves but on God, who raises the dead. He has delivered us from such a deadly peril, and he will deliver us. On him we have set our hope that he will continue to deliver us, as you help us by your prayers. (2 Cor. 1:8–11)

In the introduction to his letter to the Corinthians, Paul explains that God *rescued* him from what was most certainly a death sentence. How, we don't know—we only know that He did. In finding circumstances turned against us, we often lament on how we got ourselves in such a stew, or, if we're a "blamer," we divert our mental energy to fingering the responsible party. But for those looking for God's resurrection power, the eyes of the heart keep darting to the horizon looking for the cavalry, "I lift up my eyes to the hills — where does my help come from?" (Ps. 121:1).

Re-energized

> *But those who hope in the Lord will renew their strength.*
> *They will soar on wings like eagles; they will run and not*
> *grow weary, they will walk and not be faint. (Isa. 40:31)*

Of course we care about food, drink, and exercise, but those who walk by faith are conscious of the fact that energy, strength, perseverance, and boldness are not strictly governed by energy transfer, caloric intake, and REM sleep. God can provide strength when there is none and energy when there's no fuel to burn; He can bring vitality out of frailty.

Reversal

> *You intended to harm me, but God intended it for good*
> *to accomplish what is now being done, the saving of*
> *many lives. (Gen. 50:20)*

Wikipedia defines the Japanese martial art of Aikido this way: "redirecting the force of the attack rather than opposing it head-on." In Aikido the attacker's own momentum, anger, and aggression are the very weapons used against them. God has boundless capacity and creativity in using a similar method. He is able to flip circumstances and reverse the damage and destruction caused by the enemy even when the enemy is ourselves.

Reward

> *Rejoice and be glad, because great is your reward in heaven, for in the same way they persecuted the prophets who were before you. (Matt. 5:12)*

Perhaps the most devastating event in my life occurred when the woman I was madly in love with broke up with me. I eventually got even by marrying her. The realized *reward* of marriage retroactively transformed the trudging trials and travails of courtship into a victory march. The resurrection and reversal of some events will await us in heaven, when all "things done while in the body" (2 Cor. 5:10) will be judged, rewarded, and transformed.

Resuscitation

> *"Stop wailing," Jesus said. "She is not dead but asleep."*
> *(Luke 8:52)*

One's church, ministry, marriage, friendship, career, dreams, or health may be in a state of decline, headed for death but not dead yet. In such cases God's resurrection power is often flexed in the miraculous resuscitation of the patient.

Reassurance

> Praise be to the God and Father of our Lord Jesus Christ, the Father of compassion and the God of all comfort, who comforts us in all our troubles, so that we can comfort those in any trouble with the comfort we ourselves have received from God. (2 Cor. 1:3–4)

To comfort the downcast is to *raise* the spirits of those who have lost hope. Without removing us from our circumstances, God breathes fresh life into us through comfort and encouragement, either directly or through a friend.

Renewal

> Therefore we do not lose heart. Though outwardly we are wasting away, yet inwardly we are being renewed day by day. (2 Cor. 4:16)

While we function as a single being, we are compounds. Each of us is a union of many physical, emotional, and mental parts and processes. As such, we experience God's transformation piecemeal. We are a work in process, with some areas further along in the process than others. While parts of us may remain underdeveloped, this doesn't prevent us from seeing God's transforming power at work on other fronts in our lives.

No doubt we could list more, but these are the primary ways through which we perceive God's resurrection power operating in, around, and through us: rescue, re-energized, reversal, reward, resuscitation, reassurance, and renewal. While a future day of utter transformation awaits our mortal bodies, we really would miss the point if we failed to perceive and participate in the ongoing processes of resurrection now.

CHRIST IN US

Each death in the Christian life is an opportunity to see God's resurrection power at work and an opportunity for Christ's life to manifest in and through us. Having a valuable piece of pottery dashed to pieces would be rather disheartening—unless, of course, it was a piggy bank, which is the one piece of pottery that houses its value on the inside. It's worth a great deal more as bovine shards. It is the apostle Paul's observation that this is also the case with believers.

> For God, who said, "Let light shine out of darkness,"
> made his light shine in our hearts to give us the light of
> the knowledge of the glory of God in the face of Christ.
> But we have this treasure in jars of clay to show that
> this all-surpassing power is from God and not from us.
> (2 Cor. 4:6–7)

> We always carry around in our body the death of Jesus,

so that the life of Jesus may also be revealed in our body.
(2 Cor. 4:10)

Imagine turning on a thousand-watt light bulb inside an old clay pot. What would you see? You would see every possible crack, fracture, and imperfection. You would also see a gloriously blinding light, but only through the cracks and imperfections in the jar. This is how Paul envisions us: God's power manifested and made visible in and through our weakness, frailty, and brokenness. A great word picture and a significant improvement on my piggy bank illustration.

Someone recently showed me an older magazine interview with former mega-church pastor Ted Haggard. Of course his answers to certain question were ironic in light of what the future would reveal, and there were serious issues to be sure. But the article captured a deeper problem that had nothing to do with Ted Haggard: a hidden sin affecting all of us—more deceptive and far more systemic.

Alongside the article was a typical photo of Haggard, only it looked like it had been taken in the Oval Office. Light streamed through the windows, creating a backlit halo around his head. He was laughing, an apparently approachable potentate with just a touch of graying wisdom at his temples, a handsome suit, a power tie, and the gravitas to bring warring nations together. Had Mitt Romney been standing beside him, he would have appeared a vagrant by contrast. The heavy mahogany desk that he presided over bore several books and the weight of the free world. The magazine was Christian; the image, not so much. It embodied regality, dignity, power, wealth, intelligence, confidence, and strength—everything my flesh could hope for. It would have made a great cover for *Forbes* or *Money* magazine.

Perhaps I've exaggerated the photo a bit, but not the problem it represents. Those who took and placed the image in the article were quite unconscious of its intended meaning, which is what makes it such an accurate portrait of our Christian worldview. The image portrays "the successful Christian life," as this is what some think it should look like. The picture oozes success, power, strength, confidence, invulnerability, wealth, and control. We can safely assume the power of Christ is not manifest in situations where we are either drawn to asking for an autograph or signing one. We're all affected by this distinctly American narrative of the abundant Christian life, one that's constantly transmitted consciously and unconsciously.

In 1938, De Beers Consolidated, owners of the global diamond monopoly, approached the New York advertising agency of N. W. Ayer and Son. De Beers was in crisis, and if it couldn't open up the American market, it would be ruined. So N. W. Ayer took them on as a client and produced one of the most successful advertising campaigns in history. We all remember it, but not as advertising; the narrative they invented was so successful that we remember it as history.

In America, prior to 1938, people did not generally give diamonds as engagement rings. As Tom Zoellner, author of *The Heartless Stone*, makes clear, the ads were "a brazen denial of three centuries of American cultural history, in which diamond rings were generally regarded as foppish extravagancies."[7] Year after year, in ad after ad, we heard the tale that engagements were incomplete without diamonds, that diamonds were an essential part of the American history of love. It was all a story, told so well that we didn't even realize it was a story. And some seventy-plus years later, here we are, our perceptions and understanding of love and engagement deeply, irreparably flawed.

However such devilry came about, we've all been similarly affected by an alternate narrative of victorious Christian living. The only remedy is to return to the words of Jesus, His narrative of discipleship, His vision of faithfulness, His definition of "normative," and His cross. We need reminding again and again, even as Paul did:

> Three times I pleaded with the Lord to take it away from me. But he said to me, "My grace is sufficient for you, for my power is made perfect in weakness." Therefore I will boast all the more gladly about my weaknesses, so that Christ's power may rest on me. (2 Cor. 12:8–9)

If we want Christ's life to shine through us, we must be willing to be humbled, to be vulnerable, imperfect, bruised, rejected, misunderstood, unsuccessful, and weak. And each of these, in one way or another, is a form of dying: the death of ego, reputation, status, or control. Their value is the open door they provide to experience and manifest the glory of Christ.

I remember delivering a series of talks to Christian Ivy League students some years ago. During the first evening's talk, I intentionally threw in a specific large and sophisticated word, and I did this so they would think I was smart. I can't remember what the word was—*automobile*?

The following morning I was praying about the next talk I was to give, praying that God would bless it and use it powerfully in the lives of those listening. Then came the answer to my prayer. As clear as a bell—as opposed to a large and sophisticated word—God brought to my mind the spectacle of the previous evening and my blustering use of the aforementioned polysyllabic word (maybe the word was *polysyllabic*?). What God was asking me to do became clear.

So—*and I'm cringing just remembering this*—I began my talk by telling the students that the previous night I had used a big word, and that I had done so because I wanted them to think I was smart. I even told them the word I used. And there, in brokenness and humiliation, God was able to use me, to shine through my frailty and radiate through my flaws and cracks.

There are abundant daily opportunities to acknowledge our sin, to share our failures, embrace criticism, *invite* criticism, leave our reputations open to attack, refuse to manage our image, apologize, give thanks to God for our weaknesses, and so on and so on.

There are a million ways for Christ's resurrected life to shine through us.

PETER'S MISCONCEPTION

I want to come back to Peter as we leave this section, for he manifests all the symptoms of someone who completely missed the point (at least initially). Peter saw the cross as something to be avoided at all costs, and about this he was badly mistaken. The cross is something to be embraced in every way.

The gospels show Peter defending Jesus with a sword and boasting that he will never desert Him. From this depiction we might conclude that Peter understood the meaning of "carry the cross" primarily as martyrdom. He was mistaken in this assumption as well. Jesus is talking about a life characterized by death, and a path or lifestyle *of* death that leads to life.

Later, fearing death, Peter denies that he even knows Jesus. As Jesus had yet to be raised from the dead, it's difficult to imagine that Peter had a particularly clear understanding of the resurrection. His willingness to die came from a love and commitment to Jesus that, in the end, was not sufficient. He believed that through sheer will and passion he could successfully lay down his life for the sake of Jesus, and again he was mistaken. Without the motivation of resurrection and the empowerment of the resurrected Christ, we are incapable of carrying the cross. We cannot submit to death without the power of the resurrection in us and the promise of resurrection before us. Peter was disabused of these misconceptions, and I trust that you see these principles clearly.

The contours of what follows are already visible in Jesus' inaugural address, in His declaration of the democracy of death. And as the rest of the New Testament teaching fills in and details this life of death, we will do the same, rendering important facets in much greater detail. We'll begin with a closer study of the death in faith, witness, trials, courage, humility, and love, in this order. There are indeed a million ways to die, but every death flows from one of these six.

SECTION TWO
THE WAKE OF FAITH

CHAPTER FIVE

THE ANATOMY LESSON

From an artistic perspective, literary themes in a story are equivalent to design elements repeated throughout a book, or magazine. You likely won't come across a cyan border, background, flourish, or whatever on page 118 unless it appears somewhere between pages 1 and 117. This is the elegance of repeating patterns: Each iteration may be nuanced or embellished, but the soothing repetition is there, stroking our senses and telling us all is harmonious in the universe.

Designers do this because we consumers find it beautiful and desirable. *Designers find it beautiful because God does.* God has encoded certain recipes for beauty into His creation. It's not just electrons that orbit atoms, but moons that orbit planets, and planets that orbit suns, and galactic arms that circle around galactic centers, and we who (spiritually speaking) orbit God, and so on.

This is why a city looks like a human cell, or why highway systems are like vascular networks and why trees branch like rivers branch, like roots branch, and like veins branch. Scientists call these patterns morphological or scalable redundancy, which is why they are scientists and not poets.

Furthermore, you're not likely to come across the color cyan without it being chaperoned by one of its color complements—say, magenta. This, too, is another element of design—the principle of complements.

In 1965, signage in the New York Subways switched from a Gothic font to Akzidenz-Grotesk, which is about the same time Akzidenz-Grotesk switched its name to Helvetica for obvious reasons. The typographical engineer was Massimo Vignelli, who explains the philosophy of type this way: "Type is not black, it's white. What defines type, what is pleasing to the mind is the space between the letters."[1] It is the interchange between black and white, the complement of background to foreground, that gives a font its balance and beauty.

Such design abounds in Scripture—fractals upon fractals of concept and thought that, when viewed as a whole, capture the beauty of Christ. Our goal in this book has been to identify and trace "death" as a prominent theme: as a design element of our walk with Christ. But here too we find both a repeating pattern *and* its complement: death and resurrection, like foreground and background, magenta and cyan.

Faith is enormously complex, composed of more redemptive patterns than the human eye can see, but our focus will primarily be on the "death in faith"—that is, the role death plays in the growth and maturing of faith. To this end I'm going to structure this chapter around one particular text: the raising of Lazarus in John 11.

In 1632, Rembrandt painted *The Anatomy Lesson of Dr. Nicolaes Tulp*. It's a ghoulish scene of the good doctor showing his Flemish medical students (a group of pilgrims not unlike those on a Dutch Masters cigar) the interior of a cadaver, apparently instructing them in the machinations of life. What's odd about the painting is that Dr. Tulp is looking over and beyond the students pictured in the painting to a broader audience not captured in the picture. Though the identity is unknown, this is perhaps the world's second most famous cadaver, Lazarus being the first. And while Mary and Martha are the original attending students to Lazarus, this anatomy lesson is meant for all would-be disciples. Lazarus is dead because some lessons can only be taught using a cadaver. Jesus doesn't heal Lazarus right away because He needs him dead to teach a lesson. This is a lesson about faith and the God who raises the dead—and to truly grasp the workings of God's resurrection power, we need a corpse. Someone really, really dead.

DEAD, NOT DYING (JOHN 11:1-11)

> *Now a man named Lazarus was sick. He was from Bethany, the village of Mary and her sister Martha. This Mary, whose brother Lazarus now lay sick, was the same one who poured perfume on the Lord and wiped his feet with her hair. So the sisters sent word to Jesus, "Lord, the one you love is sick." When he heard this, Jesus said, "This sickness will not end in death. No,*

it is for God's glory so that God's Son may be glori-
fied through it." Jesus loved Martha and her sister and
Lazarus. Yet when he heard that Lazarus was sick, he
stayed where he was two more days. (John 11:1–6)

I'm Not Interested in Healing Him

The text makes a point to tell us that Jesus, upon hearing the news of Lazarus' condition, promptly remained where He was until Lazarus was not just dying but thoroughly dead. This leads us to one of two conclusions. The first is that Jesus was not as good a friend as Lazarus thought He was. Some believed this to be the case: "But some of them said, 'Could not he who opened the eyes of the blind man have kept this man from dying?'" (John 11:37). This is certainly understandable. When we pray for something as dire as the life of a loved one and those prayers seem to lack sufficient postage, it's easy to harbor suspicions and insecurity, taking "no" or "wait" as an insult rather than an answer. But John goes several blocks out of his way to tell us that, "Jesus loved … Lazarus" (John 11:5), so this can't be the right answer. And that leaves us with only the second alternative: The reason for Jesus' delay is that He doesn't want to heal Lazarus because He wants to raise Lazarus.

This sounds like a great idea unless you're Mary or Martha. They are going to have to suffer through the mourning and the death, as well as the confusion as to why Jesus did nothing to prevent it. The problem from our end is that for something to be resurrected, it must first die, and that means we must endure the process of death and mourning. The problem from God's end is that resurrection power is better demonstrated on a corpse than on something that's merely dying. You may, for example, appreciate the claim that, "I'm the world's greatest reconstructive surgeon," but it's not a claim you'd want to have to learn about as a patient.

Whose Idea Was it to Raise Lazarus?

To appreciate what it was like to be Jesus, I think you'd need to open a free supermarket in Calcutta, or a free hospital in Darfur, or sell any DVD in Shanghai a month before the movie's legal release. Everywhere He went people clung to Him, and many of His miracles were performed at the behest of a needy soul. This tended to foster the illusion of passivity on Jesus' part, as if His miracles were only a response to a request and not the product of His own creative initiative. God clearly desires for us to pray and responds to our prayers, but He also knows what we are going to ask before we ask it, and He knows exactly what He's going to do about it before He does.

It's important that we not see God as a *passive* benefactor, a Daddy Warbucks of sorts. If you bring your paralyzed friend to Jesus, you should not be shocked if He decides to forgive his sins when that wasn't what you asked for (Mark 2, Luke 5, Matthew 9), or raise him from the dead when you'd specifically requested that he be healed (John 11). God is moved by our true need, not by our counsel. God has His own mind on the matter and on every matter.

The incident with Lazarus allows us to see the inner workings of a miracle. Because of His intentional two-day delay, we know that raising Lazarus is the conception of Jesus and not Mary or Martha. It's an initiative, not a response.

In fact, in the only other story in the gospels where Jesus raises someone from the dead, we observe a similar delay. In Mark 5, one of the leaders of the local synagogue, Jairus, pleads with Jesus to come to his home and save his little girl. But in the process of accompanying Jairus to his home, Jesus is sidetracked by a hemorrhaging woman:

> *So Jesus went with him. A large crowd followed and pressed around him. And a woman was there who had been subject to bleeding for twelve years. (Mark 5:24–25)*

By the time Jesus is done tending to the woman, the daughter of Jairus has already expired. Apparently His delay cost the little girl her life. But Jesus is never late. Let me amend that: Jesus is never later than He intends to be, or as Gandalf observed in *The Lord of the Rings,* "A wizard is never late, nor is he early. He arrives precisely when he means to." Having been uncharacteristically distracted, and arriving with a certain nonchalance, we're already led to suspect that Jesus was planning this all along.

Jesus' delay in both of these narratives (Jairius and Lazarus) has the intended effect of transferring our attention. We are no longer impatiently waiting for Jesus to get on with the requested miracle, but intrigued to discover what Jesus intends to do. The text forces our eyes to look in a new place for the Author of the miracle—much as the four-word message contained in Samuel Morse's first telegraph ("What hath God wrought?") was intended to spotlight God as the inventor, and he only the discoverer.

God Is My Dentist

God's forethought and creative initiative in response to our needs and prayers came as both a revelation and gift to my wife and I on our wedding anniversary some years ago. It was the day before our anniversary (which is December 8, honey—no sir, would never forget that), and because we have three kids and it falls near Christmas, there's never much to spend on our anniversary (which is on December 8), so we usually just give our kids Christmas gifts for our anniversary on December 8. But this particular year I happened to have five dollars in my pocket. Seriously. And so I went out in faith, praying that God would lead me to the perfect five-dollar gift. I didn't find anything, at least not for five dollars. But there I was driving home, when I began to ponder, *If I could give Katie anything and price was no object, what would I give her?*

The answer was teeth—caps, actually. *She has teeth.* My wife, Katie, is in fact beautiful: drop-dead, cover-of-*Glamour*-magazine, Angelina-Jolie-but-with-human-lips beautiful. She never had braces when she was young, and so she had these small gaps between her teeth, prompting her to put her hand over her mouth whenever she smiled or laughed. But new caps would have put me over my five-dollar budget by about $2,995. We did, however, have about that much in savings, which I had invested with a friend. So I threw out this fleece to God: "If Dave calls today, Lord, I'll take that as confirmation to spend that money on Katie." I was, and am, aware that this is quite spiritually reckless, but I hadn't talked to Dave in well over a year, so, like, what would have been the odds of him calling me that day, right?

Well, when I got home, Katie said, "Hey, Dave called. Said to call him back." I was beyond shocked, which accurately portrays the degree of faith I had in God answering this prayer. I called my friend Dave back, and as it turns out, the reason he had called was to tell me that my humble little investments were drowning in the Chinese market. Now I didn't know what to do. I had no idea what God was saying through these contradictory circumstances.

At this point I tell Katie everything. I mean, if I can't get her new caps, I might as well get the relational points for having tried. So we prayed together, and afterward I suggested, "Why don't we at least call the dentist and find out how much it would cost?" So I called our dentist, and he said this to me: "You're never going to believe this, Rick, but a few days ago, someone from your church called and said that if Katie should ever want to have work done on her teeth, they would pay for it entirely."

You always think that it would be really cool for God to do something so outrageously miraculous, but when it actually happens it's simply paralyzing. I just remember staring at the floor and thinking, *I better never sin again.* But as the shock wore off and I thought through the wild faith-ride of the day, I was left to reconcile similar chronology problems as those found in the story of Lazarus. If this person from my church had called several days *prior* to my call to the dentist, several days prior to *my* idea to fix Katie's teeth, then whose idea was it? Through intimate prayer God was somehow able to communicate what *He* wanted to do in and through me, and I found myself walking in one of those good works that God had planned in advance for me to do (Eph. 2:10).

No one ever prays for a resurrection while that person or relationship or job or dream is still alive. We, of course, pray to be rescued, or saved, or salvaged. I don't think that's sinful, just human, the result of living strapped to a one-dimensional time line.

But as we mature in our faith, we'll see that there are times when God may want to resurrect something we wanted him to heal or fix. We need to know this about Him—He might very well want us to experience a bit of a resurrection. And when that thing we wanted healed or fixed ends up dying—whatever it was—we need to be open and willing to trust God for how He will transform that death into life. Our faith pursuit should not automatically end when the object of hope dies. As we see in the Lazarus account, Martha's doesn't. Even after the death of Lazarus, her faith beats on and on—an Energizer bunny that will simply not turn off.

CHAPTER SIX

WAITING AND WAITING

In the world of campus ministry, student groups sprout up of their own accord. Of course there are not enough full-time ministry workers to send to every campus, so instead we make periodic visits to guide and encourage the student leaders. I used to visit some of these indigenous ministries on campuses in Pennsylvania. I'd stay for a day or two, lead some Bible studies, do some teaching, counseling, encouraging, and provide direction to the student leaders. These were all, to my recollection, gratifying, ministry-rich visits.

But while some of these ministries grew and thrived, others fizzled. Making all the difference was not what happened during my visits, but between them. Everyone seemed equally "jacked," to borrow a word from the student lexicon, when I was there. But in my absence some students stepped up in leadership, responding to the challenge and growing in their capacities, while others shrunk back.

On one campus, for example, a surprise visit to check on a scheduled student outreach revealed handwritten signs leading to a classroom where a TV on an AV stand played an episode of *Veggie Tales*. Not exactly what you'd classify as a compelling outreach to lost students. I've seen God bless dorky outreach, but not apathetic outreach.

And this is why Jesus' absences or delays in the gospels are every bit as significant and intentional as His miracles. When Jesus is detained, the action is not pause—we are not waiting for Jesus to do something, He *is* doing something.

And so it is that the real action in the story of Lazarus is actually going on before Jesus arrives in Bethany, as Mary and Martha wait.

THE STRETCH OF FAITH

On his arrival, Jesus found that Lazarus had already been in the tomb for four days. Bethany was less than two miles from Jerusalem, and many Jews had come to Martha and Mary to comfort them in the loss of their brother. When Martha heard that Jesus was coming, she went out to meet him, but Mary stayed at home. "Lord," Martha said to Jesus, "if you had been here, my brother would not have died. But I know that even now God will give you whatever you ask." (John 11:17–22)

And Waiting and Waiting

Martha and Mary have been waiting for Jesus to arrive, but this doesn't mean their faith sat idle—quite the opposite, in fact. In the days of waiting, Martha's faith has been stretched—two, three, four times its original size. But having any part of our person, including our faith, stretched out of its sockets is quite excruciating. It's been a grueling few days for Martha. Yet even after the death and burial of her brother Lazarus, "even now" the text says, she still believes Jesus can do something. Her faith feels weak, but only because it's been stretched so thin. It's actually stronger, and surely it took a great deal more of faith to "believe" at the funeral of Lazarus than it did standing at his sick bed.

However, in the same time period, Mary's faith has atrophied. Her faith had initially stretched as she awaited Jesus' arrival, but it snapped back like a severed Achilles tendon when He didn't come. The horizon of her faith slipped lower and lower and lower until, at last, it merged with the horizon of reality: Lazarus was dead.

We observe here a somewhat paradoxical principle about how faith grows and how it's tested. The paradox could be stated this way: *The battle of faith is often fought while waiting for the battle to begin.* The battle of Jericho, for example, was won "by faith" in the six days that preceded the battle itself. On the seventh day the city was taken by sword and by sight. On day seven, eyes of faith were superfluous, a vestigial organ. You could simply look and see the rubble that was Jericho and the ever-growing pile of Canaanite casualties and know the victory had already been won.

During the wait—*whatever it is you are bound by faith to wait for*—faith must wake each morning, put on its combat fatigues, and head off to the front lines. Only this is a "cold war." No heroics, no medals, no glorious or bloody battles, just a stalemate—holding the line, manning the watchtower, guarding the wall, making sure East never mingles with West. Here, in this waiting, faith must hold its ground against the onslaught of common life, the daily and deterministic march of pedestrian existence that undercuts faith's belief in an alternative reality.

The problem with daily life is that it's so daily, so unspiritual, so unremarkable, so mundane. It's casuistic, fatalistic, deterministic. Visible reality—the appearance of things—denies everything that faith holds dear. It taunts faith, not with violence or a raised voice, but with an even whisper: "This is the only reality. Accept it. What you see is all there is, all there ever will be." And every day that passes, every day of waiting, simply strengthens doubt and erodes faith's resolve. The enemy is everywhere and in everything. A box of corn flakes, a tube of toothpaste, a broken dish, a migraine headache, a trip to the grocery store, a plumber's bill—all spies, carrying the message that visible reality is the only reality, and that faith is merely wishful thinking.

It is quite possible my metaphors have obscured rather than clarified my point, so let me state it bluntly: In the struggle of faith, waiting is not just waiting. It is during the waiting that the battle of faith is fought and won. If faith is victorious it does not simply survive the wait but emerges stronger. The waiting of Mary and Martha is not simply waiting but a war, *a struggle of faith*. The delay of Jesus is not a delay but a tactic, a vehicle for stretching their faith. If Martha's faith endures the struggle, she'll be well on her way to garnering the faith prerequisite for raising Lazarus from the dead. If not, Lazarus is a dead man.

At some point in all the waiting, Mary ceased to hold out hope, probably when Lazarus died. And who of us could blame her? I mean, why wouldn't you give up the ship when it's sunk and sitting on the bottom? So Mary comes to terms with reality and embraces the unblinking truth: "Lazarus is dead and nothing can change it. Accept it; God's not going to save him. I was naive to have believed otherwise." But even after the verdict of death has been rendered, Martha's not ready to surrender. Her faith continues to struggle to define reality in terms of what God says it is, will be, or may be, *not* by what her senses are telling her.

The Greek word *hupostasis* occurs precisely twice in Scripture, with the rough English translation being "essence" or "reality." Hebrews 1:3 states that Jesus is the "essence" or "reality" of God and the "exact representation of his being." Hebrews 11:1 says that faith is the "essence" or the "reality" of things unseen. Same word.

If you combine the notion in the verses, here is what you get: Jesus defines reality, not circumstances or the appearance of things. Faith seeks to take hold of true reality in the terms Jesus has defined. For example, if Jesus tells me that my sin is killing me, then that's reality, even if my senses tell me, "I've never felt better in my life." Our faith must take hold of that truth, *that reality*.

There's an old sermon illustration (which is a nice way of saying it may or may not be true) that goes like this:

> *It's a close baseball game. There's a runner on third base, and the batter hits a deep fly to left field. The left fielder goes back, catches it, and fires it home to try to get the runner tagging up from third. It's a perfect throw and the ball, the catcher, and the runner all arrive at home plate at the same time. The umpire, Bill Clem, hesitates with the call. One bench is screaming, "He's out! He's out!" and the other, "Safe! He's safe!" Bill Clem looks at both benches and says, "He ain't nothin' till I call it!"*

As Martha runs to Jesus, she is appealing to the umpire of reality: "I know what the situation looks like, but you're the one who defines reality. You make the call. You tell me what reality is in this situation, and I'll believe it."

I don't think it's accidental that a similar delay, and corresponding faith-stretching, occurs in Jesus' raising the daughter of Jairus. It appears that the faith prerequisite for day-to-day living isn't robust enough to lift a dead body off the floor. This doesn't make the miracle impossible; it only delays the miracle until one's faith is prepped for the heavy lifting.

Through the days of Jesus' absence, the ligaments of Martha's faith have been stretched taut. Unfortunately, Jesus' arrival provides about as much relief as a visit from a Russian gymnastics coach.

THE DANCE OF FAITH

> "Lord," Martha said to Jesus, "if you had been here, my brother would not have died. But I know that even now God will give you whatever you ask." Jesus said to her, "Your brother will rise again." Martha answered, "I know he will rise again in the resurrection at the last day." Jesus said to her, "I am the resurrection and the life. He who believes in me will live, even though he dies; and whoever lives and believes in me will never die. Do you believe this?" "Yes, Lord," she told him, "I believe that you are the Christ, the Son of God, who was to come into the world." (John 11:21–27)

I Need Assurances

Some have suggested that you need to find out what God's doing and get involved. Good advice. Some have suggested that you need to tell God what you want and *believe* that He will give it to you. Dangerous advice. Both suggestions, however, miss the idea of walking by faith, which is a romantic stroll, not a sprint to catch up with God or God running to catch up with you. Rather, as we abide intimately with Christ, God communicates to us the good works He wants us to trust Him for. This we do confidently because we truly believe we've heard them from Him and not just made them up.

If, for example, you asked me to give money to the cause of missions, I would not simply check on what happens to be in my pockets, nor would I invent a rather large "faith goal." No, I would pray and attempt to discern what God was asking me to trust Him for. Neither my current reality nor my own imagination are solid grounds for biblical and confident faith. If your missions budget were based on what I could afford, well that's simple: Round it up to zero dollars. If it were based on what I could "imagine," I don't know, I have a pretty active imagination—let's be conservative—put me down for 1.6 million dollars. Or I could just arbitrarily choose a number between the two, but then my giving would be based on the principles of lottery, not faith.

Rather, the exchange between Jesus and Martha provides a picture of the intimacy and reciprocation of the dance of faith: We communicate our hearts to God, and He communicates His desires to our heart, what He wants us to trust Him for. In John 11:21–27, Jesus and Martha are waltzing. Martha is no longer attempting to lead or trying to talk Jesus into something He doesn't wish to do.

She's responsive, anticipating His movements, allowing herself to be led by the Lord. She has no idea where the dance will lead, but her intimacy affords her the intuition of knowing the next step, knowing where it's headed.

Jesus desires to raise Lazarus from the dead, but He requires a nail of faith on which to hang the miracle. He is communicating to Martha what He desires to do so that she can supply the nail.

This communication makes all of the difference in the world. It means that Mary is not wrong in believing Lazarus to be irreversibly dead because Jesus has not told her any differently. To believe that Lazarus would rise without being informed of it by Jesus would be delusion, not faith. It would certainly not be wrong for Mary to ask Jesus to raise Lazarus; it would, however, be wrong for her to expect it. But at this point Jesus revealed His intentions to Martha, and it would be wrong for *her* to shrink back from believing. She is the recipient of the promise and therefore bears the responsibility of believing it. And it is the communicated promise that provides the reinforcement and rebar within the gelatin-like substance of faith.

Listen, I know how this is going to sound, but I can't help but say it anyway: "This reminds me of the time God raised my daughter from the dead."

Okay, I'll explain.

When my wife and I decided to have kids, we realized we couldn't. We never found out why, and my male ego would desperately like to believe it wasn't due to any lacking on my part. So we tried for several years, and though *trying* to have children isn't exactly back-breaking migrant work, it was still discouraging to come away with no baby for the effort.

One day, a week before we were scheduled for some tests, we discovered that Katie was pregnant. We were as thrilled as, well, parents expecting a child. But about six weeks into the pregnancy Katie was put on full-time bed rest due to complications. Things worsened, and a few days later Katie began bleeding and clotting so severely that there was only one thing that could explain it. When we called and described what had happened, the doctor told us it was a miscarriage and scheduled us to come down and complete an ultrasound to confirm it.

As we drove to the doctor's office, praying all the way, I felt this overwhelming sense that God was telling me to trust Him; I felt that He had the power to bring life from death. It was a strong desire to exert faith in Him. I wasn't pleading or asking Him to save the baby. I believed we had already received the final verdict, but I had this sense that "even now" God could do something about our state of affairs—I believed and felt confident that whatever the result, God could do anything, and I sensed He was going to do something.

As Katie sat in the chair having the ultrasound, I saw a puzzled look on the technician's face. She turned the monitor toward us and pointed to a little blinking light and said, "That's your baby's heart beat." We were surprised, sort of. Because of what happened on the drive there, I had come with a sense of expectation and confidence. It was a faith I couldn't have mustered if not for God's initiation and disclosure.

Katie and I had always liked the name Avery, so when our baby girl arrived in October of that year, we named her Avery. Sometime later, while shopping for names for our second child, I came across the name "Avery" in a book of baby names. It means to "confirm a promise." Pretty cool, no?

I am not saying that such communication and certitude is essential to our day-to-day walk of faith. For example, I just left this paragraph to drive my son to a friend's house. I did so prayerfully but I don't have a strong sense about it. I have not heard a voice from God, still, calm, or otherwise, nor do I need one. If my intuiting of God's direction turns out to have been wrong, I've wasted eighteen minutes, not a marriage or career. But all of us are engaged, or should be, in longer-range faith projects. If the Author of these faith projects is indeed God, then we should expect certain assurances, for how else is our faith to be sustained under great pressure and over vast duration? Put another way: If God provides us such promises, assurances, and certitude, then we're certainly going to need them.

We've seen that sometimes God's intention is to raise the dead, although our hearts may hold out to the bitter end praying for rescue or healing. We've seen that our faith must stretch in order to accommodate such a feat. We've also seen that waiting is one of the ways God stretches our faith. Whether you're Israel awaiting the Messiah, Noah awaiting the rain, or Martha awaiting Jesus' arrival, the battle of faith is fought in the *waiting*. Faith must choose to believe God's promises through the daily drip of the mundane, which can slowly erode at faith. What strengthens and fortifies faith in the midst of the struggle is the confidence that comes from the clearly communicated promises of God, be that from Scripture or those communicated through the intimacy of our personal walk.

This is the course in faith that Martha has just passed, and passed quite swimmingly. But the homework was abbreviated, so the question is this: Has Martha's faith stretched enough to believe Jesus will raise Lazarus? I would have said yes—poor girl's had a heck of a week. But Jesus knows otherwise. Such potent faith passes to us with the ease of a gallstone. And so Martha must stretch just a little bit further.

GROWING THROUGH DOUBT

> When Mary reached the place where Jesus was and saw him, she fell at his feet and said, "Lord, if you had been here, my brother would not have died." When Jesus saw her weeping, and the Jews who had come along with her also weeping, he was deeply moved in spirit and troubled. "Where have you laid him?" he asked. "Come and see, Lord," they replied. Jesus wept. Then the Jews said, "See how he loved him!" But some of them said, "Could not he who opened the eyes of the blind man have kept this man from dying?" ... "Take away the stone," he said. "But, Lord," said Martha, the sister of the dead man, "by this time there is a bad odor, for he has been there four days." Then Jesus said, "Did I not tell you that if you believed, you would see the glory of God?" (John 11:32–40)

Growing Doubts

Okay, picture this scenario in your mind: Jesus and the disciples finally show up four days after Martha and Mary originally sent word to Him. As verse 18 makes clear, Jesus was only two miles from Bethany, where Lazarus was. In other words, it would have been obvious to everyone that Jesus had been delayed for some reason or another.

So what happens when Jesus and His disciples show up? Wouldn't Martha or Mary or someone have asked, just as a matter of conversation, what had delayed them? I imagine an inquiry by Martha going something like this:

> Martha: "Was Jesus embroiled with the religious leaders in Jerusalem? Was that what kept you?"
>
> The disciples: "Uh, no."
>
> Martha: "I guess the crowds were keeping Jesus so occupied that He couldn't get away?"
>
> The disciples: "No. Not really."
>
> Martha: "Was it the sick? Was He overwhelmed having to heal them all?"
>
> The disciples: "No, not that we recall."
>
> Martha: "So what took Him so long?"
>
> The disciples: "Nothing. After we got your request we just kind of hung around Jerusalem for a few days before coming here."
>
> Martha: "What?"

Something to this effect must have surely taken place, for the passage tells us that accusations were spreading concerning Jesus, that His love and commitment to Lazarus (and Mary and Martha by implication) were not what they appeared. "Could not he who opened the eyes of the blind man have kept this man from dying?" See, the problem with this question is that the answer is, "Yes, He most certainly could have." This is hard to swallow: a large uncooked piece of meat that Martha's faith will have to digest and metabolize if she is to overcome the doubts that it raises.

If you're Martha, you've been struggling for days with grief, as well as faith, clutching desperately to the hope that Jesus can, and will, do something. But what is her confidence based on? It's based on the belief that Jesus loves and cares for her—but all the rumors and gossip needle at Martha's confidence in the goodness of Jesus, the very thing she's been using as a personal flotation device. And hope does not float; it sinks like a rock if it is left with nothing to cling to.

Growth through Doubt

But doubt and confusion aren't always irrevocably negative entities. In fact, they provide the resistance that causes faith to grow.

Faith is like a muscle. And as any adolescent male could tell you, muscle grows by lifting weights. The resistance of the weight forces the muscle to expand and grow in order to accommodate the strain. Resistance creates strength, mass, and resilience in the muscle—*eventually*. Weight lifting actually breaks down the muscle only so that it can rebuild in a form that more amply fills out a T-shirt.

Doubt and confusion are the barbells of faith. Pressing down upon faith are the weighty doubts of, "God is absent. He doesn't care. He's forgotten me. His plans are to hurt and punish me." Faith has to bench-press these off the chest so the weight doesn't crush the heart. The conscious decisions to reckon and act in light of faith, and not doubt, are the repetitions that build the muscle of faith.

Doubt gains traction when God seems nowhere to be found; confusion presides when He *is* found, but in a way contrary or disturbing to our sensibilities. Both are essential to the growth of faith. When God wants to produce a great man or woman of faith, He typically throws them into a jail cell without explanation and pretends to lose the key. *Nice work, Paul! Go to jail. Great choice, Joseph! Go to jail. Well done, Jeremiah! Go to jail. Good work, Isaiah! Go sit in a cistern!*

There, in the dark, isolated, confused, and apparently forgotten, faith has nothing else to do but go out to the "yard" in its orange jumpsuit and pump iron with the other inmates: "God does have a plan for me. God hasn't forgotten me. This isn't a punishment. God will rescue me."

Here is where the promises and truths of God become prison tattoos, permanent and inseparable parts of us. We own God's goodness because we've had to fight every hour of every day to believe it when everything around us screamed that it wasn't true. By the time we get our civilian clothes back and the door to the outside world swings open, God's prisoner emerges as a muscle-bound behemoth, barely squeezing through the door jam—*spiritually speaking.* And it is through such a muscular faith that God can lift or raise anything He so desires: a marriage, a church, a ministry, an addict, a family, a career.

This prison cell of doubt and confusion can be a literal prison, as it has been and still is for many persecuted believers, or it can be taken figuratively for those extended periods of spiritual dryness; mental, social, or spiritual isolation; spiritual oppression and attack; constraining circumstances; depression; or emotional bondage—and the list could go on. The results are the same whether it's an actual prison, one of our own making, or even the four walls of our own mind.

I think John the Baptist's experience attests to the fact that no one is exempt from the jail cell of doubt and confusion. Though Jesus provides this endorsement of him, "Among those born of women there is no one greater than John" (Luke 7:28), John himself begins to capitulate to doubt, needing additional confirmation of Jesus' identity. He asks Jesus, "Are you the one who was to come, or should we expect someone else?" (Luke 7:20). It's a trifle unsettling to see the greatest of those born to a woman lose his faith and confidence to the inquisition of doubt.

God clearly allows the presence of doubt and confusion in our lives since even the smallest sign or communication from Him would send them packing, and yet He withholds such signs. He does so for our growth and for our good. But this does not guarantee that every dear soul emerges from this prison, spiritually sane and clothed in his or her right mind. The work of faith must be done daily, hourly, and it must persevere, or Satan will surely use it for evil. The battle of faith is real and so are its causalities.

Endure!

Jesus, no stranger to torment, sent along assurance to John that he might endure his stay in the dark: "Go back and report to John what you have seen and heard: The blind receive sight, the lame walk, those who have leprosy are cured, the deaf hear, the dead are raised, and the good news is preached to the poor" (Luke 7:22).

Jesus does the same for Martha, repeating again His promise and intent: "Did I not tell you that if you believed, you would see the glory of God?" (John 11:40).

In the Batman movie *The Dark Knight*, Bruce Wayne, played by Christian Bale, wrestles with self-doubt and stands on the brink of both revealing and renouncing his hidden identity. In his struggle with doubt and confusion, he asks his mentor and confidante, Alfred (played by Michael Cain), "What would you have me do?" To which Alfred replies, "Endure, Master Wayne. Take it."

Confusion and doubt paralyze. We know we should do something about our situation, but what? What we are to *do* is endure. Jesus wants Martha to endure in her faith; He wants us to endure because "the testing of [our] faith develops perseverance. Perseverance must finish its work so that [we] may be mature and complete, not lacking anything" (James 1:3–4).

CHAPTER SEVEN

WELCOME BACK

"Lazarus, come out…. Take off the grave clothes and let him go." If you ponder these words and, as typographer Massimo Vignelli suggests, you notice the white space between the letters, you should see the shapes of your own salvation: the time that Christ summoned you out from the spiritually dead to be alive with Him.

What we share in common as believers, we also share with Lazarus: We were all raised from the dead. The resurrection of our own salvation was no less staggering—indeed more so—than the physical raising of Lazarus.

The growth of faith is not learning something new, but living out in the day-to-day what we have already experienced, and what we already know to be true, every day. Maturity in the Christian life is the wisdom of the aged coupled to the faith of a child. The Christian life is learning more and more about Christ while unlearning self-sufficiency. As our faith matures, grows, and stretches, it regains some of its youthful elasticity.

The challenge of faith is to take the great object lesson of our salvation, our own personal resurrection, and to apply it in every area of our life, to experience the gospel every day.

RECEIVING BACK THE DEAD

> *So they took away the stone. Then Jesus looked up and said, "Father, I thank you that you have heard me. I knew that you always hear me, but I said this for the benefit of the people standing here, that they may believe that you sent me." When he had said this, Jesus called in a loud voice, "Lazarus, come out!" The dead man came out, his hands and feet wrapped with strips of linen, and a cloth around his face. Jesus said to them, "Take off the grave clothes and let him go." Therefore many of the Jews who had come to visit Mary, and had seen what Jesus did, put their faith in him. (John 11:41–45)*

The Victory of Faith

It's easy to skip over the emotions attending this miracle. Familiar with the outcome, sometimes we can greet Lazarus emerging from his tomb with the same awe and wonder we give the Punxsutawney groundhog emerging to check its shadow. This miracle was so potent that John tells us, in an easily missed footnote, that "the chief priests made plans to kill Lazarus as well, for on account of him many of the Jews were going over to Jesus and putting their faith in him" (John 12:10–11).

The raising of Lazarus sparked jealousy and anger in Jesus' enemies, and awe, wonder, and faith in His followers. Yet amidst the festive array of colorful emotions and reactions, Martha was alone in her experience of victory and relief—it's finished! Jesus said the miracle would be predicated on Martha's faith, and she endured even as her faith was pinched, pulled, and kneaded, providing the raw ingredients to bring Lazarus back.

ABRAHAM, FATHER OF FAITH

It's strange to say that anything about raising the dead is normative, or standard operating procedure. But in the relatively few narratives of the dead being raised in Scripture, faith-stretching is standard practice. We see it in the raising of Lazarus and in the raising of Jarius' daughter. I think if we look closely, we can spot it in the account of Abraham when he trusted God to bring his son Isaac back from the dead, figuratively speaking:

> *By faith Abraham, when God tested him, offered Isaac as a sacrifice. He who had received the promises was about to sacrifice his one and only son, even though God had said to him, "It is through Isaac that your offspring will be reckoned." Abraham reasoned that God could raise the dead, and figuratively speaking, he did receive Isaac back from death. (Heb. 11:17–19)*

Picture Abraham's journey up Mount Moriah to sacrifice his son Isaac as the Lord had requested. As Abraham loads up his donkey and sets out with Isaac, he tells his servants that, *"We* will worship and then *we* will come back to you" (Gen. 22:5).

In this single line, the writer of Hebrews has ascribed faith to Abraham. Though Abraham knows he's been called to ascend the mountain to sacrifice Isaac, he firmly believes that Isaac will accompany him on his return. He has no idea how God will do this, but he does believe it will happen. We know this much from the text.

But what we don't know is the myriad thoughts that must have been buzzing in Abraham's mind as he made his journey, and here I shall engage in some conjecture.

I would imagine that as Abraham heads up Mount Moriah he is looking—by faith—for the divine vehicle through which both he and his son will return. Abraham has walked with God for many years and knows him as his "deliverer," his "protector," and his "provider." By this I mean Abraham has experienced, on more than one occasion, God's deliverance, protection, and provision. And so on his ascent up the mountain, Abraham's eyes are probably darting about and scanning the horizon for deliverance as they've been trained to do. But as the boy and the father get closer to the top of the mountain, the number of possible ways by which Abraham might have imagined God rescuing him have begun to dwindle. Options have narrowed considerably. He may well have hoped the exercise would have been called off long before he reached the top, and yet here he is, on the top of the mountain with his son and a knife. Yet he's still walking by faith.

> Isaac spoke up and said to his father Abraham, "Father?" "Yes, my son?" Abraham replied. "The fire and wood are here," Isaac said, "but where is the lamb for the burnt offering?" Abraham answered, "God himself will provide the lamb for the burnt offering, my son." And the two of them went on together. (Gen. 22:7–8)

When Abraham says, "God himself will provide the lamb," he is either continuing to express faith that God will intervene, or he's being intentionally vague and deceptive in order to keep Isaac in the dark. I don't believe Abraham is trying to deceive Isaac. This isn't the story of Hansel and Gretel, where the children are intentionally deluded so they'll walk quietly into the oven. The emphasis on "God himself will provide" signifies a confidence that provision is forthcoming. The next verse finds Abraham hog-tying Isaac on the altar. Come on. How clueless do you think Isaac was? I think Abraham still believed what he said—even in that moment he believed that God would provide.

So as Abraham arranges the wood on the altar and binds his son to the heartless stone, God's intervention must have become increasingly difficult to imagine.

But there's still hope, still faith, still a chance that God will avert what now seems inevitable. There's still a chance, until Abraham raises the knife to twelve o'clock. Now all the alternatives have narrowed to one. It's at this point that Abraham's faith makes a leap. It's irrelevant at this millisecond if God can save, protect, deliver, or heal. If Isaac is to descend the mountain with Abraham, it will only be because God is the God who raises the dead. And he believes it. At that moment "Abraham reasoned that God could raise the dead, and figuratively speaking, he did receive Isaac back from death" (Heb. 11:19).

This leap of faith can be clocked fairly precisely to the moment that Abraham raised the knife. God's actions flow with Newtonian economy: excess energy neither gained nor lost. If Abraham raised the knife, then Abraham needed to raise the knife. This was the extreme measure required to push the limits of his faith over a cliff, removing all boundaries and limitations. At that moment faith and circumstances were irreconcilable, much as they were when Martha went running out to meet Jesus. *Almost irreconcilable.* Both could be retained if and only if God is the God who raises the dead, if Isaac and Lazarus could die and yet live. And this is what happened.

> But the angel of the LORD called out to him from heaven, "Abraham! Abraham!" "Here I am," he replied. "Do not lay a hand on the boy," he said. "Do not do anything to him. Now I know that you fear God, because you have not withheld from me your son, your only son." Abraham looked up and there in a thicket he saw a ram caught by its horns. He went over and took the ram and sacrificed it as a burnt offering instead of his son. (Gen. 22:11–13)

To say that Abraham's faith was significant is like saying the death of Christ was useful. Adjectives cannot convey the far-reaching effects of Abraham's choice to reckon "that God could raise the dead."

> The angel of the LORD called to Abraham from heaven a second time and said, "I swear by myself, declares the LORD, that because you have done this and have not withheld your son, your only son, I will surely bless you and make your descendants as numerous as the stars in the sky and as the sand on the seashore. Your descendants will take possession of the cities of their enemies,

*and through your offspring all nations on earth will be
blessed, because you have obeyed me." (Gen. 22:15–18)*

The results of this kind of faith in the kingdom of God always seem to be massive. What is often overlooked is the impact of Martha's resurrection faith, which left its own not-so-insignificant dent in redemptive history.

*Meanwhile a large crowd of Jews found out that Jesus
was there and came, not only because of him but also
to see Lazarus, whom he had raised from the dead. So
the chief priests made plans to kill Lazarus as well, for
on account of him many of the Jews were going over to
Jesus and putting their faith in him. Now the crowd that
was with him when he called Lazarus from the tomb
and raised him from the dead continued to spread the
word. Many people, because they had heard that he had
given this miraculous sign, went out to meet him. So
the Pharisees said to one another, "See, this is getting
us nowhere. Look how the whole world has gone after
him!" (John 12:9–11, 17–19)*

RESURRECTION RESULTS

In the movie *Field of Dreams,* Iowa farmer Ray Kinsella (Kevin Costner) hears a strange voice, its meaning uncertain: "If you build it, he will come." Against all reason, Ray listens to the voice. As the voice bids him to plow his cornfield under and create a baseball diamond, Ray willingly and blindly surrenders life, livelihood, and the appearance of sanity to build it. Though certainly not intended as one, it would be hard to find a better metaphor for the life of faith. Unfortunately the metaphor breaks down when we find out the voice is coming from the ghost of a shoeless baseball player named Joe Jackson.

In a heart-tugging scene at the end of the movie, Ray thanks Shoeless Joe for having come to play on the field that faith built, and Jackson looks at Kinsella and says, "No, thank you, Ray," for without Ray's journey of faith there would be no field, no game, no baseball in that place.

With assurance from Jesus that "if she builds it, He will come," Martha, through her faith, builds a field for Lazarus, but not Lazarus alone—her friends, family, village, and a good bit of Israel. As John 12:11 says, "For on account of [Lazarus] many of the Jews were going over to Jesus and putting their faith in him." Indeed, the effects of the miracle and Martha's faith continue to ripple out from Scripture, as the Pharisees pronunciation, "Look how the whole world has gone after [Jesus]," was rather prophetic.

So was all the convulsive twisting and wrenching and stretching of faith worth it? In detailing the results of the miracle, Scripture demonstrates the answer is yes. When death is swallowed by faith, God transforms it into life—and the life that emerges is directly proportional to the amount of death swallowed and the faith it took to consume it. In no place is this proportionality more visible than in the cross, which translates the death of mankind into life eternal for all who believe in Him. The raising of Lazarus took enormous faith but the results were commensurate.

Even if no one came to Christ or was outwardly affected, it would still be worth every drop of faith spilled. Why? Because it pleases God.

The days of Jesus' ministry were amazing, so it comes as little surprise that the word *amazed*, or some derivative of it, is used roughly forty times in the gospels—only two of which are ascribed to Jesus, and they both concern faith:

> *He was not far from the house when the centurion sent friends to say to him: "Lord, don't trouble yourself, for I do not deserve to have you come under my roof. That is why I did not even consider myself worthy to come to you. But say the word, and my servant will be healed. For I myself am a man under authority, with soldiers under me. I tell this one, 'Go,' and he goes; and that one, 'Come,' and he comes. I say to my servant, 'Do this,' and he does it." When Jesus heard this, he was amazed at him, and turning to the crowd following him, he said, "I tell you, I have not found such great faith even in Israel." (Luke 7:2–9)*

> *Jesus said to them, "Only in his hometown, among his relatives and in his own house is a prophet without honor." He could not do any miracles there except lay his hands on a few sick people and heal them. And he was amazed at their lack of faith. (Mark 6:4–6)*

Both instances of Jesus' amazement are emotional reactions to faith (or a lack of faith): Jesus stood amazed at the faith possessed by a Roman centurion and the apparent lack of it in His own home-town. We walk by faith to please Jesus, indeed to amaze Jesus.

THE DEATH IN FAITH

In an attempt to avoid excess or unintended consequences, allow me to clarify: I'm not saying that Jesus always wants to perform resurrection in our lives. I'm not saying that just because something dies we should assume it's because God wants to raise it back to life. In fact we should assume that death is God's answer to our request unless we hear otherwise from Him. While I do not doubt God's ability to raise the dead, I believe our experience of "resurrection" is intended to be far less ostentatious and far more organic (though no less miraculous), such as God bringing a dead friendship, dream, hope, church, marriage, vision, or career back to life.

But as Jesus could find only one worthy candidate with which to perform this miracle, it seems to me that it is entirely possible that there is much God desires to do, but doesn't, because of the lack—or immaturity—of our faith: "And he did not do many miracles there because of their lack of faith" (Matt. 13:58).

It is God's desire to lead us along on a faith-stretching journey, one that will, at times, entail waiting, confusion, and doubt. Over time we will come to experience the Lord as our rescuer, provider, comforter, protector, defender, and strength in very deep, tangible, and meaningful ways. But this is not the end of the journey. At some point God will seek to reveal Himself to us as the One who raises the dead. And once we've come to see God in this way, we will never see anything as necessarily dead or final until Jesus says it is. We will have a faith that God can call on for any and every good work. This is the death in faith.

SECTION THREE
THE LIFE
OF MARTYRS

CHAPTER EIGHT

THE DEATH IN WITNESS

The author of the English *Book of Common Prayer*, which is still used by Episcopalians today, was a man named Thomas Cranmer. He was a leading figure during the English Reformation and had the dubious distinction of serving as archbishop of Canterbury during the reign of King Henry VIII.

When Queen Mary I, also known as Bloody Mary, took the throne in 1553, she brought Catholicism back to England, which logically meant Protestantism needed to be disposed of. Among her first initiatives to that end was to arrest the leaders of England's Protestant movement, and this included Thomas Cranmer. She ordered Cranmer to sign a confession and recant of all his teachings. Though for a while he was able to dance around the issues and postpone his execution, in the end, Cranmer complied. On February 24, 1556, broken in body and spirit, he wrote out a complete and thorough recantation repudiating all he had believed and taught. He fully embraced Catholicism, including the pope, and stated that there was no salvation outside the Catholic Church. Cranmer was a beaten man—*or so it seemed.*

His recantation, however, didn't earn him a reprieve from execution, and he was given the opportunity to make his confession public before he burned at the stake. So there he is, standing at the pulpit with everyone expecting this somber apology, and Cranmer *goes off.* He renounced his recantations, lambasted the pope, and announced that the first thing to burn in the pyre would be his hand for writing the coerced confession. They yanked him from the pulpit and hauled him away.

True to his word, as the flames plumed around him, he jabbed his right hand into the heart of the flame and expired with these final words: "Lord Jesus, receive my spirit.... I see the heavens open and Jesus standing at the right hand of God."

I was in Staples some time ago and the guy behind the counter had the name Thomas Cranmer on his name tag. I asked him, "Are you related to the famous martyr?"

"What martyr?"

"Thomas Cranmer."

"Who's that?"

"I'm guessing one of your relatives."

"Huh. Never heard of him."

"Perhaps your parents named you after him."

"I dunno, they never mentioned it.... Do you have a Staples Card?"

Thomas Cranmer is no doubt in heaven along with his reward,

his recognition, and I hope a little more respect than he gets at Staples these days.

It's easy to forget our lineage, the long line of martyrs from whence we came. Yet not one of us would have the gospel if someone in the not too distant past wasn't willing to pay a price to make sure we got it.

Death and *evangelism* have been bound together since the beginning of Christianity—inseparable, inescapable. It's in the blueprint: Jesus came "preaching the good news of the kingdom, and healing every disease and sickness among the people" (Matt. 4:23), and He was killed for it.

Since the commissioning of the very first missionaries, disciples have gone forth believing the best, yet expecting the worst:

> But be on your guard. For they will deliver you over to councils, and you will be beaten in synagogues, and you will stand before governors and kings for my sake, to bear witness before them. And the gospel must first be proclaimed to all nations. And when they bring you to trial and deliver you over, do not be anxious beforehand what you are to say, but say whatever is given you in that hour, for it is not you who speak, but the Holy Spirit. (Mark 13:9–11 ESV)

In His teaching, Jesus would often use hyperbole to sharpen His point: There is not a "splinter" in our eye that needs removing, rather an entire "plank" sticking out like a diving board. Perhaps His disciples secretly hoped that all of the cryptic talk about being "arrested" or "handed over" was just classic Jesus hyperbole—you know, Jesus*isms*.

It wasn't. Jesus' descriptions were actually understatements, as Jesus informs them they'll be "handed over" but doesn't tell them to *what*, or to *whom*. The "what" and the "whom" would include lions, crucifixion, gladiators, torture, stoning, burning, and beheading, but no need to get bogged down in details they'd discover soon enough. So gruesome, in fact, was the treatment of the early Christians that the Greek word for "witness" (*marturion*) became synonymous with death, giving us our word *martyr. Martyr* equals *witness.*

But the semantic migration of the word *witness* into *martyr* isn't merely historical irony; it's precisely how Jesus meant for *witness* to be defined. It is how He Himself defined the role: Witnesses are willing to die (even if they are never called on to do so) proclaiming the truth so that others may live.

> But before all this they will lay their hands on you and persecute you, delivering you up to the synagogues and prisons, and you will be brought before kings and governors for my name's sake. This will be your opportunity to bear witness. (Luke 21:12–13 ESV)

> And I will grant authority to my two witnesses, and they will prophesy for 1,260 days, clothed in sackcloth.... And when they have finished their testimony, the beast that rises from the bottomless pit will make war on them and conquer them and kill them, and their dead bodies will lie in the street of the great city that

> *symbolically is called Sodom and Egypt, where their*
> *Lord was crucified. (Rev. 11:3, 7–8 ESV)*

The church has grown and the gospel has gone to the nations through the steady march of witnesses, beginning with the disciples.

THE THEORY OF MARTYRDOM

As followers of Christ, we've all heard stories about, and recognize the potential for, martyrdom … at least in theory. Few of us have ever faced the possibility of dying as a result of our witness. I never have. At least that I know of. Perhaps I've foisted myself on some unwilling listener and while pontificating them into submission, they've secretly schemed to bludgeon me with a shoe or puncture my voice box with a pen.

Actually, there was a time when I thought I might die, but it turned out that the only present danger was my paranoia. When I used to work in New York City, I commuted home at night from Grand Central Station. Back then, Grand Central became Mayberry Central after midnight, as it was virtually vacant, with trains running only every other hour.

So there, in a secluded narthex of (yet to be renovated) Grand Central Station, at two in the morning, I sat among the homeless sleeping on the benches. Shortly after I sat down, a man the size of a mountain—wearing mechanic's coveralls, the casual attire of serial killers—sat down next to me. And I mean right next to me—you couldn't swipe an ATM card between us.

He proceeded to pull out a badly folded piece of paper from his pocket and, for whatever reason, told me that it was his prison release papers and that he had just gotten out of prison a few weeks ago. He was older—about forty-five—which, as I quickly did the math, meant he might have served a sentence of fifteen to twenty years. *Hmm,* I thought, *I wonder what crime you gotta commit before they give you fifteen to twenty years.*

I remembered I had a gospel booklet in my bag, and I somewhat frantically pulled it out. Besides fear, I remember feeling compassion, though it would not be inaccurate to say that I was using evangelism as self-defense, figuring that if he had some kind of church background he'd be less likely to kill me. I mean, if you kill a minister you'd probably get … fifteen to twenty years.

I asked him if I could go through the booklet with him. I don't think he spoke, just nodded, but I could be remembering this much creepier than it actually was. The first Bible verse I read from the booklet was John 3:16, "For God so loved the world," and he pointed to the verse with his bear claw of a hand and said, "That verse … that verse and the Lord are the only things that kept me going in prison all these years."

He then called over some of the other homeless people from other benches, and had me keep reading the booklet, but louder so everyone could hear. When I finished reading, they all began to talk about Jesus, and one of them pulled out a bottle of gin and said, "Let's have communion together." This was not the time to point out aberrant theology, or even to wipe the mouth of the bottle before drinking from it. Such moments allow you to view your convictions on such matters with crystal clarity—apparently I don't have any.

Apparently I was never in danger at all. In fact, surrounded by my new entourage of disciples, I'd probably never been safer. As my own dear mother, whom I allowed to read the manuscript of this book, wondered if I might be embellishing this story just a bit, I feel the need to affirm to you that this—no joke—is exactly what happened.

The truth is, most of us have never faced the threat of violence or physical death in proclaiming the gospel and most likely never will. This can leave us feeling quite removed from the whole notion of martyrdom and even excluded from the great company of saints, but not because we have a narrow view of evangelism. I think the problem is that we have a narrow view of death.

THE DEATH IN EVANGELISM

Just as the concept of love is not reducible to a wedding, the concept of death is much bigger than a funeral. This is the point I've been trying very hard to make. If we can stretch our understanding and see death more broadly, more dynamically, and more biblically, I think we'll find that we've already experienced a form of death in some of our attempts to share Christ and be His witnesses. A martyr's death is simply a larger-than-life example of what it means to live as a witness, which necessitates that our ego, reputation, dignity, and status continually brush up against death in our efforts to give testimony to Christ.

What is it that makes evangelism so difficult? *The possibility of rejection.* And what does rejection feel like? It feels like a small death: the crippling of our pride, our reputations being dragged through the mud, our egos deflated, our feelings hurt, our confidence wounded. And in a sense, dear friends, this is how we all get to be martyrs.

I'll begin by narrating a recent experience I had when sharing my faith—a sort of director's cut with commentary, allowing me to point to the ways in which death is at work even in an ordinary, nonviolent, evangelistic encounter.

Dying in the USA

Recently we called a plumber in to fix a toilet in our home. The toilet, for some scientific reason beyond my grasp, would not flush correctly. As a man, it's always difficult to have someone come into your home to fix your stuff; it's sort of an indictment of your manhood. You stand around feeling like a boy, wondering if you should hand the workman his tools like he's your dad fixing your go-cart. A hundred dollars an hour is not enough to assuage white-collar guilt.

So as he worked on the toilet, I hung around the bathroom, and we naturally began to talk about sports. It was a wonderfully manly conversation, and if he harbored any ill will regarding my lack of testosterone to fix my own toilet, it certainly didn't show. He genuinely seemed to like me, and vice versa.

Whenever we experience feelings of acceptance, admiration, or affection we, in effect, experience the sensations of life rummaging through us: motivation, energy, positive sense of self, and the like. Once you've experienced that caffeinated jolt of life from a conversation, or friend, or relationship, it's difficult to turn from it—it makes us clingy. The stronger the connection—the more life reverberating through it—the more difficult it is to sever.

As we continued to talk, the plumber eventually asked what I did for a living, and I told him I was in ministry. Since I already knew what he did for a living, a natural segue for me was to ask him about his spiritual background, or where he went to church, or something pastoral like that.

But let's pause, because this choice to begin moving the conversation toward the gospel has some implications. The choice to point the discussion in a spiritual direction—*toward Christ*—typically involves a *willingness* to sever an emotional, or relational, connection, a willingness to cut yourself off from a source of life. Hmm … this sounds similar to the definition of death. *Precisely.* In a small but significant way, it is a death—at least in the emotional, social, and relational sense. If in just under thirty minutes I had an IV line dripping life into my soul from a visiting plumber, how much greater is that lifeline flowing to me through friends, family members, or coworkers? How much greater the risk? Anyway, the risk seemed bloody real enough even with the plumber, and yet the dying of my dignity wasn't over.

The next problem we encounter in sharing our faith is that there's no seamless or easy way to transition to the gospel that will allow you to retain either your dignity or the other person's admiration and respect. Once you're down on one knee holding out the engagement ring, you can't pretend your shoe is untied. You're fully committed. And once you move from nebulous chatter about feeling "blessed" and "all things happen for a reason" to actually talking about Jesus—well, you simply must regard your reputation as a casualty should that person reject it.

Seriously, what sort of silky transition could you possibly devise to share Christ with the plumber? Maybe something like, "Just as there are four rolls of toilet paper in a package of Charmin, so there are four spiritual laws?" or, "Just as there is refuse that clogs this toilet, so our lives are a cesspool of sin that only God can flush"? There's just no way to normalize it. Often times it *is* weird to share the gospel, and you can't always create the illusion that it's not.

Now, we could lament the irrationality of this, how silly it is that talking about spiritual things should be so weird when people talk so candidly about politics and sex and nervous breakdowns. But what would be the point? The answer is both simple and obvious: We are in a spiritual battle, and Satan has made it this way. *It simply is.* Mention Jesus in a crowded elevator and it's transformed into a dentist's waiting room: The tension is palpable. There exists, at least in this country, a powerful emotional and spiritual wall that everyone senses, and it doesn't go away by observing that it shouldn't logically be there. Our struggle is not against illogical social norms, but against spiritual powers that have created an invisible wall. This elevates the degree of sacrifice, the risk of reputational loss involved in evangelism—and that's the intent. Satan knows precisely what we fear; he's the Wicked Witch of the West, and he's saying, "How about a little fire, scarecrow!"

But if you can't ignore it or pretend it's not there, how do you transcend the powerful social and spiritual barriers to sharing the gospel? The answer is this: You willingly walk into the wall knowing it could knock you senseless, that people may snicker at the spectacle, and that you may be left with the dignity of Benny Hill. We all have a public or social self, an inflatable "us" that everyone sees, and it's a painful thing to have our bubbles burst in public. If a person is not interested in talking about God or knowing Christ, how can he not think you're foolish? In that person's mind you have an imaginary friend.

The plumber thought that I was a great guy. But if I was to talk to him about Christ, I had to anticipate that if his heart is hard, he was going to think I was peculiar, ignorant, unstable, needy, deluded, or … take your pick. Unless, of course, his heart was open to the gospel, in which case I would have become the most blessed person he's ever had the fortune to meet.

But we're not done yet. Before the clock tolls and the evangelistic opportunity expires, there are yet a few more opportunities for our ego to turn into a pumpkin. What if the person asks questions we don't know the answer to? What if we get tongue-tied? That could be, um … what's the word … *humiliating.* What happens if the conversation takes place between you and a family member or a good friend, and afterward, your relationship isn't the same?

When you expand the definition of death to include emotional, relational, or social death; the death of a career or academic advancement; the death of your reputation, your respect, your influence, or your authority; the death of a friendship or social circle—this is when you realize that it isn't necessary to move to Algeria in order to be a martyr.

SUCCESSFUL WITNESSES

If you're curious about the encounter with the plumber, he wasn't much interested in talking about God or faith or prayer—or anything, for that matter, except the Philadelphia Eagles. As both a Christian *and* a New York Giants fan, that pretty much shut the door on our conversation.

I include the results because we are naturally interested in how any story ends, especially one about salvation. But if you review all the places in the gospels where Jesus prepared His disciples for the missionary enterprise, you'll notice something quite odd: Rejection and mistreatment *were* the expected results.

Whenever you are arrested and brought to trial, do not worry beforehand about what to say. Just say whatever is given you at the time, for it is not you speaking, but the Holy Spirit. (Mark 13:11)

If people do not welcome you, shake the dust off your feet when you leave their town, as a testimony against them. (Luke 9:5)

Then you will be handed over to be persecuted and put to death, and you will be hated by all nations because of me. (Matt. 24:9)

If the world hates you, keep in mind that it hated me first. (John 15:18)

This should redefine how we view a successful witness. We are pragmatic to a fault. How do you know if you're doing something right? If it works, if people respond, revenue goes up, call centers get inundated, focus groups approve. But in Jesus' many words about evangelism, the responsiveness of the audience is never mentioned as a metric of success. Rather, He affirms that when people reject us (and therefore the gospel), we are being successful witnesses, faithfully proclaiming the truth, refusing to compromise it.

As life is always entwined with death, there is a joy unique to the experience of sharing one's faith. The truth we believe seems truer, the good news better—the bread of life stays fresh as long as we're ripping off hunks and feeding it to others. But Satan is a thief, and there's nothing he loves to steal more than our joy. It is the greatest of tragedies that, having risked the death of our reputation, we should feel like failures because the person didn't believe or responded negatively. Jesus wants us to know that the success of witnessing lies in the telling, not in the response; the success lies in the willingness to die, *not* the willingness of the listener.

Apart from people coming to Christ, our witness has immeasurable value to God. Telling others about the good news is a vehicle of worship, a public declaration of our love for Him, and a demonstration of our willingness to suffer for that love. Sacrifice is the ultimate expression of devotion.

And here's a mind bender: The more negative the response, the more pure and potent the devotion. The greater the rejection and personal sacrifice we endure, the greater the act of worship. When we see someone respond and come to Christ, our joy is, to some degree, mingled with the results. When no one comes to Christ, our joy is solely in the act of worship, our satisfaction only in obedience. When the gospel is rejected, faith continues to flow when we choose to believe that God's Word will not return void, that He will still use it in that person's life. When someone responds to the gospel, faith moves on to pick another fight, as victory is clearly in sight.

SAY ANYTHING

The words *witness* and *evangelism* are often used interchangeably; I've used them this way throughout this chapter. And while these concepts overlap, I think there's value in drawing a distinction in emphasis. In evangelism, the emphasis falls upon communication: proclaiming the good news of Jesus Christ and proclaiming it boldly and clearly, "in season and out of season" (Acts 19:8; Col. 4:4; 2 Tim. 4:2). In being a witness, the emphasis is upon our identification as followers of Christ: "He who listens to you listens to me; he who rejects you rejects me; but he who rejects me rejects him who sent me" (Luke 10:16).

To be a successful witness is to be willingly identified as a follower of Jesus. It's a simple test, no studying required. As success in witnessing is not based upon results, neither is it assessed by how clear or compelling our presentation of the gospel. Therefore it's quite possible to be a successful witness but a lousy evangelist (in the communication sense of the word). Being a witness is required of every follower and is therefore something every follower can do.

Failure as a witness, however, is an unwillingness to be identified as a follower of Christ. Also a simple test. Scripture's label for this failure is "ashamed." Either we are willing to be identified with Jesus or we're ashamed to be associated with Him. The concept of being ashamed speaks to the willful choice not to be seen with Jesus" However, if you have feelings of fear and humiliation, this does not mean that you are ashamed of the gospel; the difficult feelings are part of what makes our witness a most precious sacrifice.

Jesus knew that fear for our lives would incline us to disassociation, and for this reason we find stern warnings that our love relationship with Him is not to be hidden and hushed-up like an illicit affair. Jesus is not Marilyn Monroe. In the economy of words that is the gospel of Luke, the writer repeats Jesus' warning, presumably because Jesus repeated the warning.

If anyone is ashamed of me and my words, the Son of Man will be ashamed of him when he comes in his glory and in the glory of the Father and of the holy angels. (Luke 9:26)

Don't be afraid; you are worth more than many sparrows. I tell you, whoever acknowledges me before men, the Son of Man will also acknowledge him before the angels of God. But he who disowns me before men will be disowned before the angels of God. (Luke 12:7–9)

Some time ago around Easter, I spoke at a campus on the topic of evidence of the resurrection. On that particular campus there is a large student ministry as well as a significant faculty fellowship, somewhere between seventy to eighty Christian professors, provosts, and university workers. Being a Christian in the academic world is not exactly a career booster, as it signals to the magistrates a view of the world less than wide-open and more than atoms and molecules. It can, in fact, be a career-ender. Which is why it was no small thing when I asked the Christian faculty to occupy the front rows of the lecture, to stand at the conclusion, and then to be willing to talk to anyone who came to the front with questions.

I wasn't asking them to be evangelists, just witnesses willing to be identified as followers of Jesus Christ. I don't know if all of them came, but many of them did. At the end of the presentation I asked the professors to stand, then invited anyone with questions to seek out one of the faculty. And stand they did, willingly and faithfully in front of their academic community, declaring their love for Jesus even though it could have meant the loss of reputation, tenure, publication, salary, position, job, or what amounts to death in the academic community.

As the event wrapped up and the audience trickled out, the faculty remained, talking among themselves. They were ecstatic, wired by a spiritual adrenaline rush, a special grace reserved for martyrs: "But you will receive power when the Holy Spirit comes on you; and you will be my witnesses" (Acts 1:8). They said, "We need to do this again." The Christian students had been just as excited. You could hear them say things like, "I never knew she was a believer; I had her for English my freshman year." I'll tell you, it was no small thing for the students to see one of the deans of the university stand to answer questions about his faith in Jesus Christ.

They were, each one of them, successful witnesses. They did all that God could have asked from them, and that "all" was being willing to be identified with their Savior. As I listened to some of the conversations that played out, I'm not sure how I would rank them as apologists or evangelists. In most cases, the faculty simply professed a love for Jesus and not much more. But I ask you, what's wrong with that? The answer is "absolutely nothing" when you see that there is value in witness beyond conversion. Hopefully it's been both encouraging and cathartic to acknowledge the personal risks and sacrifices organic to evangelism, if for no other reason than it's an honest accounting of what many of us have experienced for years as we share Christ—"Hi, my name is Rick, and I am one of evangelism's silent victims. Hear my screams."

Far from being ashamed of these social disasters and public embarrassments, it's cause for celebration. Note the honor and privilege that's ascribed to paying a price for the sake of Jesus and the gospel. Witnesses are fools in love:

> *The apostles left the Sanhedrin, rejoicing because they had been counted worthy of suffering disgrace for the Name. (Acts 5:41)*

> *For it has been granted to you on behalf of Christ not only to believe on him, but also to suffer for him. (Phil. 1:29)*

Recognizing the risk and sacrifice in evangelism allows us to see that even for us (the unpersecuted church), proclaiming the gospel involves a willingness to die. And even if our words are welcomed or received well, or the experience turns out to be just plain enjoyable, well, we certainly couldn't have known that going in, and thus we *were* ready and we *were* willing to experience the alternative.

And even if our version of death is like Martha Stewart's version of prison, it is not to be taken lightly. We cheat death by embracing it in faith, not by avoiding it. And there are as many ways to avoid the death in evangelism as there are ways to die, so to that we must turn.

CHAPTER NINE

THE POWER OF EVANGELISM

REPENT OR PERISH

On 42nd and Broadway there was, once upon a time, a man holding a megaphone and wearing a placard that read, "Repent: Hell is Real." He may still be there. On a personal level this is about as far from the way I approach evangelism as … well, something that's really far away from something else. But in the mid-eighties, evangelicals were about as numerous as Incas in New York City, so I went over to say hello. His personality was unlike anything you would have anticipated. He was about the kindest, most soft-spoken, gracious person you are ever likely to meet.

After we had introduced ourselves, he said to me with the greatest of urgency, "Brother Rick, we must warn these people. They don't know; they don't see it. We must tell them of the love of the Lord Jesus. Here are some flyers. You go on that side [of the street] and hand them out, and I'll stay on this side and hand them out. Blessings to you, Brother Rick."

If his placard was startling, the flyer was even more "eye catching."

I worked in an ad agency on Madison Avenue a few blocks away, and as I handed out the flyers, I desperately prayed that no one from my office would walk by. Perhaps the Holy Spirit would have given me the words to say, but I cannot fathom how I would have explained my behavior short of, "An alien has taken over my body."

If there ever was a living stereotype of the guy with the megaphone, placard, and thumping Bible, it was this guy because, well, he had a megaphone, a placard, and a Bible that he thumped.

Evangelism done well (or not so well) raises questions about effectiveness and appropriateness, as well it should. Even in the book of Acts we are exposed to both successful and less than successful missionary initiatives:

> Now at Lystra there was a man sitting who could not use his feet. He was crippled from birth and had never walked. He listened to Paul speaking. And Paul, looking intently at him and seeing that he had faith to be made well, said in a loud voice, "Stand upright on your feet." And he sprang up and began walking. And when the crowds saw what Paul had done, they lifted up their voices, saying in Lycaonian, "The gods have come down to us in the likeness of men!" Barnabas they called Zeus, and Paul, Hermes, because he was the chief speaker. (Acts 14:8–12 ESV)

Being worshipped as Zeus and Hermes was not Paul and Barnabas' desired outcome. Somewhere their message broke down. Given the outcome, I wonder if they would have approached the city of Lystra differently if they had it to do over again. Maybe the whole misunderstanding was avoidable. Maybe, maybe not. This is always the question, isn't it: Could we have been more effective in our witness? Unfortunately, the answer is always yes. I've rewritten this paragraph three times and could have done it another thirty— there's always a better way to say everything.

SPIRITUAL POWER

I spend a disproportionate amount of time thinking about such questions as I work alongside the research department of an evangelistic organization. I've noticed a disturbing trend in my thinking, and I see it becoming pervasive in the broader Christian community. In a desire for greater ministry effectiveness, our efforts and attention have focused almost entirely on improving relational and communication skills in evangelism to the neglect of the more important question of spiritual power and effectiveness. And there is a difference. We have reasoned that poor relationships, lack of compassion, dismal listening skills, and insensitive communication are the sources of the problem. They are a problem, no doubt about it, but they're not *the* problem.

In John 12:24, Jesus stated that "unless a kernel of wheat falls to the ground and dies, it remains only a single seed. But if it dies, it produces many seeds."

While Jesus has His own death in mind as the initial inference here, the statement is also a general description of how the kingdom grows. How does the church grow? A kernel of wheat falls to the ground. What is the secret of evangelism? A kernel of wheat *must be willing* to fall to the ground. What is the power of evangelism?

When that kernel of wheat falls to the ground. What will keep the gospel from spreading? When the kernel of wheat refuses to fall to the ground. And here we find ourselves once again, in our willingness to die. In our little deaths, spiritual power and life is unleashed.

If this thesis is correct, if this is the primary source of spiritual power in evangelism, then we should expect to find someplace in the New Testament where it tells us to think less about the relational and communication issues of evangelism and more about the spiritual dynamic. Well, take a look at this passage:

> *When I came to you, brothers, I did not come with eloquence or superior wisdom as I proclaimed to you the testimony about God. For I resolved to know nothing while I was with you except Jesus Christ and him crucified. I came to you in weakness and fear, and with much trembling. My message and my preaching were not with wise and persuasive words, but with a demonstration of the Spirit's power, so that your faith might not rest on men's wisdom, but on God's power. (1 Cor. 2:1–5)*

Paul willingly divested himself of status, becoming a fool so that God's Spirit might shine through him. This is what endowed his evangelistic efforts with spiritual power. Notice the correlation Paul draws: It is the willingness to suffer emotional, social, and intellectual death (being seen as an idiot and a fool) that escalates the power of the Spirit. John the Baptist, whom I suspect wasn't much of a talker, states this evangelism principle more succinctly: "He [Jesus] must become greater; I must become less" (John 3:30).

It makes perfect sense. I mean, none of us would say that conversion is a human endeavor, right? God has to work, God must persuade, God must awaken, and God must convict—*agreed*? From what we know of God's character, does it make more sense to think that He would choose to bless eloquence and emotional intelligence, or faith, humility, and a willingness to die to self?

By going to the heart and soul of evangelism, Paul completely flips our perspective and priorities. The things that make an evangelistic approach socially or relationally ineffective can be the very things that make it spiritually potent, allowing divine power to shine through all the rips and tears in our human fabric.

To awkwardly transition to the gospel and stutter our way through our words may lose us points on the social scorecard, but in faith, humility, and death, we've amplified our own spiritual potency. This is the crux of Paul's point. This is not an argument against using Greek philosophy or rhetoric, as some commentators suggest, but an argument for "first principles first," the notion that spiritual effectiveness is more important than communication effectiveness. Paul's argument shows that a lacking in the latter can actually enhance the former, keeping our focus and reliance on the power of God and not the skills of man.

Conversely, to the extent that we try to hold on to our reputation and status, manage our image, and seek to mitigate personal sacrifice, our evangelism loses its true effectiveness in terms of spiritual power. We cannot simultaneously seek to hold onto our lives while attempting to give life away. I mean, we can, but the two end up canceling each other out, netting a sum of spiritual power somewhere around zero.

There is clearly evangelistic anemia in America. We've all sensed it. People seem inoculated and immune to the gospel. Ironically, after all our research, we extrapolate from the data that the answer to our evangelistic impotence is even better communication, strategies, and relationship skills. It's important to remember that the reason Paul defended his oratory mediocrity to the Corinthians was because they had twisted things around, overemphasizing personality, communication skills, and sophistication. They saw these as the power of ministry, and therefore ministry ineffectiveness could only be attributed to their absence.

An important word of clarification: As faith and stewardship are complements, the physical and spiritual are meant to work together. God's power in evangelism is supposed to work with our careful handling of the gospel. That's why effectiveness in communication *is* important. Paul is not pitting one against the other. Rather, he is attempting to rebalance the equation, reminding them of the all-important spiritual principles that are at play in evangelism, in which weak is strong, and incapable means dependent on God. He redirects their priorities away from effective communication and toward *spiritual* effectiveness, where God's resurrection power freely flows as we, His witnesses, willingly die to ourselves. We can actually compromise evangelism's effectiveness when we seek to save our lives in the process of giving the gospel away.

RISK AVOIDANCE

I saw a commercial for some abdominal "blasting" mechanism that was guaranteed to give me the abs I've long admired on the male mannequins at the department store. The motion of the gizmo seemed to mimic the reclining of a La-Z-Boy. Apparently, if I play on this toy for thirty minutes a day, rippling hills of muscle will emerge from the flabby layers of my midsection. I haven't consulted a trainer, but I'm pretty sure muscle develops through pain, not from lounging. And yet we all want to believe in the existence of pain-free shortcuts.

This way of thinking is something we need to recognize in ourselves. We won't grow in our faith without dying to ourselves. So we need to be suspicious of our motives, especially in areas of our faith that *require* sacrifice, suffering, and discomfort. Evangelism is such an area. In fact, within our culture, it's perhaps the only area where Christians pay a price for kingdom membership and privileges.

And therefore it is in this area that we need to be the most distrustful and paranoid of our flesh. We should assume that our flesh seeks a shortcut, a way that a kernel of wheat can produce a crop without letting the kernel actually fall to the ground (John 12:24).

Why am I so paranoid of our flesh? As there are a million ways to die, there are at least that many ways to avoid it. The following are tactics I've used over the years to avoid the death in evangelism. My research on myself has produced one profound observation: We are all geniuses in at least one area, and that is *saving our own skin*.

Apologetic Armor

Apologetics is a field of Christian study that explores the reasons for belief and teaches how to defend one's faith against philosophical attack. Like most people, my interest in apologetics came out of my own struggles as well as a need to answer the questions friends asked about my faith. But whenever you bulk up intellectually or physically, you run the risk of becoming a bully. It feels good not to be pushed around, and it feels good to kick sand in someone else's ideology.

Over my years of study and ministry, I got rather good at winning debates, defending the faith, and frustrating critics. People wanted to take me with them to do ministry in the way you want a defensive lineman with you in a bad part of town.

But I became convicted regarding my dependence and desire for logic, persuasion, and bullying when I thought deeply about this text.

> He told them, "The harvest is plentiful, but the workers are few. Ask the Lord of the harvest, therefore, to send out workers into his harvest field. Go! I am sending you out like lambs among wolves. Do not take a purse or bag or sandals." (Luke 10:2–4)

What struck me about this passage was how intentional Jesus was in equipping His disciples with absolute vulnerability: no food, no place to stay, no lineman to protect them in the bad parts of town. He basically sent them out in their underwear. It dawned on me that I had used apologetics to avoid this kind of vulnerability, as a pelt or hide to protect me from the harsher elements of evangelism. Now why would I do that? Because I wanted to avoid the death of my reputation, and I didn't want to be seen as foolish or ignorant. The way I saw it, if someone wanted to reject Christ, they were going to be the one who looked like an idiot—not me.

Further adding to my warped perspective was the respect and admiration my apologetic armor garnered from the Christian community. Not only did I refuse to die to my reputation, I fed it. I wasn't simply avoiding the *l* of "loser," I sported a large *s* on my chest.

I still struggle with the temptation to save myself in this way. But I now recognize in it the stench of self-preservation, as well as its ultimate fruitlessness. In seeking to save my life, I'm actually draining life from the power of my witness. These days, when I find my thoughts and motivation heading down this path, I simply share something that decreases me in the eyes of my listening audience.

For example, I was invited to a public debate with the head of the New Jersey Atheists Network on the campus of what was then Kean College. As the debate began, we each made our opening comments, and at first I was wonderfully reliant upon the Lord. But the more points I scored and the more penetrating my insights, the more difficult it became to keep my ego stuffed behind the podium. The next thing you know, I'm quoting Kant and Hume as if I've actually read them (which I haven't). I felt very much alive—larger than life, in fact—and growing larger by the moment. I was ballooning into the marshmallow man in *Ghostbusters*, Garfield in the Macy's Day Parade.

Then it hit me: *What difference does any of this make if people don't come to Christ? And how is God's power going to be released through my pride and arrogance?*

So in my closing argument I elected to put away the footnotes and say something simple and intentionally deflating, something to the effect of, "I think what's really important here is Jesus. He longs to have a relationship with each and every one of you." In the intellectual debate-hall environment, I'm sure I sounded like a moron. I know I did. I fell on my sword, but God's Spirit was much more powerfully at work in and through my dead carcass than He was when I was alive, resplendent, and clothed in glory.

Apologetics has its place, but that place is not as a fire wall between us and death. Apologetics is not a means to bring greater glory and life to ourselves, but greater glory to Christ—and life to others.

A Marginal Audience

Now, take a moment to reimagine my scenario of sharing Christ with the plumber from chapter eight, but this time picture me talking to a homeless man instead. If you were able to imagine it, perhaps you sensed an emotional downshift. Sharing the gospel with a homeless person isn't as threatening as sharing with a friend, neighbor, or coworker, and the reason is as tragic as it is true.

In all honesty, I care significantly less what a homeless man thinks of me than what an active member of my social circle thinks of me. Furthermore, there are none of the traditional social norms to contend with, so there's no awkwardness or embarrassment. What could possibly be socially inappropriate to someone who lives in a box on the streets?

Since I derive no life from this man, I derive no death if rejected. And this is why these types of outreach and ministry have always been easiest for me. I don't think I'm alone in feeling this way, for it's been my observation that these dear souls hear the gospel quite a bit more than the average businessperson, and quite a bit more than my *actual* neighbors. Part of the reason it's easier, of course, is the great compassion of God's people. However, when I take a close look at my own heart, part of the reason is also a desire to serve Christ while minimizing personal risk.

In no way am I suggesting we do less outreach to the homeless; please do not hear me saying that. This wonderful means of ministry has only surfaced a less than wonderful tactic of self protection: that I avoid evangelism in the relational networks where I have the strongest bonds and greatest platform because it is in these spheres that I also have the most to lose.

I Am Relevant

I've always held to a belief that evangelistic engagement with the culture means speaking to that culture in a language it understands. I still do. If wearing a T-shirt over my thermal undershirt and letting my facial hair seed into a sensitive aesthetic of virility gets you to listen to me, then dude, *that's how I'll roll.*

Access to students is everything in campus ministry, and the username and password to gain that access is "dorm programming." Resident-hall directors must provide educational programs for their students, and they're desperate for content. But if you want students to actually attend, the big attraction in dorm programming is the self-defense class. Learning how to gouge the eyes out of a would-be attacker with a set of car keys is quality programming. From a misspent youth, I actually had the credentials to teach martial arts, and so I offered to teach a self-defense program—*free of charge*—on dorm floors all over the campus on which I worked. I gave impressive demonstrations. (This was several decades ago, before I looked like Elvis in my karate suit.) Students loved it. Students loved me. I was Jack Bauer and I was relevant, and this gave me a unique platform for ministry to students.

But along with making it onto the student playlist came an increasing sense of spiritual emptiness. Everyone wanted to talk to me, just not about Christ. My confidence was brimming, but it was flowing from my newfound relevance. While this helped to connect me to my audience, it unplugged me from humble dependence upon God.

I often hear young believers say, "I want people to know you can still be cool and be a Christian." I understand what they're saying even though I'm only relevant these days in my obsolescence—cool and hip and handsome in the way Woody Allen is cool and hip and handsome. While the motivation for this kind of thinking is endearing, it misunderstands the difference between being worldly cool and spiritually cool. Humility, brokenness, love, and grace are what God's spiritual in-crowd are wearing this year and every year. Spiritual cool unleashes the power of the Spirit to convict, convert, and point toward Jesus, while worldly cool points you to my hip rectangular reading glasses and SIGG water bottle. As Jesus said, "A student is not above [or cooler than] his teacher," and our teacher proclaimed the gospel from a platform of weakness, brokenness, and death (Luke 6:40).

Relevance can better connect you to the audience you're trying to reach, and there's not a darn thing wrong with that. But we have to be sensitive to our desire for others to find us cool and attractive, as this goal can override the true power of evangelism, which is the power of death. *Peace out.*

Strawmen, Stereotypes, and Over Sensitivities

The fact that those who engage in initiative evangelism, in which a person walks up to strangers with a tract, script, or quiz and shares the gospel, are lampooned is neither here nor there. Those who engage in it, as I have at times, know what they've signed up for and have been blessed with sufficiently thick skin. More problematic to me is that the ghosts of Charles Finney and Billy Sunday provide a rationale *to avoid evangelism altogether*, to avoid a type of death. It's not like we're lining up for lethal injection, excited to die for our faith to begin with. So when you come to believe that evangelism is actually counterproductive or harmful to the gospel, why in the world would you do it? You wouldn't.

I know there are "zealots" out there, but I think there are more rumors about zealots than *actual* zealots. I just don't personally know of anyone bowling people down with a Sam's Club-sized Bible, do you? I can't think of anyone in my church wagging a finger at the evils of whoredom, demon moonshine, and moving-picture shows. The reality in my community is that there are only a couple of churches that seem to believe in evangelism, and even those don't tend to do it.

Yet the specter of this "evangelist" stereotype seems to haunt most discussions about evangelism and outreach. He's everyone's excuse and scapegoat. He's the excuse that unbelievers cite for wanting no part of the church and the excuse believers cite for not sharing with them. It's hard to get at the truth. Statistics show that vast numbers of unbelievers have been "turned off" by Christian evangelism. But then again I view every salesman as an annoyance unless I want their product.

Perhaps the reality of the caricature is immaterial, as the shadow of it is real enough—and this is all that matters. This is the only excuse my flesh needs to keep my head safely tucked down, out of harm's way, and away from anything that may cause social or emotional discomfort.

In the Name of Effectiveness

My daughter just returned from one of her missionary endeavors to the homeless in downtown Philadelphia, where she dispensed food and blankets, as well as conversation and companionship. I am proud that she was involved in this amazing ministry of compassion, and by proud I mean my flesh would in some way like to take credit for it or her, though I can do neither. My daughter also loves to share her faith, and on this day of outreach, someone suggested to her that talking about Christ to the homeless was not such a wise idea. This person suggested that it could compromise the "effectiveness" of the outreach if there was an "evangelistic agenda" or if the food was not given completely "in love."

This is not the book to thoughtfully explore this. But what I want to point out is the many presuppositions about evangelism that can lead to doing no evangelism at all. Do we really know, for instance, that having an agenda for someone's spiritual well-being is a negative thing (or that Jesus doesn't have such an agenda Himself)? That it's not possible to love someone and have an agenda? That it's not loving to be concerned about a person's soul? Who says that giving a person physical food has less of an agenda than providing spiritual food? I think you get the point.

For me, "greater effectiveness" can be just the excuse I'm looking for to avoid putting my life on the line—including my reputation, honor, status, and dignity. I would love to believe that any form of evangelism that causes me fear, anxiety, or social stress is ineffective and therefore unnecessary. But I always sober myself up with the fact that the Corinthians profoundly believed Paul's manner, approach, and presentation of the gospel to be terribly uncouth. Like the Corinthians, we are often enamored with physical reality—what works, looks good, sounds good, and has style. The spiritual kingdom is inverted—weakness is a strength, servanthood is leadership, humility is powerful. In the spiritual kingdom death is the key to life, and this is why those who proclaim life are always in some way martyrs, and therefore *witnesses*.

In the end, why we fail in our witness is not nearly as important as how we might succeed, how we might acquire the coveted label of "faithful witness" (Rev. 2:13).

CHAPTER TEN

READY AND WILLING

In his book *Principles of Psychology,* William James writes, "Everyone knows what attention is. It is the taking possession by the mind, in clear and vivid form, of one out of what seem several simultaneously possible objects of trains of thoughts."[1] This certainly describes *attention,* but it doesn't answer the more important question: *What gets our attention?*

The dynamics of attention, what does and doesn't attract it, can be field-tested quite easily by hopping in your car. According to Tom Vanderbilt, author of *Traffic*, getting in your car, turning on the ignition, and pulling out requires some 1,600 distinct skills, none of which require your attention. In fact, hardwired, or "overlearned," actions (like driving a car or swinging a golf club) are best ignored because we can get stage fright when we turn our attention to these actions. When you swing a golf club, it's precisely the wrong time to think about swinging a golf club.

Perhaps you glance over and turn on the radio as you're driving. The average driver adjusts the radio 7.4 times per driving hour. If you're driving a new car with a new radio, it takes, on average, 1.5 seconds of attention to adjust it. Attention requires a medium workload or it gets bored. Since driving the same stretch of road we've driven a million times isn't much of a workload, we typically add to it (10.8 times per hour) by playing with the radio or the inside of our noses, searching for Tic Tacs in the glove compartment, or gathering change for the next toll.

Redistributing some of your attention to smaller distractions can actually be helpful, provided you don't take your attention from the road for more than three seconds. A lot can happen in three seconds, including 80 percent of car crashes.

Yet having nothing to hold your attention is equally hazardous. With precious little going on and a view that never changes, the experience of "time gap" is common. A time gap is that sensation of, "I was just driving for the last fifteen minutes, and I don't remember any of it." This is the lowest threshold of attention, ideal for long drives and piano recitals.

New drivers don't tend to get "time gap" because they rely heavily on "foveal" vision, their eyes darting around paranoid. Foveal vision requires attention, unlike the blank stare of an experienced driver whose focus is five miles up the road.

So you made it home and got there in one piece. By the way, that stop sign back there—had it said "spot" instead of "stop," you wouldn't have noticed. If you paid close attention to everything you saw while driving, you'd go out of your mind. You gave it the amount of attention it required, and that's the first golden rule of attention.[2] The second golden rule of attention is this: You see clearly that which you are looking for and everything else registers as a stop sign.

Our spiritual attention functions in a similar way. There are many things that capture our attention, but what matters, what is absolutely determinative to our witness, is whether we are actively looking to be used by God. If we're not attune to being used by God, we'll never notice the signs as they fly past us.

Of course you won't be looking to be used by God unless you are *willing* to be used by God. Willingness entails an agreement to pay a price or to do something that you may find uncomfortable. It may not come to this—the experience may be quite pleasant, perhaps euphoric, but you'll only find that out if there's a fundamental willingness to break out of your comfort zone should the situation require it. Are you willing to be used? Are you open to being used?

I've created quite a drumroll for this decision, but we make this decision in the blink of an eye, at the onset of each day, as we flick on our blinkers and merge out into the world. We either do so open, willing, and expecting God to use us, or not open at all. Our eyes are either darting to the horizon, looking for options and opportunities, or darting around right in front of you like a new driver, thinking only about the next ten feet, the next thing on the agenda.

I learned this lesson in a sobering way. I used to commute into New York City, and I had an hour ride on the train both to and from New York. I resourcefully used this time to hibernate. The city can do that to you: You're either running in circles barking and panting or curled up for a nap. It turns you into a dog.

One particular morning I got on the 7:15 train with an open mind, my attention focused on how God might use me. I found myself sitting next to an elderly man, a retired lawyer named Oren who still did some consulting work in the city. We got to talking, and I had the opportunity to share my spiritual journey with him. As we continued to talk, God seemed to open the door for me to explain the gospel. Oren didn't kneel on the train and pray a prayer, but he did listen to every word, nodding thoughtfully, and told me how much he appreciated me sharing with him.

That was that. I never saw him again after we disembarked in Grand Central Station. Months later Oren wrote me a letter saying how much he had enjoyed our conversation, and over the years we stayed in touch through Christmas cards. Twelve years later he called me on the phone. He was eighty-five years old and wanted me to know he was dying of brain cancer. He thanked me for what I had meant to him and assured me he trusted Christ. He also told me that he had shared the gospel with his children and grandchildren, and that many of them had come to know Christ. We were both crying as we said good-bye, and indeed I'm tearing up now as I write this. His last words to me were, "So … I guess I'll be seeing you in heaven." Six months later I got a card from his wife telling me he was gone.

I loved Oren.

All of that came from a thirty-minute conversation on a train. It was a sobering lesson because stepping back from that event, I am struck by how many opportunities I must have missed on the hundreds of train rides while I slept. The thing about not being open and available to God is that He can't direct or divert your attention short of a visible manifestation of Himself. It's like you're a cell phone outside of the network—you simply can't be reached.

Whenever I leave home for any extended period I usually take my laptop with me. Wherever I open my computer, I am reminded that as I sit there occupying a space in the physical world, there is an invisible highway of communication going on around me, messages and images flying through my head. (Though I haven't checked with my tech friends as to the veracity of the claim that images are literally whizzing *through* my head—they wouldn't know to go around me, right?)

So I have a choice to make: Do I connect to the Wi-Fi network or do I live in peaceful obliviousness to it? The question is always answered through cost analysis: Sometimes I'm willing to pay to be in the hot spot, and sometimes I'm not.

Whenever I venture out into the world of people, the simple question that appears on my screen of consciousness is this: Are you willing to be used … or not? If I say yes to the offer, I'm "online"; I'm open and awake, my eyes of faith panning everywhere, looking for God to lead, open to however He might use me. I actually have a great picture of this mind-set still sitting in my inbox.

My friend Warren and I have known each other for a good number of years. For the last five of those years, Warren has spent his summers trying to get a church planted among the Cypriots, that is, the people of Cyprus. After his most recent trip to Cyprus, Warren stopped off in Europe before heading back to the U.S.

He sent me this e-mail from Moldova:

> Hey, check this out! I'm in Moldova; I came a day earlier than the rest of the team because of a mix up with my ticket. So I had to stay in a hotel last night. I got up this morning and went downstairs to have a coffee and to pray. I was sitting in the little breakfast area reading my Bible when another guy walked in to have breakfast. When the waitress asked him if he wanted coffee or tea, he said tea. I looked up from my Bible and when I looked at him, I sincerely heard the Holy Spirit say to

me, "That guy is a Cypriot. Talk to him." So when he sat
down, I said, "Where are you from?" He said, "London."
He said, "Where are you from?" I said, "Virginia, but I
just came from Cyprus." He said, "I'm Cypriot, but I live
in London." We started to talk. The Holy Spirit told me
clearly that I was to share the gospel with him. Ahhhh
it was so easy; it was as if he was ripe for this moment.

To live your day completely open to God's Spirit can be just like that, like a page out of the book of Acts. But the question, "Am I open and am I available?" is one of cost. There's a price to be paid for being in the hot spot. The question is not just, "Do you want to be on the spiritual network?" The question is, "Are you willing to *pay* to be on the spiritual network?"

THE JOY OF DEATH

It's always difficult to shift our thinking, and it does take a shift in thinking to see the little deaths and mini-martyrdoms that are a part of being a witness for Christ. As it's not wise to jerk someone's head around too much, it is with some hesitancy that I bring up this additional—and I promise the last—shift in perspective. Not only should we think of evangelism in terms of death, but we should think of our deaths in terms of joy. Let's preface this discussion with a wonderful John Piper quote:

And I pray for awakening and revival. And I try to preach
to create a people that are so God-saturated that they
will show and tell God everywhere and all the time.[3]

Piper uses "saturated" because it describes the concept he is trying to convey like no other word. Actually, the word *passion* does, but it's been gutted of meaning due to overuse, which is why I suspect he has swapped in "saturated." The essence of *passion* is this: If you're passionate, you're not just *willing* to sacrifice for Christ, you *want* to sacrifice. You are so utterly consumed, so intensely saturated, so brimming with joy in the person of Christ that sacrifice and suffering are the only vehicles adequate to express it, satisfy it, spend it, or satiate it. You're not simply willing to die—you can't wait for someone to pull the trigger.

The death integral to passion will be the focus of another chapter, but we cannot completely ignore it here or our perspective would be badly skewed—especially if we saw our sacrifice as something to be given reluctantly or as something manufactured by an act of sheer will.

When we are saturated and brimming with Christ, joy overflows its banks, surging with an impulse to talk to others about Christ and fueling a desire to suffer any of the attending consequences. This is passion: a moth deliriously happy and headed for the flame.

Not too long ago I was at a commissioning service for a missionary headed to serve in a Muslim country. She was a Muslim who came to Christ in the U.S. and was heading back to her native country to share the gospel. Several western missionaries were recently martyred in that country, and someone asked her if she was scared. She said, "No, just excited," and then repeated three times, "I just love Jesus. I just love Him so much. I just love Him." That wasn't really the question, but it was certainly the answer.

When we are truly passionate, choices to sacrifice are perceived as opportunities, as they were for this young woman: a way to spend or satiate our consuming passion. But we are not always so gloriously consumed, and choices will sometimes need to be made out of convictions and commitments that were forged when passion was in a molten state. So be it.

Bill Bright once observed that you will never meet an unhappy person who regularly shares his or her faith. I believe that observation to be correct. The most alive people you will ever meet are witnesses who are willing to die. Those who avail themselves to be vessels of grace enjoy the benefits of being grace's repository, the Spirit bubbling up within them and carbonating every area of their lives.

All of which is to underscore the point: Our willingness to die is fueled by our experience of life. It's not fueled by the raw, unaided power of our wills.

Josef Tson, leader of the spiritual revival in Romania in the seventies and eighties, said that the secret to the revival was the willingness to die and declared that what was hindering it "was our desire to survive."

"Sometimes," said Tson, "the Lord wants you to stand up and die and through your death bring revival." As a courageous victim of numerous interrogations and beatings under the Romanian dictator Ceaușescu, Tson certainly knew what he was talking about. He preached a message of martyrdom, and young people embraced it, declaring, "We do not want the compromise of our parents. It is either or. Totally with Jesus or without Him." It was at that moment when they were willing to die, said Tson, that revival came to Romania.[4]

"There are, aren't there," said C. S. Lewis, "only three things we can do about death: to desire it, to fear it, or to ignore it."[5] Those who desire it we call witnesses.

CHAPTER ELEVEN

THE SECRET LIFE
OF TRIALS

I'm staring up at the ceiling praying, "Dear God, please don't let the tree fall on our house."

This moment was the culmination of an eight-week ordeal that began when we moved to Orlando in the summer of 2004. We had already been through two hurricanes, lost our power for several weeks, and needed to replace the roof on our home. For unrelated reasons, our toilets didn't work, so we were using a toilet in a small shed in the backyard. Our porch started to fall off the house, but that was easily explainable: The foundation of the house underneath it had disintegrated. The fix was easy; we just needed to spend twenty thousand dollars to jack up the house and fix the foundation. Then the repairs on the porch went like clockwork. The construction left

149

our home somewhat exposed to the elements, which I take it is how we acquired the rat infestation. But they might have come simply to feed off of the termites—*it's hard to say*. Our kids hated the new schools, and twice we called the police asking them to find one of them who had run away. While fixing our home we were going into debt at the rate of four thousand dollars a month. There I was, staring at the ceiling under the newly constructed roof, desperately praying that the nightmare would end and Hurricane Charlie would simply pass us by.

As over-the-top as all this sounds, it seriously isn't the half of what took place. Perhaps this will in some way capture it for you: I remember heading up to bed one evening, glancing at the big picture window in our living room, and thinking, "Well that's about the only thing in the house that hasn't broken." When I woke up the next morning and came downstairs, there was a duck in the middle of our living room—*a duck!* I had no explanation as to how it got in the house, but as I walked over to it, the duck turned and flew right *through* that picture window, destroying it.

I believe God had a great purpose for these trials, but for the life of me, I still can't tell you exactly what it was. I don't doubt, however, that whatever it was definitely needed doing.

THE SECRET LIFE OF TRIALS

Trials are rather involved spiritual operations. Well, what God does in and through trials is "involved." The trials themselves are simply the instruments, the blunt tools used to open us up. As Puritan Thomas Brooks observed, "Trials bring up the scum of the soul."[1] They open us up so disease can be found and removed.

But we need to persevere through these trials if we are to derive benefit from them. Like a half-completed surgery, a half-completed trial is of zero value—even less than zero. It would have been better to have never begun the operation than to have the bloody mess of aborting it. So God goes to great lengths, encouraging us through His Spirit and through the Word so we stay on the operating table long enough to accomplish His good purposes.

As counterintuitive as this may sound, I think the biggest reason we don't persevere through trials is that we don't realize when we're in one. Back to our worn medical analogy: If I don't know that you're operating on me with all those sharp, pointy instruments, I'll assume I'm being tortured. Then I'll desperately search for a means of escape.

And this is precisely what happens when we don't recognize a trial for what it is. We mistake divinely ordained hardships for bad luck, bad friends, a bad year, bad breaks, bad government, a bad choice, bad advice, bad genes, or a bad hair day, and quite naturally we run. A scalpel is just a knife with a medical motive, and if you hold it to my throat in any scenario other than during an operation, I'd be insane *not* to run. The only intelligent reason we'd ever embrace our calamities is if we recognized them to be *divinely conceived trials* and not unfortunate happenstance.

But identifying a trial *as* a trial is extremely tricky, since all that separates a God-ordained trial from random misfortune is the sender. Unfortunately trials arrive quite anonymously as parcels of adversity left on our doorstep without labels, return address, handling instructions, or explanation. Lacking such vital information, we can make some dreadfully wrong assumptions about the contents, the intention, and the origination of our mystery gift, diverting all our energies toward trying to send the damnable thing back.

Of course no adversity that enters our life is ever really random. It's always there by God's consent and design, as C. S. Lewis observes:

> My general view is that, once we have accepted an omniscient and providential God, the distinction we used to draw between the significant and the fortuitous must either break down or be restated.... If an event coming about in the ordinary course of nature becomes to me an occasion of hope and faith and love or increased efforts after virtue, do we suppose that this result was unforeseen by, or is indifferent to, God? Obviously not.[2]

So anything that stretches us and stretches our faith is a trial. Nothing enters our life or has any bearing upon it without God having foreseen and permitted it, and this includes temptations as well as trials. But this rather important fact does not seem to keep us from making wrong assumptions about the source or intent of our trials. Such misdiagnosis will more than likely be the reason—or excuse—behind our failure to persevere.

Perhaps the greatest form of animal humiliation is the medical e-collar, those plastic funnels that encase a dog's head like daisy petals and keep them from gnawing at the site of a medical procedure. I think they should make them for humans. If we are going to persevere and allow our trials do what they were intended to do without sabotaging the operation, we need to turn our heads to the Scriptures for discernment so we can understand the wisdom of trials and the clever ways in which they conceal and disguise themselves.

DISGUISED AS GOD'S ANGER

To test the power of perception, a rather simple experiment was performed in an MIT classroom. Students were told there would be a substitute teacher. They were also told that as this substitute was a relatively new faculty member, the department was soliciting their feedback on his performance. Students were each given a short description of the teacher. One half of the classroom was given this description:

> Mr. _____ is a graduate student in the Department of Economics and Social Sciences here at MIT....This is his first semester teaching Ec. 70. He is 26 years old, a veteran, and married. People who know him consider him to be a very warm person, industrious, critical, practical, and determined.

The other half of the classroom was given this description:

> Mr. _____ is a graduate student in the Department of Economics and Social Sciences here at MIT....This is his first semester teaching Ec. 70. He is 26 years old, a veteran, and married. People who know him consider him to be a rather cold person, industrious, critical, practical, and determined.[3]

Exactly two words separated the descriptions: the words "very warm" on the first, versus the words "rather cold" on the second. After class, students were given an identical questionnaire to complete. Those students who received the first description described the substitute as good-natured, considerate, popular, informal, sociable, humorous, and humane. Those receiving the second description described the teacher as self-centered, formal, unsociable, unpopular, irritable, humorless, and yes, even ruthless. The preconceptions formed by the description determined whether the students saw the teacher as Ellen DeGeneres or Joseph Stalin.

So how do we perceive God? That depends. Have we sinned recently? Have we been having our daily devotions? Are we stuck in a habitual pattern of sin? Were er raised in a dysfunctional family? Such contexts form our preconceptions about God and how He's feeling about us. I mean, we know He *loves* us, but does He *like* us? This is the question our preconceptions try to answer, *and they often get it wrong*.

So when a package of hardship, seemingly sent from God, sits ambiguously on our doorstep lacking any explanation, our preconceptions decide whether we see the parcel as having been sent with care and concern or as payback for sins: past, present, real, and even imagined.

Ambiguity raises preconceptions to the conscious level, determining whether you see a smirk or a grimace, a nod or a snub. This is also why God removes all ambiguity regarding His motives in our trials.

> *Because the Lord disciplines those he loves, and he punishes everyone he accepts as a son. Endure*

hardship as discipline; God is treating you as sons. For what son is not disciplined by his father? ... But God disciplines us for our good, that we may share in his holiness. No discipline seems pleasant at the time, but painful. Later on, however, it produces a harvest of righteousness and peace for those who have been trained by it. (Heb. 12:6–7, 10–11)

Trials come from the heart of God, not from His fists. Trials are never, ever sent in anger. *Propitiation* is the technical term for the magnificent truth that Christ not only absorbed our sin, but removed God's wrath and anger toward it. If God got angry with you over a specific sin, that would negate what Christ did to pay for that sin. What would be true to say is that Christ propitiated it; He propitiated the heck out of it; He propitiated it to death. God admits each one of your hardships into your life with motives of love, care, and protection.

DISGUISED AS RANDOM MISFORTUNE

Innocent children evaporating from shopping malls, airplanes cartwheeling down runways, stray bullets gunning down unintended targets—the bad news is never-ending. There's life in the universe, and it's random.

On this morning's news I saw a story about a mother who was convicted of killing her three-year-old child. I couldn't hear all of the details over my crunchy cereal. Not to be jaded, but what am I supposed to do with this "news"? What *can* I do but keep eating my cereal like I never heard it? But I did hear it, and it does affect me. Without any knowledge of the people, circumstances, or context, the only message conveyed by the story is that "life is random and unfair." This is what we learn, every day, from our "news."

Like a horror film, the news isn't really scary when you're watching someone else's shocking tragedy unfold. Later, when you're alone and tragedy touches your own life, you're haunted by the prospect of randomness, of being alone in the universe with no sovereign hand to filter out calamity or screen rogue comets from colliding with the earth.

What can create a trial is its perceived randomness. Trials are like runaway tornadoes, terrifying because it appears as if no one's driving them. It's with these fears in mind that the apostle Peter wrote this:

> *In this you greatly rejoice, though now for a little while you may have had to suffer grief in all kinds of trials. These have come so that your faith—of greater worth than gold, which perishes even though refined by fire—may be proved genuine and may result in praise, glory and honor when Jesus Christ is revealed. (1 Peter 1:6–7)*

The operative phrases are: "for a little while" and "may have had to."

"May have had to" is meant to communicate that God sees your life—has seen its future, its weakness, its underdevelopment—and He's deemed this particular trial at this particular time necessary. It comes to you with premeditation and forethought, designed specifically for you, which is to say that it is not random.

"For a little while" communicates that though God allowed Thing One and Thing Two to turn your life upside down, He has never let them off their leash. The ordained trial is divine medicine, bringing spiritual wellness. The syringe carries a precise dosage, its duration carefully measured.

Think of it: This passage is both the affirmation of our greatest hope and the denial of our greatest fear. Peter confirms that everything in our life happens for a reason: "And we know that in all things God works for the good of those who love him, who have been called according to his purpose" (Rom. 8:28).

Or think of the opposite. Think of the wispy condolences offered by those who don't know God when someone is suffering: "You're almost out of the woods," "It's always darkest before the dawn," "Tomorrow's a new day," "Everything will work out," "You're in our thoughts," and so on. It's babble. Such words, without the backing of omnipotence, crumble into platitudes and empty sentiment. The afflicted sense this and are not consoled.

All trials, hardships, and suffering come into the life of the believer with divine permission and forethought; they'll last exactly as long as they were planned to last. In essence, there is a white picket fence around all of our yards.

As Natural Consequence

It was the early nineties in New Brunswick, New Jersey. I had taken the campus minister job at Rutgers University. My wife, Katie, was seven months pregnant, and my daughter, Avery, was two. It was mid-August when the clock started on three of the most hellacious months of our lives.

It began with a series of partial paychecks. The financial support for our ministry bottomed out, so we had to put everything on a credit card: bills, groceries, diapers—*everything*.

Then my wallet, along with my credit card, was stolen. I found out when the Visa people called and asked why I had purchased six thousand dollars worth of audio equipment and an Ab Blaster. (A thief with a six-pack?) Understandably, the credit card company found it difficult to believe that a person who puts his groceries, diapers, and bills on a credit card wouldn't impulsively buy out the inventory of an entire Radio Shack. The mortgage company had the same doubts. We were trying to buy our first home, and I think the mortgage company asked themselves the question, "Do we really want to loan money to someone who gets partial paychecks, puts their groceries on a credit card, and every now and then purchases six thousand dollars worth of audio equipment?"

The answer was no.

So we went to another mortgage company. But by now Katie's purse had been stolen, and more inexplicable charges showed up. I needed to replace my stolen driver's license, but New Jersey wouldn't give me one because apparently there was a criminal with my name running loose in the state purchasing audio equipment. Then I had a hernia, Katie got an ulcer, and our daughter began having intestinal problems.

Next I got taken to court for throwing a box in a corporate Dumpster. (Should you happen to make the same misjudgment, don't discard a box with your name and address on it.). Let's see … what else happened? Our car was towed from a poorly chosen parking space and would not be returned to us until I could prove I was not the Richard D. James of New Jersey who had a record of repeat felonies.

This was difficult to prove, as my identification had been stolen. We borrowed a student's car so that Katie (nine months pregnant at this point) could drive me back and forth to the DMV forty minutes away to try to clear my name. The car worked wonderfully once the cloud of oily smelling exhaust cleared. We would pull away from the smoke with Katie at the wheel trying not to focus on what might very well be contractions—little Avery sat buckled into the back seat, me on the passenger side, emasculated and demoralized, my arm hanging out the rusted car window like some criminal in a getaway car.

If you notice, there was nothing overtly "spiritual" about any of this mess. It was just stuff, the common indigestion life belches in your face. But that doesn't disqualify it from being a trial. God wants us to recognize that trials come in packages of every conceivable shape and size, and He doesn't want us to expect them to arrive with some kind of "spiritual" label attached.

> *You may have had to suffer grief in all kinds of trials.*
> *(1 Peter 1:6)*

> *Consider it pure joy, my brothers, whenever you face*
> *trials of many kinds. (James 1:2)*

The common emphasis of these verses is variety: trials of "many kinds." God alerts us to something critical about discerning trials: There is no reason not to consider the common, everyday, garden-variety hardship to be a trial. There is no other criteria, no special application or status; this is not an exorcism for which ecclesiastic verification is required. If a situation stretches you, stretches your faith, and taxes your emotional, mental, or spiritual resources, then by all means, it's a trial.

Disguised as Personal Issues

Regarding the aforementioned trial, did I mention the reason my wallet was stolen was because I had left it on the roof of my car? I got in the car and drove away with my wallet and a Taco Bell chalupa sitting on the roof. And did I explain that my hernia was caused by not using my legs when moving exceedingly heavy boxes, or that the sign on the corporate Dumpster said "no dumping"?

Are these details relevant? Actually, no, but we sure feel that they are. I am reluctant to label something a trial whenever I am the one who caused it. But trials are routinely organic to our lives. God, I suppose, could bring a drifter from Reno or someplace into town on a Greyhound bus to steal my credit card, but why? There's already more than enough raw material in my life to make use of.

As a parent I desire to see my children develop and grow, but I've never once had to fabricate reality to accomplish these ends. I've never needed to pay actors and stage a dramatic reenactment where my kids are faced with a hard situation. Life's taken care of that for me.

And while it may be true that I was the source or cause of my trial, it was God who delivered it. He didn't have to. In fact, many times God graciously allows the consequences of our actions to pass by, forwarding them on like a Dear Santa letter to some location in the North Pole, never to be seen by anyone but Him.

So even if we are the source of our suffering, and our trials were self-inflicted, it's only because God has lovingly allowed us to experience these consequences.

Disguised as Hindering Obstacles

One of the things that make kids *kids* and not miniature adults is their perception that anything that's difficult or painful in life is an obstacle. Broccoli is not a means to health, but an obstacle to dessert. School is not the path to a good education, but a roadblock to recreation. And I doubt any young child has ever seen their bedtime as an opportunity to sleep.

Most of us outgrow this perception. And if we don't outgrow it in our spiritual lives, we will always perceive trials as those things that keep us from our goals, not the way by which we arrive at them.

We often set goals for our life with the best of intentions but fail to see trials as the necessary fuel needed to accomplish those goals. As a young believer, the first area of my life where I felt convicted was my crude mouth. The day I began to censor myself was the day of a thousand bee stings, stubbed toes, and parking tickets. My mouth *got worse*, not better, so how else could I have perceived these irritations but as obstacles to my holiness?

But they were not; they were vehicles to the intended destination. No one swears at Disney World, and a change of habit required exactly this difficult set of circumstances. Trials help us get better even though our performance during trials can carry the illusion of getting worse—fix my golf swing and I guarantee that I'll gain five strokes before I lose any.

I recently tried my hand at the video game Halo, and it was a rather humiliating debut. I was killed twenty-six times in less than ten minutes. There were many reasons for my spectacular failure, but most significant was my habit of running *away from* the power pills instead of running toward them. I thought they were bombs—they looked like flashy, blippy things—*how is that not a bomb?* Well, without the juice from the power cells, my player basically fainted at the first sight of an enemy, and thus I died twenty-six times. The point is this: Trials are often disguised as obstacles to our spiritual progress when, in fact, trials are the very fuel our progress requires.

And, Oh Yeah, Him

While granting these helpful warnings and specifications provided by Scripture, it would still seem that God could make both the trial and His intentions clearer. This is where we really need to remember that we're in the midst of a cosmic struggle. In the song "Sympathy for the Devil," The Rolling Stones eerily capture the confusion that both surrounds and camouflages our enemy. "Please to meet you, hope you guess my name, but what's puzzling you is the nature of my game." Well said, and we shall not inquire about where they derived such insight.

Satan further confuses an already confusing set of circumstances, making it very difficult to discern who's doing what to whom and for what possible reason. It's a war, and bullets seem to come from every direction. There's no telling what's friendly fire or what's enemy fire.

While God seeks to transform a trial into spiritual growth, Satan leverages our flesh, attempting to turn the trial into a temptation. And this is when it really gets confusing to tell all the players apart—this is when the accusations start. Remember that other line from the same song? "I shouted out, 'Who killed the Kennedys?' Well, after all, it was you and me." Satan's accusations stir up confusion—you did it, he did it, God did it, they did it. In all the confusion—never mind being able to recognize the trial for what it is—you'll be lucky to remember what day it is.

This dimension of spiritual warfare is a final backbreaking layer of complexity, further obscuring our understanding of what's really happening.

DON'T I KNOW YOU?

In the opening minutes of the movie *Terminator II*, John Connor comes face-to-face with cyborg/Terminator/Arnold Schwarzenegger. It's a tense meeting, as a terminator's job is typically to snuff out human life. But this terminator has been redeemed. Its purpose now is to rescue humanity, which it can only do if John Connor will recognize it as an angel sent to help, not as a devil sent to destroy. Connor, by faith, must choose to believe that this killer is a benevolent friend; he must somehow recognize its true identity despite the confusing appearance.

If we fail to recognize the purpose of trials, if we fail to recognize their benevolent source and intention, and if we fail to recognize when we're in one, it's quite likely we will fail to persevere. We will run from it rather than embrace it—and a trial must be embraced, must be allowed to "finish its work so that you may be mature and complete, not lacking anything" (James 1:4).

We must allow trials to fully live out their natural lives, and we must stay with them to the bitter end—and the end, or death, in a trial is indeed bitter.

CHAPTER TWELVE

DEATH OF A THOUSAND CUTS

The French have a phrase, *la petite mort,* or "the little death," which is roughly defined as "the period of melancholy resulting from having spent one's life force." The expression actually refers to the emotional lull following sex. I apologize for the bluntness, but one must make certain allowances for the free expression of artists, poets, and the French. Life is a series of little deaths, a million black dots, major and minor, of varying duration, culminating in a glorious crescendo— "Precious in the sight of the LORD is the death of his saints" (Ps. 116:15).

In his letter to the Corinthians, the apostle Paul describes his trials in similarly poetic terms, though not with the innuendo of the French. In stating that "death is at work in us" (2 Cor. 4:12), Paul refers to his trials as a series of little deaths, or an ongoing experience of death. But Paul was a poet in the way that George W. Bush was a poet, that is to say, not at all. Besides an occasional doxology or engrafted creed, issues of clarity, not aesthetics, govern Paul's word choices. So if Paul observes that trials are like "little deaths," it's because there are important reasons for seeing them this way, not because it sounds poetic. Here, then, is Paul's description of trials as "perpetual dying" or "little deaths":

> *We always carry around in our body the death of Jesus, so that the life of Jesus may also be revealed in our body. For we who are alive are always being given over to death for Jesus' sake, so that his life may be revealed in our mortal body. So then, death is at work in us, but life is at work in you. (2 Cor. 4:10–12)*

I believe one of Paul's reasons for using death and dying as symbols of the trials we face is that he wants us to see that trials deprive us of life in the way that death deprives us of life. Trials don't have the finality of death, but they do share some significant family resemblances. Paul's choice of words throughout this passage of 2 Corinthians highlights the symbiotic relationship between these homely twins—trials and its uglier sibling, death. Paul offers us three of their more repugnant similarities: Both trials and death carry with them feelings of despair, a lack of life, and a sentence of death. A typical trial won't kill you—*it just feels like it will.*

THE DESPAIR OF LIFE

What exactly does death feel like, even if it's a little death? Paul's 2 Corinthians phrase, to "despair even of life," certainly seems to get at the meaning. Trials are like death in that they take us to the very end of ourselves and then proceed further.

Life is outdistanced.

As long as you can say the words "I can't go on," you usually can.

When you can't go on, you don't. Everyone has a point of no return when it's not just the fuel gauge that's on empty, but the tank itself. Hope springs eternal until it doesn't. Then we despair of life; we wish we had never been born.

Paul puts it this way:

> *We do not want you to be uninformed, brothers, about the hardships we suffered in the province of Asia. We were under great pressure, far beyond our ability to endure, so that we despaired even of life. (2 Cor. 1:8)*

The Will Smith film *The Pursuit of Happyness* shows the process of a man reaching the point of despair. The movie relates the more-or-less true story of Chris Gardner. Gardner possesses boundless energy and ideas. This is important to understand, for it would take unimaginable trials to bring such an energetic person to the end of himself. But the unimaginable happens *and keeps happening*. Gardner's business venture fails, and he can't pay his rent; his wife leaves him alone with their five-year-old son; his car is impounded; he loses his bank account; he's dragged off to jail for unpaid parking tickets.

Then his problems begin.

Gardner is kicked out of his apartment and is forced to live on the street with his son while he completes an unpaid internship with a brokerage company. Gardner studies for his exams on a bus, on the subway, or on a filthy cot in a homeless shelter, all while his son sleeps next to him.

At the emotional breaking point, Gardner barricades himself into the public restroom of a subway station. As he and his son sit curled on the bathroom floor, someone begins to pound on the door. All Gardner can do is keep his foot jammed in the door and weep as he cradles his sleeping son in his arms.

I cried. I think most of the theater cried, and not just out of sympathy, but empathy. Everyone has this matching swath of emotion; everyone can place a time when they reached the end of themselves, when their life went from the margins to off of the page. Trials can take us to this point, the place where our selves end and nothing impedes our view of despair.

As moving as this dramatic scene is, it doesn't end there. The footage keeps rolling, and the camera drifts up to the ceiling. Now we're looking down on the entire bathroom, down on Gardner and his son, seeing it from a bird's-eye view, as a third-person observer. The cinematographer captures an ethereal quality, but remains true to the experience of death and despair—*and total detachment.*

When tragedy strikes it can feel like time stops, can't it? You hear every ticking of the clock; you feel like you're in a shell and cut off from the living world, a spectator of life. Life has left you, and you've left it behind. When life ceases to inhabit us, we cease to inhabit it.

In Dietrich Bonhoeffer's poem "Night Voices" (his last recorded words from prison before being executed), you can clearly see this haunting detachment:

> *In the stillness of the night,*
> *I listen,*
> *Only footsteps and shouts of the guards,*
> *A loving couple in the distance, stifled laughter ...*
> *Twelve cold, thin strokes of the tower clock awaken me.*

There is in them no music, no warmth, to shelter and comfort.[4]

Back in everyday life, the crucible of a trial may be as trivial as a bee sting or stubbed toe. I'm not saying we can sit with an ice pack on our foot and claim solidarity with Bonhoeffer, but trials, *to the degree of their severity*, do mimic the sights and sounds of death. Paul's trial, at least the one described in 2 Corinthians, did not end in death, but he did experience the despair of life.

THE CESSATION OF LIFE

The sensation of life flows to us through many outlets. My living room, where I'm sitting, is filled with them. There's my cell phone sitting on the table that connects me to my relationships. If I were to pick it up and dial any name from the directory, I'd immediately feel more alive. Photographs of my wife and kids reflect the life I derive from my family. Some things I've written are lying around, artifacts of accomplishment that supply feelings of worth. A shelf full of books, running the length of the room, is the source of my mental, intellectual, and creative stimulation. Paintings and beautiful decorations pump aesthetic life into the atmosphere (if you're sensitive to that kind of thing). And there's my television and computer, both of which connect me to ideas, news, and the outside world. Every few feet there's another outlet to plug into. This is why it's called my living room.

Trials pull the plug on life in the same way death does. But while trials yank out a power cord, death rips the entire fuse box off the wall. Paul's description of trials is intentionally categorical. As we derive life from many sources, we experience the death that comes with trials in *all* categories of life: We are hard-pressed on every side, but not crushed; perplexed, but not in despair; persecuted, but not abandoned; struck down, but not destroyed.

There are mental deaths ("perplexed"), emotional deaths ("hard-pressed" by stress and anxiety), relational deaths ("persecuted but not abandoned"), and physical deaths ("struck down"). These are large, sweeping categories meant to express comprehensiveness without being, well, comprehensive. But the basic idea here is "variety": If you're looking for a trial, one can be found in the death of your finances or the death of a dream, a goal, your pride, your health, a relationship, a job, your reputation, your security, your happiness— just look for the dead body stuffed in a closet.

I recently had lunch with a good friend who experienced a cancer scare the week prior. Of course we all know someone who has had a cancer scare, but my friend is only twenty-five years old, and he values his health enough to work for a health-food company. It turned out to be a false alarm, a scare. But as the word *scare* conjures up mental images of trick-or-treaters dressed as Pokemon, it was most certainly more than that.

I asked what God had taught him through all the anxiety and fear of the week, and his answer was simple: "I never realized how much life I derived from my health and from being healthy." It's as if God came into my friend's living room, walked over to the plug in the outlet, and said, "Hmm, wonder what this leads to." The momentary loss of life felt like death—only smaller.

Whatever type of difficult trial you go through, you will feel as though a lifeline to the land of the living has been severed, making the label *la petite mort* quite—how do the French say it?—*à propos.*

THE SENTENCE OF DEATH

> *Indeed, in our hearts we felt the sentence of death. But*
> *this happened that we might not rely on ourselves but*
> *on God, who raises the dead. (2 Cor. 1:9)*

The lawyers of convicted murderer and death-row resident Michael Ross made a rather unique argument for their client. Ross was no longer interested in appealing for his release and instead had acquiesced to his inevitable death. His lawyer argued that such acquiescence was "death row syndrome" at work, and that appeals for his release should still be made whether Ross was interested in filing them or not.[5]

The problem with Michael Ross, besides being an accused serial killer and convicted murderer, was that he lost hope. His death sentence made him lose hope.

To feel the "sentence of death" is to experience as surety the verdict of death before it is rendered. There's another name for living life as though the verdict of death has already been given, and it's called fatalism. Fatalism is a lethal strain of determinism, a belief that the die is cast; that the future is fixed, unalterable, and inescapable; and that the future is grim. If death is a black hole, fatalism is its pull of gravity.

Why don't slum dwellers just hitchhike out of urban squalor? Why don't abused wives just leave their marriages? Why don't the homeless get a job at McDonald's? Why don't oppressed masses overthrow their dictators? Why not just leave behind a self-destructive lifestyle? Besides the fact that some face illness on multiple levels, fatalism is a major reason. Some suffer from the suffocating belief that the future has already been determined, defeat is inevitable, and resistance is futile.

In the gospels, it's easy to miss the profound faith expressed by the blind, lame, and leprous who came to Jesus for healing, for it's likely they all suffered under the added affliction of theological fatalism. To be in such a state, in the words of the chief priests, meant that "you were steeped in sin at birth." Do you see the satanic checkmate? How can you believe God will heal you from a condition He determined you to have? It's not simply that you're blind; it's that you believe you were *meant* to be blind.

As Paul expresses, Christians *are*, and at the same time *are not*, exempt from the sentence of death. We are not immune to the feelings of despair or to hearing fatalism's verdict; we are free, however, not to believe it. Because we know that God can redeem any situation and has the power to save and rescue, hope abides (as does His Spirit) in any and every circumstance, protecting us from fatalism and its pull toward the flame. We are not exempt from hearing voices and verdicts, but because of hope—because of Christ—we never have to join our voice with theirs. *Never.*

SLUM DOGS

If this is what a trial can feel like, what's to keep us from running away instead of enduring? Absolutely nothing. Absolutely everything.

When we were new parents, Katie and I read a ton of books on parenting. Actually, Katie read a ton of books on parenting; I just displayed them prominently on my night stand. One book instructed us to let our baby cry at certain times and only pick her up once she'd stopped, thus teaching her that mom and dad can't be manipulated and crying will not help her.

The book promised this would establish a pattern that would last for life, and it certainly has. We put our daughter down, she cried, and I ignored it; she cried again and I crumbled; I ran to her crib and rocked and cooed her until she was happy; and this I believe has been our pattern for the last twenty years.

Supernanny is one of those guilty-pleasure shows that let you derive some pleasure from someone else's drama. The premise of this reality show is simple: Parents struggling with renegade children get an emergency visit from "the Supernanny:" a delightful, highly skilled, Mary Poppins type of woman named Jo Frost.

The typical scenario finds parents using an appeasement strategy on their children, hoping that giving them what they want will bring tranquility to the home. It doesn't. Jo Frost brings structure and authority to the picture. What's instructive to watch is the children's reaction to immovable boundaries and an authority figure who will not be manipulated. The children all have the same basic strategies, innate, I suppose: They try arguing, bargaining, manipulating, and self-pity, and when all else fails, they act out destructively.

I say all of this because the death within a trial is also the breaking point of the trial. It's here that the trial is doing the most good, and it's here that it's the most painful. Everything in us wishes to escape, and typically our adolescent strategies resurface. We attempt in some way to manipulate God: to bargain with Him, try to make Him feel sorry for us; perhaps we throw a temper tantrum.

With little effect and with the pain acute, we are at this point most likely to sniff around the garbage dumps of old habits and patterns of sin: those things that used to coddle and comfort us and help us to cope. You can see Peter's pastoral concern over this very thing as he writes to believers under extreme duress:

> Therefore, prepare your minds for action; be self-controlled; set your hope fully on the grace to be given you when Jesus Christ is revealed. As obedient children, do not conform to the evil desires you had when you lived in ignorance. (1 Peter 1:13–14)

So what's to keep us from running away? As I said, one unfortunate answer is "nothing." We can and sometimes do run away from trials. And when we fail to persevere, we unwittingly reestablish old behaviors rather than create healthy new ones. I'm not saying all is lost—with God all is never lost—but we can sabotage some of His grander purposes for the trial and therefore miss out on all of the good He has intended for us.

What's to keep us from running away? *Everything.* And I think *everything* is expressed in this verse:

> Humble yourselves, therefore, under God's mighty hand, that he may lift you up in due time. Cast all your anxiety on him because he cares for you. (1 Peter 5:6–7)

Why should we humbly submit ourselves and persevere through a trial that God has ordained for us? Because our all-knowing, all-powerful Father knows what's best for us, knows precisely what we need and how best to produce it. Because He cares for us, and everything He does for us flows from perfect, unyielding love. And because God, in due time, will lift us up. A resurrection of some sort awaits us in every trial, and it's now to the resurrection of trials that we turn.

CHAPTER THIRTEEN

FLIGHT TO PHOENIX

In his second letter to the Corinthians, Paul describes trials as deaths in order to communicate the similarities, in order for us to see death as a process continually at work in our lives. Question: Why would Paul tell us this? Answer: So we'll recognize how God's resurrection power is at work in our trials.

If you've ever thought that Listerine tasted like floor cleaner, that's because it sort of is. In the twenties Listerine was sold as an industrial-strength floor cleaner until some marketing genius discovered the obscure medical term *halitosis*. By inventing an imaginary halitosis pandemic, marketers created the need for mouthwash, and they positioned Listerine as the cure.[6] The idea of halitosis needed to be ingrained in society's consciousness if it was ever to comprehend why it needed Listerine.

In 2 Corinthians, Paul rebrands trials as "little deaths," and he does so to seed our thinking, to prepare us to see the power and the process of resurrection at work within them.

> *We always carry around in our body the death of Jesus,*
> *so that the life of Jesus may also be revealed in our*
> *body. For we who are alive are always being given over*

to death for Jesus' sake, so that his life may be revealed
in our mortal body. So then, death is at work in us, but
life is at work in you. (2 Cor. 4:10–12)

In the movie *The Shawshank Redemption*, Tim Robbins plays Andy Dufresne, a messianic figure wrongly accused of a crime and sentenced to life in prison. If you don't immediately see the symbolism, it becomes clear when Andy's first miracle is to convince the guards to give the prisoners beer, much like Jesus' first miracle of turning water to wine.

The movie builds up to Andy's miraculous escape in which he crawls five hundred pitch-black yards through a rotting, fully operational sewage pipe. It is a powerful—indeed redemptive—scene as Dufresne emerges from the sewer covered in the stink of death into a cleansing rain—transformed, washed clean, and purified from human stain. All this while narrator Morgan Freeman eulogizes, "Andy crawled through a river of s*** and came out clean on the other side."

It's a great picture of redemption; it's a great picture of the resurrection in our trials—crawling, clawing, and feeling our way through the dark and the stink and the sewage, but expectant, always anticipating the resurrection, the new life, the freedom, and transformation that lies just ahead.

As the death of trials takes on many forms, stretching beyond the literal definition of death, so too does the resurrection of trials. What our eyes of faith look for is God's resurrection power at work in our trials, bringing life out of death. The process of resurrection is like the process of creation in Genesis: life out of death, light out of darkness, form out of void. The manifestations of God's resurrection power are manifold, but the Scriptures, and this chapter, give primary attention to three particular manifestations: how God brings life out of trials, how God ministers life to us in the midst of our trials, and how God rescues us from our trials.

TRIALS TRANSFORMED INTO LIFE

To Paul's way of thinking, death (our trials) is the raw fuel God uses to generate life. Paul wants us to see trials as a consumable resource, like firewood that's burned and transformed into heat. I'm not sure if you've ever read a Bible translation that paraphrases the Scripture like *The Message* or *The Living Bible,* but they're quite useful for spelling out difficult concepts. This is one of those concepts. So allow me to provide my own, somewhat uninspired, very loosely paraphrased version of 2 Corinthians 4:10–12 so you can see the concept clearly.

> *I endure many hardships. But I think of my trials like "little deaths" because I see how God brings life out of them. You, Corinthians, are the ones who will benefit from this, so I don't mind if God uses my life and faith as an engine to convert death into life. In fact, once you realize that trials are firewood to be burned and transformed into life, you will no longer run from them but embrace them. Notice also that your hardships are proportional: the more trials or "little deaths" you endure, the more life that comes out the other side. In fact, this is the major reason why I rejoice in the*

severity of my trials, persevere in them, and embrace
them by faith. I never think, "Oh, no, another trial."
Instead I think, "Bring it on. These are simply more
logs for the fire."

The ancient alchemists invested much time and genius trying to transform waste into gold. Noting its bullion color, Hennig Brand, for example, left sixty buckets of urine to evaporate in his cellar, hoping a residue of gold would remain. It didn't, though we can thank Brand and this vile experiment for the discovery of phosphorus.[7]

The idea of turning raw sewage into something as precious as gold was not insanity. The idea that man could do it, however, was insane. Few things allow us a vantage point from which to view God's glory and power than the transmutation of life's sewage (our trials) into actual life.

The Role of Faith

In the early seventies some dubbed Boston Harbor the "harbor of shame," as over two million people's untreated sewage dumped into it daily. The festering stew of toxins and E. coli was not only fatal to fish and other sea life—if a human fell in, health officials called for a mandatory trip to the hospital for a battery of shots, tests, and screenings. Today, not only can you swim in the water, but you can drink it. (*You first.*) The transformation did not occur naturally, nor did it happen overnight. It was the result of the construction of a massive sewage treatment plant on Deer Island, dubbed by histori-cally minded locals as Fort Poop. The miracle of Deer Island is that it transforms roughly 390 million gallons of sewage a day into both drinkable water and gas-powered energy—imagine that![8]

In the same way, it is God's power—and His alone—that transforms the death that comes with trials into life. Yet just as in the process of salvation, faith plays a significant role in this transformation. Faith serves as a Deer Island of sorts in the process of transforming life's sewage (trials) into life. Faith is how we access God's resurrecting and transforming power. Faith is the divinely energized catalyst. And faith is our mandatory participation in the process, without which the trial will remain dung.

Gasoline, for example, cannot transport me to Boston any more than a bucket of waste can yield gold. Gasoline is just a smelly combustible fluid unless an engine converts it to mileage. A log cannot keep me warm in the winter unless it's burned, and the tornado-force winds of a trial remain destructive if not harnessed by faith and transformed by God's power into life.

As Edith Schaeffer observed in *Affliction,* her wonderful treatise on suffering, "There is also a day-by-day, moment-by-moment victory which Christ died to make possible … meant to take place over and over again in the period of time we are still in the land of the living."[9]

In context, Edith Schaeffer is talking about the moment-by-moment processing of our struggles through the eyes and heart of faith: an attitude that confronts trials at the door and welcomes them in saying, "Lord, I entrust myself to you. I trust you to bring life and growth from this. I believe you will work through this for good."

There's a good example of this in Acts 16 when Paul and Silas are thrown into prison while preaching in the city of Philippi.

Upon receiving such orders, he put them in the inner cell and fastened their feet in the stocks.

About midnight Paul and Silas were praying and singing hymns to God, and the other prisoners were listening to them. Suddenly there was such a violent earthquake that the foundations of the prison were shaken. At once all the prison doors flew open, and everybody's chains came loose. (Acts 16:24–26)

In obedience to a vision, Paul and Silas go to Philippi to proclaim the gospel. As a result of their faithfulness, they wind up in prison. It sounds painful, difficult, dark, and confusing. Yet they take it all in and process it by faith. Faith digests their trial and metabolizes it. There are a variety of ways we could respond and allow our faith to metabolize the trial. We could respond to the trial with thanksgiving and praise, or we could remain silent, prayerfully entrusting the circumstances to God. The common thread is faith.

The opposite would be to respond to the trial with bitterness, blame, complaining, whining, resentment, or self-pity. Should we choose this direction, there should be little or no expectation of life emerging from it (though God, as is His prerogative, may elect to do otherwise). Without faith, trials are just trials, sewage remains sewage, and we continue to swim in the harbor of shame.

I say all of this with a caveat: Trials keep. They don't go bad or grow stale. If you begin walking by faith today, the trials of the past can begin filtering through the treatment plant even now, becoming redemptive fuel.

The Normative Life of Death

It's easy to write off the trials of the apostle Paul. He was an apostle, his letters became Scripture, and he saw Jesus, all of which make Paul unique. He's not like other Christians we know. He's not like anyone we know. But as he writes to the Corinthians about his struggles, he feels the need to squash any "oh, that's just Paul" talk. He feels compelled to tell them that this life of trials, this life of living though dying, is not his life—it's the Christian life:

> We have been made a spectacle to the whole universe, to angels as well as to men. We are fools for Christ, but you are so wise in Christ! We are weak, but you are strong! You are honored, we are dishonored! To this very hour we go hungry and thirsty, we are in rags, we are brutally treated, we are homeless. We work hard with our own hands. When we are cursed, we bless; when we are persecuted, we endure it; when we are slandered, we answer kindly. Up to this moment we have become the scum of the earth, the refuse of the world....Therefore I urge you to imitate me. (1 Cor. 4:9–16)

In literature, satire is a genre that is the literary equivalent of the political cartoon or Weekend Update on *Saturday Night Live.* Its shrewdest and most effective use is to point out blatant hypocrisy when people can't see it or simply refuse to see it. By turning it into a joke, satire pushes the issue over the top, allowing everyone to see it and respond; they can either laugh, cry, repent, or all three. The Corinthians didn't see the disparity between Paul's own trials and their lack of hardship, so Paul uses a bit of satire in this passage to reveal it. And as our experience of trials is often equally at odds with Paul's, we should acknowledge that the joke is also on us.

The Zeroth Law of Proportionality

The first and second laws of thermodynamics are not really the first and second laws of thermodynamics. Prior to the first law, we find the zeroth law of thermodynamics (that temperature exists).

My spell-checker is politely reminding me that *zeroth* is not a word anyone uses anymore … for any reason, and it wants me to change it. While I know my spell-checker has only my best interests at heart, *zeroth* is a real word—actually it's the perfect word for a principle that comes before all other principles.

Therefore, the *zeroth* principle of trials is the death and resurrection of Christ.

Christ took upon Himself eternal condemnation and transformed it into eternal life. It is because of this principle that our trials are now redeemable. But there is another replicating pattern here: the symmetry or proportion of death to life.

Comedian Steven Wright makes a joke about having a map at a one-to-one scale. That, of course, would be a map equivalent to the size of a state. That's a one-to-one correspondence, and it's a one-to-one correspondence we see in the cross. You have *eternal* death on one side of the equation yielding *eternal* life on the other side—the cross performing the operation. The amount of life derived is proportional to the amount of death incurred or suffered.

This is why the apostle Paul does not simply rejoice in his trials, but rejoices in their quantity and intensity. Greater trials yield greater life.

It's important to see this symmetry in our own suffering: the death, sludge, and manure on one side of the equation will be proportional to the life that emanates from the other. Tertullian's famous observation on the suffering of the early church, that "the blood of the martyrs has become the seed of the church," is nothing more than a restatement of this equation.

While the point seems abstract, it is immensely practical. Such an understanding of proportionality changes our perspective of the amount or intensity of our trials, just as it did for Paul.

If, for example, you've experienced more trials than anyone you know and it doesn't seem fair—well, it's not fair. You've been given twice as much fuel, which can be transformed into twice as much life. Perhaps Satan has harassed you to a degree far exceeding the experience of others. Well, that's a calculated risk on his part. If you don't give out or give in, he's actually provided you with excess fuel that can be processed by faith and transformed into life. If Satan sends you a bomb and it doesn't explode (that is, if you don't give up), he's actually given you a weapon.

Conversely, very little death equals very little life. You cannot squeeze copious amounts of spiritual life from the rinds of a trouble-free existence. In the kingdom of God, you cannot escape the physics of proportionality and faith.

LIFE IN THE MIDST OF TRIALS

God is not only the God who raises the dead, He's also the divine resuscitator. When everything in us desires to quit and surrender to our trials, God breathes new life into us.

The grammatical structure of 2 Corinthians is complicated, to say the least. Yet there is a structure, and even Paul's meandering are not a journey without purpose. His roughly four-chapter digression (chapters three through six) provides us with the most comprehensive account of how God imparts life to us in the midst of our trials.

Following the switchbacks of his thoughts, Paul's narration of his travels and itinerary trail off in 2 Corinthians 2:12, right after he shares of a terribly fragile state of mind resulting from Titus' absence.

> *When I came to Troas to preach the gospel of Christ, even though a door was opened for me in the Lord, my spirit was not at rest because I did not find my brother Titus there. So I took leave of them and went on to Macedonia. (2 Cor. 2:12–13 ESV)*

This narrative will not pick up again until chapter seven, when Paul shares of his reunion with Titus, "But God, who comforts the downcast, comforted us by the coming of Titus" (2 Cor. 7:6). The intervening chapters catalogue Paul's struggles and trials: a list so torturous it reads like an addendum to the Geneva Convention. Yet the reason for the litany is neither bombast nor boasting, but to itemize the variegated ways that God imparted life to him and kept his heart pumping through all his desperate and despairing circumstances.

In this section you'll see the oft-repeated phrase "therefore we do not lose heart," which is Paul's way of pointing to the specific promise or provision of life that kept his heart from fainting. Here are some of the provisions and promises from 2 Corinthians 3—6, in no particular order.

Life Lines

To give someone purpose is to give someone life. Purpose gets me out of bed in the morning and propels me through the challenges of the week, month, and year. God appointed Paul as His ambassador, entrusting him with the gospel, the very message of life: "Therefore, since through God's mercy we have this ministry, we do not lose heart" (2 Cor. 4:1). The thing that protected Paul's heart and kept his arteries from hardening with despair was the privilege and purpose of the mission. Paul, of course, shares these truths because they are equally true for us. But should our pulse slow, there are other reasons not to lose heart.

The apostle Paul carried a burden reserved for those who get to see the Lord face-to-face. But Paul never lost heart because these two truths circulated within him:

> Therefore we do not lose heart. Though outwardly we are wasting away, yet inwardly we are being renewed day by day. For our light and momentary troubles are achieving for us an eternal glory that far outweighs them all. (2 Cor. 4:16–17)

Through his trials, Paul was "being transformed into [Christ's] likeness with ever-increasing glory" (2 Cor. 3:18). Death was at work in him, but so was life. Spiritual growth, sanctification, and the experience of transformation propelled him, but so did the promise of future reward and future transformation: "For our light and momentary troubles are achieving for us an eternal glory that far outweighs them all" (2 Cor. 4:17).

When Paul stood before the Lord, he knew he would receive a reward commensurate to his suffering and faithfulness. But there's more....

"For Christ's love compels us" (2 Cor. 5:14). Yes, it most certainly does. Love is life. Love empowers, energizes, and overcomes. It's the reason to sacrifice anything and everything. And if that were not "compelling" enough, there is yet another motivator here: the promise of our eternal dwelling and our future home, which injects us with life in the form of hope:

> *We are confident, I say, and would prefer to be away from the body and at home with the Lord. So we make it our goal to please him, whether we are at home in the body or away from it. (2 Cor. 5:8–9)*

Paul finally states, "I have great confidence in you; I take great pride in you. I am greatly encouraged; in all our troubles my joy knows no bounds" (2 Cor. 7:4). Children, spiritual or otherwise, are a source of life and a motivation to persevere. When our bones wish to disassemble, our children are the ligaments that hold us together.

This is how God keeps our hearts beating amidst the deaths that we experience in trials. These are the promises and the provisions that impart life in the midst of death.

DELIVERANCE OUT OF TRIALS

There seems to be no end to the wizardry God can perform through our trials. He can take the death of a trial and bring life from it. In the midst of a trial, He can impart life to us and keep us from losing heart. Finally, He can flat-out rescue us from the situation altogether.

Moses' parting of the Red Sea is more than just a miracle or an example of God's power to deliver His people. It's a paradigmatic picture of salvation; it's iconic of God's deliverance; it shows God's power to swoop in, rescue, and save us; it's the refrain of deliverance echoed throughout the Scriptures; it's a theme park ride at Universal Studios.

That's right: You can ride right through the very waves that Charlton Heston split in two in the movie *The Ten Commandments*. And *this* is paradigmatic, iconic, and all of that, especially in light of our tendency to shrink, control, and trivialize God's power to deliver.

God can, period. God can rescue us from any circumstance— any malady, any problem, any pain, any obstacle—wherever, whenever. While Jesus ultimately offered Himself up to the cross when His time had come, until that time, the gospels tell us that He simply walked through the riots of people without anyone laying a hand on Him.

It is reflexive for us to declare our belief that God can do anything, but such affirmations can blind us to the ways that we don't believe. "I believe that God can" is sometimes just a contraction for "I believe that God can, but I doubt that He will."

Paul begins his second letter to the Corinthians with this resounding affirmation of God's ability to rescue us, for such assurance is foundational to a life gregariously adorned by trials.

"He has delivered us from such a deadly peril, and he will deliver us. On him we have set our hope that he will continue to deliver us" (2 Cor. 1:9–10).

Again and again and again, God delivers us from both fire and frying pan and will continue to do so.

This, then, is the power of resurrection at work in our trials: God turning death into life, God injecting us with life in the midst of our deaths (trials), and God rescuing and delivering us out of the grasp of death. As we walk through our trials by faith, we should do so with assurance that the Son will rise in and through them and resurrection *will* overcome death, though exactly how and where life will emerge retains a shroud of mystery.

LOOKING FOR LIFE

Some time ago I was sharing with another Christian about a particular season of trials in my life. I remarked that I saw a ray of hope when someone very close to me came to Christ, and that I felt the two events (the person coming to Christ and my trials) were connected.

My friend was genuinely excited for me, affirming that "it's a powerful testimony when unbelievers see Christians going through trials." I agreed, then clarified that the person who came to Christ actually lived several hundred miles away from me and was unaware of my trials. I received a stare of incomprehension from my friend, a look of, "Then how could these two events be related?"

I suggested that cause and effect in the spiritual world was complicated, and that sometimes you don't know how things relate, *only that they do*. I got no response—I might as well have been speaking tongues in a Lutheran church.

This person understood the concept that someone could observe me going through trials and desire to know Christ, but they were unable to comprehend that the cause and effect in the spiritual realm could be any more complicated than this.

Weren't Job's friends guilty of a simplistic understanding of this spiritual cause and effect? They simply couldn't conceive of an equation beyond sin equals suffering. The message of Job is not that cause and effect aren't in action in our suffering, but that the causes are far more complicated than we can imagine or predict.

You would have had to have slept through the last couple decades not to have heard the conversations and debates about topics like global warming, tipping points, threshold effects, chaos theories, swarm theories, and butterfly effects—lots of effects, lots of theories. Fundamentally, it's a discussion on the nature of cause and effect. In complex systems (like weather or the environment) with an enormous amount of variables, cause and effect seem to follow different principles than previously assumed.

In complex systems, change is imperceptible until it hits a certain threshold. Then change happens rapidly and dramatically. One moment you're out in the yard throwing a stick for your pet mastodon, and in the next you're in an ice age. This is quite different than, say, aging, in which change is as consistent and gradual as the rise of a forty-five-degree angle. We can't point to a single day when we got old (fortieth birthdays notwithstanding).

The threshold model of cause and effect is probably closer to what we witness in Scripture: long periods of *apparent* inactivity followed by swift, dramatic change. For example, in Genesis 15:16, God says to Abraham, "The sin of the Amorites has not yet reached its full measure." So how long will it take the sin of the Amorites to reach its full measure? How long will heaven remain static? About four hundred years. But every sin registers, accrues, and accumulates. Every indiscretion, every lie, every immoral act has a ripple effect, and when it hits a divine threshold, judgment is swift and change is rapid.

The ways of God are complex just like the weather, a common metaphor for God's ways in Scripture. There is certainly cause and effect in His dealings with us, but correspondence is rarely simple. All of which is to say this: Always expect life to come out the other side of a trial that you've walked by faith, but never look for life in simple correspondence, obvious places, or expect that you'll always be able to see it. Life will spring up somewhere—the grass will inevitably push up through the pavement.

A Tree Grows in Nairobi

I was speaking at a church some time ago. A young man approached me afterward and asked, "Were you ever involved in a ministry at Rutgers University?" I told him yes, and he informed me that his younger brother had gone there and came to know Christ because of me. How cool. I asked for his brother's name to see if I could mentally place him, but he replied, "You wouldn't know him. Actually, after you shared the gospel with him, he told you to leave. I think he even slammed the door behind you. But then he immediately called me—we talked—and then he gave his life to Christ over the phone."

It was a wild connection, like playing "six-degrees of Kevin Bacon" with God. I think God orchestrated this meeting as a reminder and a promise that life *always* emerges, whether I'm there to observe it grow or not.

Time is one of those things that separates spiritual cause from spiritual effect. Our intuition tells us that the prayers of a long-deceased Christian matriarch may have had everything to do with the spiritual vitality of a distant relative in a distant generation. It's like dropping a pebble in water: The "effect" of the waves radiates outward, traveling far and wide.

By faith we reckon the equation to be true: Our trials are fuel, and as we endure them by faith, life will emerge by God's power in some way, shape, or form—in us and in others.

The Scriptures call our attention to the death that comes with trials neither for poetic or dramatic reasons. In seeing the death in trials, we ought to recognize the many ways that God brings life from them and through them.

CHAPTER FOURTEEN

TAPS

MICE AND MEN

In April 2008, President George W. Bush awarded the Medal of Honor posthumously to a Navy SEAL by the name of Michael Monsoor. Monsoor had been killed in Iraq in September 2006. Beneath his shirt, Bush wore a gold replica of Monsoor's dog tags, and as he brought Monsoor's parents to stand beside him, he could hardly hold himself together as he struggled against tears.[1]

In May 2006, Monsoor had been the hero of another rescue—one he survived, saving the life of a teammate while risking his own. Bush gave this description of the event:

> *With bullets flying all around them, Mike returned fire*
> *with one hand while helping pull the injured man to*

192

safety with the other. In a dream about the incident months later, the wounded SEAL envisioned Mike coming to the rescue with wings on his shoulders.[2]

But in September 2006, Michael Monsoor gave up the last of his spare lives, saving two fellow soldiers by throwing himself on a live grenade. As Bush describes,

Mike and two teammates had taken position on the outcropping of a rooftop when an insurgent grenade bounced off Mike's chest and landed on the roof. Mike had a clear chance to escape, but he realized that the other two SEALs did not. In that terrible moment, he had two options—to save himself, or to save his friends. For Mike, this was no choice at all. He threw himself onto the grenade and absorbed the blast with his body. One of the survivors put it this way: "Mikey looked death in the face that day and said, 'You cannot take my brothers. I will go in their stead.'"[3]

War is a billion acts of courage and cowardice—and this is just on the battlefield. What about a surviving spouse or parent? You couldn't say that the moment of "looking death in the face" takes more courage than having to see it every day on the face of a son or daughter, could you?

On the day Bush awarded Monsoor the Medal of Honor, our nation honored true courage. But courage hasn't always enjoyed this kind of approval rating. For the decades prior to September 11, 2001, America's stock in the moral commodity had been on a steady decline—and in no place was this more visible than on the battlefields of Hollywood.

Catch 22 probably started it all, but the honor might need to be shared with *All's Quiet on the Western Front.* Then there was "M*A*S*H," *Apocalypse Now,* and *The Deer Hunter.* After that, Hollywood spit them out with semiautomatic regularity: *Full Metal Jacket, Born on the Fourth of July*—reload—*Hamburger Hill, The Thin Red Line, Tigerland*—reload. While some of these movies occasionally salute noble values, many scenes give us an alternative narrative and an alternate definition of bravery.

Though war was often the intended target of these films, courage was often the casualty, with some scripts presenting a definition more disturbing than the last: courage as the dolt-eyed nationalism of mindless cattle; as a suicidal impulse; the despair of nothing left to lose; a mind drugged with revenge, prejudice, and terror; or an aberrant pathology that just happens to love the smell of napalm in the morning.

Before September 11 the conceptual framework of courage in this country was in decay. But as the Twin Towers crumbled, selfless servants rushed in, risking everything. In doing so they transformed the ash and rubble of Ground Zero into a towering memory of modern courage. September 11 changed the national perception, definition, and value of this virtue. How could it not? We saw with our own eyes people who had everything to lose give their lives for those they'd never even met. Courage had returned to its place in the forefront of American consciousness.

THE FORGOTTEN HERO

I've taken this historical back trail because I believe courage has likewise vanished from Christian consciousness, though for altogether different reasons. We are, after all, free from persecution, so we can afford to keep courage boxed in the attic like an old tuxedo—should times and trends change, we're optimistic it will still fit.

However, I think the predominant source of our neglect is that we don't have a file folder for courage. It doesn't fit into a category of spiritual disciplines like Bible study, prayer, or daily devotions, and it never made it to our top-ten list of Christian virtues. It was even snubbed as a nominee for "fruit of the Spirit'" (love, joy, peace, patience, kindness, goodness, gentleness, and self-control). It is as if courage sort of fell between the seat cushions, *out of sight, out of mind*. But Scripture puts an extremely high value on courage, and there's nothing Scripture highly values that we can afford to ignore. Yet we probably haven't even noticed it's gone missing.

For example, let's say I worked for the ACME box company. What if I came to you and said that I was struggling in my efforts to be an effective witness at my place of work. What would you say? What would you ask me as you sought to diagnose the problem and locate the source of my evangelistic impotence? "Are you doing devotions every morning? Have you prayed for the people at work? Have you tried memorizing evangelistic passages of Scripture? Do you know how to explain the gospel message? In what ways could you set a godly example?" All good questions. I'm sure these are things that I would ask.

I doubt, however, that you'd have the audacity (or perhaps the rudeness) to ask me if I were just being a coward, or say, "It sounds to me, Rick, like you're just plain yellow."

And yet if I don't share the gospel in any reasonable way, if people don't even know I'm a Christian, more than likely it's because fear has shut me up—fear of losing my job, of what others think of me, of not getting promoted, or of being judged or losing friends.

According to the Oxford dictionary, what I've just defined is cowardice and what I lack is the courage to face and overcome these fears in order to be a witness for Christ. I do not doubt that any and all of the spiritual to-do's I've mentioned—Scripture memory and the like—affect our boldness, but *they are not synonymous with courage*. A robust worship life feeds and inclines toward boldness, but courage is its own action, its own virtue, and must either be exercised … or not.

Think of how the Christians you know respond to an obvious sin issue. They can appear oblivious to the presence of the moral disorder, yet to those close to them it may be concealed as Tourette syndrome. Is the problem that the Holy Spirit hasn't spoken to them about this issue? Or is the problem that they don't have the courage to face the painful truth about themselves?

So when I say that courage has disappeared from the forefronts of our minds, I mean that when problems arise in our spiritual lives, we tend to look only to the traditional gauges of community, Scripture reading, prayer, fasting, unconfessed sin, et cetera. We don't have a mental warning light that says, "Coward. Running low on courage." And if our problem were cowardice, would we have the courage to admit it? "Yes, sir, I'm a coward all right. Can't run away from danger fast enough."

If as believers we haven't noticed that courage has gone missing, what hope is there for broader society? For instance, in the wake of corporate corruption and an economic crisis, business schools have been retooling their ethics curriculum—most notably, Harvard, whose illustrious alumni include Enron's Jeff Skilling. But where does the problem truly lie? Is the issue one of immoral executives doing something wrong, or is it a problem of moral coworkers doing nothing about it? Is it the avarice of one or the cowardice of many? For every greedy mastermind there are typically dozens of appeasers, enablers, and "yes men"—lieutenants who are well aware of the problem even if they might be ignorant of details.

John McCain wrote the following in his treatise on courage, *Why Courage Matters*:

> Courage is like a muscle. The more we exercise it, the stronger it gets. I sometimes worry that our collective courage is growing weaker from disuse. We don't demand it from our leaders, and our leaders don't demand it from us. The courage deficit is both our problem and our fault. As a result, too many leaders in the public and private sectors lack the courage necessary to honor their obligations to others and to uphold the essential values of leadership. Often, they display a startling lack of accountability for their mistakes and a desire to put their own self-interest above the common good. Corporate America has taken significant blows to its reputation, because too many executives don't have the courage to stand up for what they know is right.[4]

Courage, it would seem, has left the building, and we must go after it before it flees and hides. Because it has been so removed from our thinking, we are going to need to bake a theology of courage from scratch. But let's begin with a description of courage, just so we know what it is we should be running toward.

THE DEFINITION OF COURAGE

As the thesis of this book has to do with death, not courage, it's critical to see the connection between the two. Nothing could be more tightly braided than courage and death, both conceptually and practically. Whether it's risking one's life in the face of mortal danger, laying our lives down, or some act of dying to self that involves an emotional, mental, social, or relational death—whatever form death may take, courage is the moral fortitude to face it without surrender or retreat.

We find that courage, like a complex molecule, is as strongly bonded to life as it is to death. Within courage, the willingness to die is due to a powerful attraction to life—to preserve one's own life, the life of another, the life of a nation, belief, or ideal. Courage acts when it believes that greater life is to be gained through a direct encounter with death. In the case of Michael Monsoor, his calculations happened in an instant. He muffled the grenade with his body so that his friends could *live*.

In his book *Orthodoxy*, G. K. Chesterton describes his rather meandering, or perhaps loafing, route to faith. Though Chesterton described it as a "slovenly autobiography," it's a rather unique intellectual journey. For Chesterton the virtue of courage was a signpost leading *to* God and *away* from atheism, because it seemed to defy any kind of "survival of the fittest" mentality. This was also the case on September 11, when firemen willingly traded in their lives for strangers unable to save themselves.

For Chesterton, true paradoxes were clearly the fingerprint of a Creator, and Jesus as the God-man was chief among them. In his well-known description of courage in *Orthodoxy*, Chesterton beautifully articulates the paradox of courage:

> *Courage is almost a contradiction in terms. It means a strong desire to live taking the form of a readiness to die. "He that will lose his life, the same shall save it," is not a piece of mysticism for saints and heroes. It is a piece of everyday advice for sailors or mountaineers. It might be printed in an Alpine guide or a drill book. This paradox is the whole principle of courage; even quite earthly or quite brutal courage. A man cut off by the sea may save his life if he will risk it on the precipice. He can only get away from death by continually stepping within an inch of it. A soldier surrounded by enemies, if he is to cut his way out, needs to combine a strong desire for living with a strange carelessness about dying. He must not merely cling to life, for then he will be a coward, and will not escape. He must not merely wait for death, for then he will be a suicide, and will not escape. He must seek life in a spirit of furious indifference to it; he must desire life like water and yet drink death like wine.[5]*

Courage, roughly defined, is a passion for life manifested in a willingness to die; a desire for life that's so strong that one is willing to walk within an inch of death to get it; desiring "life like water" yet "drinking death like wine."

So, returning to my previous examples, courage to witness in the workplace would be driven by a strong desire for the spiritual life of others—so strong, in fact, that you'd be willing to suffer the death of your ego, status, job, or relationships in order to get it. Or in the case of the person oblivious to their own sin, courage would manifest itself in a desire for greater spiritual life, godliness, and intimacy with God. In this person, the desire for life would be strong enough to drive them from the safe cover of mediocrity and denial, into the openness of truth.

Virtue is defined as behavior deemed to be good or of a high moral standard. It would seem like "arriving on time" or "putting the toothpaste cap back on" could squeeze into such a broad definition, and of course different cultures and traditions have some significant variations. The Greeks saw justice, courage, wisdom, and moderation as the cardinal virtues. Hindus throw cleanliness into their list, and in the twenty-first century, being "green" is also highly venerated.

My point is this: Society is not a reliable gauge for determining which virtues are important and what value to place on them. For this we must turn to Scripture. But as you can find biblical support for many virtues, including cleanliness and caring for the environment, we must determine the relative value and importance conferred by God's Word. So courage is in the Bible, but just how important is it? As we'll see in the following chapters, I think the answer is "very."

While visiting a Sicilian military hospital in 1943, General George Patton came across a young soldier weeping from battle fatigue. Patton expressed his compassion by slapping the boy in the head and calling him a coward, an incident that nearly cost Patton his command. As we turn to the Scriptures and see the importance

God places on courage, perhaps we can ponder where we have failed to measure up.

However, it's quite important we not see Christ as General Patton. He is not berating us for our failures. He cares more than we can imagine about our struggles, and "because he himself suffered when he was tempted, he is able to help [us] who are being tempted" (Heb. 2:18).

CHAPTER FIFTEEN

HONORABLE MENTION

No sooner had the warm liquid mixed with the crumbs touched my palate than a shudder ran through me and I stopped, intent upon the extraordinary thing that was happening to me. An exquisite pleasure had invaded my senses, something isolated, detached, with no suggestion of its origin. And at once the vicissitudes of life had become indifferent to me, its disasters innocuous, its brevity illusory; it was me. I had ceased to feel mediocre, contingent, mortal.[6]

It's amazing what one person can experience in the single bite of a cookie. In this case the cookie was a madeleine, the writer Proust, and the novel, *Swann's Way*. This novel is often regarded as the first truly modern novel, exposing the reader with arcane detail—Proust at one point goes 356 words without a period—to the complex interior and emotional life of the characters. "Only thoughts and feelings," as Virginia Woolf put it, "no cups and tables."

This "stream of consciousness" narrative is a modern literary invention circa the turn of the twentieth century. In previous centuries, authors of fiction and nonfiction alike weren't concerned with such internal absorption. Emotional states were simplified, not dissected. People were "happy" back then. And on this account the gospels are true to their era. The gospel writers did not write about emotions in detail, so we can wrongly see the experience of the first disciples as very one-dimensional.

In Luke 7, for example, when a prostitute barges into a Pharisees' dinner party and wets Jesus' feet with her tears, wiping them with her hair, we assume that she was so overcome with remorse she didn't care what people thought. Should we assume she didn't care, wasn't embarrassed, or that this act didn't take courage? Should we assume her mind contained one, and only one, emotion?

In John 11 when Mary and Martha ask Jesus and the disciples to come to Bethany to attend to Lazarus, the text tells us, "Then Thomas (called Didymus) said to the rest of the disciples, 'Let us also go, that we may die with him'" (John 11:16). Because John doesn't choose to tell us how they felt about potentially dying, should we assume they were ambivalent or that it was an easy choice to make?

My point is that as we survey the biblical testimony on courage, we'll find courage demonstrated in many places—even when the text doesn't specifically label it so. And instead of assuming the Holy Spirit blunted all fear and trepidation like morphine, thus making courage superfluous, we should assume that the situations in which the disciples found themselves were every bit as terrifying as they appear, and that their choice to be obedient was a courageous one, neither easy nor euphoric.

BIBLICAL COURAGE
Joshua

In the opening minutes of the film *Saving Private Ryan,* you can nearly smell the fear, a mixture of vomit, seawater, sweat, and other bodily fluids sloshing around the floor of the landing craft as it nears the beach at Normandy only moments before the invasion of Nazi-occupied Europe. This is essentially the scene in the opening chapter of the book of Joshua as we wait with Joshua and Israel in the hand-wringing days prior to the invasion and occupation of the Promised Land. It is one of the most critical events in all of redemptive history.

I'm no military expert, but it seems to me that from a tactical perspective, there's got to be a hundred and one ways this mission could go sideways, spiritually as well as militarily. But Israel's heavenly commander on chief seems preoccupied with only one thing: the potential for cowardice in His general.

Issued no less than four times in the first chapter is this refrain: "Be strong and courageous" (Josh. 1:6), "Be strong and very courageous" (1:7), "Be strong and courageous"(1:9), "Only be strong and courageous" (1:18). God's omniscience means He has war-gamed every scenario. What else are we to conclude from this repetitive charge but this: As God looks out on the impending battle, there is only one way He foresees that the plan could be in jeopardy, and that is if Joshua is a coward.

Here at the most crucial moment in the most crucial battle for the Promised Land, the panoramic view of Scripture narrows to a squint at one person and one virtue. It's as if God says to Joshua, "Everything is going according to plan, and the only way this won't succeed is if you don't have the courage to pull the trigger." Now I'm sure God would have found a way; I'm not endeavoring here to reconcile the sovereignty of God and the cowardice of man. I'm just trying to make a point: There are times in Scripture, times in salvation history, when courage is unequivocally what counts.

Esther

Next we turn to Esther: supermodel, secret agent, Laura Croft of the Old Testament.

The setting of the book of Esther is during Israel's Babylonian captivity. The Persians' King Xerxes, having recently banished his wife Vashti, is in the market for a new queen. In what sounds like a reality TV show, Xerxes holds a beauty contest in order to find himself a reigning partner, and Esther emerges the winner. Unbeknownst to the king, Esther is a Jew, placed in the palace by God to thwart a plot to annihilate the Jews. As the story unfolds, time is of the essence and Esther's devout uncle Mordecai urges her to go to the king and intercede for her people. But the practice of inserting oneself into the king's itinerary without being scheduled was a social faux pas punishable by death. It was going to take enormous courage on Esther's part, and to strengthen her resolve, Mordecai gives this infamous order:

> For if you keep silent at this time, relief and deliverance will rise for the Jews from another place, but you and your father's house will perish. And who knows whether you have not come to the kingdom for such a time as this? (Est. 4:14 ESV)

Mordecai's call to courage is both a stick and carrot: If you try and save your life, you will lose it (stick); but if you act, you have a significant role to play in God's master plan of redemption (carrot). It is significant that when Jesus calls His disciples to be courageous, He carries the same stick: "For those who want to save their life will lose it" and the same carrot, "and those who lose their life for my sake, and for the sake of the gospel, will save it" (Mark 8:35).

Esther's response is essentially "bring it on." Well, perhaps another translation reads that way. The NIV account is as follows:

> Go, gather all the Jews to be found in Susa, and hold a
> fast on my behalf, and do not eat or drink for three days,
> night or day. I and my young women will also fast as
> you do. Then I will go to the king, though it is against
> the law, and if I perish, I perish. (Est. 4:16 ESV)

Hers is a remarkable story of courage, wouldn't you agree? However, if you browsed for books or study guides on Esther, you would find titles such as *Esther: Woman of Faith*, or *Esther: God's Faithful Servant*. The stories and studies rarely mention the word *courage*.

The problem is this: In Scripture, an act of courage typically manifests both faith *and* courage, but our spiritual glasses often only see the faith component. Faith and courage are *not* the same thing or else only believers could be courageous, and this is clearly not the case.

Faith, love, loyalty, passion, and commitment: All of these characteristics can create the drumroll for an act of courage, but are not themselves courage. You could have faith and still act with cowardice (think of the apostle Peter's denial) or act without faith and still act courageously. That Esther has faith is indisputable. Why else would she call others to fast? Yet the prominence, uncertainty, and resolve of the statement, "If I perish, I perish," clearly directs our attention to her courage—her willingness to die.

To recognize that we are, indeed, wearing such spiritual spectacles, consider this question: What is the greatest act of courage in the Bible?

I wonder if you thought immediately of the cross. Surely Jesus' death for our sin is the most courageous act in all of history. What is courage but the willingness to die so that others may live? Jesus died an infinite death to give us an eternal life—which was an act of infinite courage! Yet when we look at the cross, what we often see is an act of love. Having labeled it as such, we rarely see Jesus' courage. Many times, courage is simply not in our field of vision.

In light of the fact that biblical heroics typically manifest both faith and courage, and not just faith, the point of the book of Esther is the point made as well through the stories of Nehemiah, Moses, Daniel, David, Elijah, Paul, Peter, Jeremiah, et cetera. All of these are models of faith, and all of these are models of courage. They all stared down the barrel of a loaded tyrant as Esther did and walked away under their own power. If we remove the faith/faithfulness blinders as we read the Scriptures, courage clearly emerges as a predominant virtue integral to most great acts of faith and redemption.

But before we leave Esther, let me throw out this remaining thought. Esther's anthem, "If I perish, I perish," seems to pluck the same chords of "guts and glory" as the declaration of Shadrach,

Meshach, and Abednego prior to their being thrown into the fiery furnace: "The God we serve is able to save us from it, and he will rescue us from your hand, O king. But even if he does not, we want you to know, O king, that we will not serve your gods or worship the image of gold you have set up" (Dan. 3:17–18). These words highlight how uncommon their valor and undaunted their courage.

Now to my point: Both the books of Esther and Daniel speak to believers who have to live out their faith in the hostile environment of exile. I want to suggest that the Scriptures show us that courage is a prerequisite to living out our faith in the context of a fallen and godless world, especially when we venture outside the community of faith.

The Disciples

As we look at this third and final example of courage, this one from the New Testament, there are some interesting parallels with the Joshua account: a similar situation and a similar call to courage. But more on this in a moment.

If you wanted to locate the author within their writings, look for their bones—that is, their outline, the underlying skeletal structure over which the narrative is stretched. Herein we find the authorial intent. Luke buried one of his bones in chapter 9, verse 51: "As the time approached for him to be taken up to heaven, Jesus resolutely set out for Jerusalem." From this point forward in Luke we read Jesus' words and actions in the context of His final journey to Jerusalem, in the cast shadow of the cross that awaits Him. All of the events and messages from chapters 10 through 20 are injected with the urgency of catching a departing flight—last warnings, last instructions, last appeals.

One of those last messages is addressed to His disciples. In Luke 12, Jesus is more than just a little concerned about how His disciples will hold up against hostile opposition after He's gone. When the persecution starts will they be men or mice? The message won't travel far if the messengers won't come out from under the bed.

> *I tell you, my friends, do not fear those who kill the body, and after that have nothing more that they can do. But I will warn you whom to fear: fear him who, after he has killed, has authority to cast into hell. Yes, I tell you, fear him! Are not five sparrows sold for two pennies? And not one of them is forgotten before God. Why, even the hairs of your head are all numbered. Fear not; you are of more value than many sparrows.*
>
> *And I tell you, everyone who acknowledges me before men, the Son of Man also will acknowledge before the angels of God, but the one who denies me before men will be denied before the angels of God. And everyone who speaks a word against the Son of Man will be forgiven, but the one who blasphemes against the Holy Spirit will not be forgiven. And when they bring you before the synagogues and the rulers and the authorities, do not be anxious about how you should defend yourself or what you should say, for the Holy Spirit will teach you in that very hour what you ought to say." (Luke 12:4–12 ESV)*

Like the taking of the Promised Land in Joshua, we are at another critical juncture in the plan of redemption—*the* critical juncture. Everything is on the line, literally everything: mankind, the heavens, the earth, the universe, black holes, dark matter, super novas … *everything*. In the impending cosmic battle of the cross and the resurrection, any number of things could threaten the plan, but as in the book of Joshua, Jesus sees cowardice as perhaps the most menacing. Yes sir, everything is moving like clockwork: The Son of Man is heading to Jerusalem, there He'll suffer and die, and everything looks to be coming off without a hitch, unless … well, unless His disciples lack the courage to be His witnesses. This would be highly problematic.

And so with words akin to those God speaks to Joshua ("I will never leave you nor forsake you," Josh. 1:5), Jesus assures them that God's presence will go with them: "Don't be afraid; you are worth more than many sparrows," and "Do not worry about how you will defend yourselves or what you will say, for the Holy Spirit will teach you at that time what you should say" (Matt. 10:31, 19).

But while Jesus' words are encouraging, they are also unyielding. He will hold their hands—not only to comfort them, but to keep them from running away.

The movie *Enemy at the Gates* relays the story of how the Russians courageously held Stalingrad against the well-trained and better-equipped German Army. The rousing motivational speech given by the Russian commander was simple: "Deserters will be shot." While lacking the softer edge of, "There's no 'I' in team," I guess it was highly effective, communicating that cowardice was unacceptable and retreat intolerable.

While undoubtedly ruthless, this kind of motivation is necessary. If you are to climb into the ring with death, your mind cannot splinter with doubts or escape plans. Retreat cannot be an option or it will be selected, which is why Spartan women sent their sons off to war with the admonition, "Come back with your shield or on it." Jesus does not share the callousness of a Russian commander or a Spartan mother, but He does eliminate retreat as a potential alternative for His disciples. His words resonate with those spoken by Gene Kranz to Mission Control during the Apollo 13 crisis, according to the movie: "Failure is not an option."

Looking at both Joshua 1 and Luke 12, one question is frustratingly unanswered: How? How exactly are we supposed to "be courageous"? What steps do we follow? Typically virtues and vices can be broken down into constituent parts, bite-size pieces that allow us to see the building blocks of love, the steps to forgiveness, or the anatomy of a lie. Courage seems to be a singular naked act of the will with no stutter steps or stepping stones. You simply choose to act, jump, fight, or throw yourself on a live hand grenade.

I imagine the creative team at Nike arriving at this realization: "Okay, so what moves a person to push themselves, pressing their bodies and minds beyond physical limits, enduring agony and the prospect of failure, humiliation, and defeat?"

"I don't know. They *just do it.*"

On this account, even William Miller, author of the courage tome *The Mystery of Courage,* offers little advice. In a humble and good-natured response to the question of how one learns to be courageous, Miller suggests, "It helps to read stories." Miller basically shrugs and says, "Not sure. You might try picking up a biography on Lincoln or something."[7] Any number of things can propel one to act courageously, but courage is a distinct act and a distinct virtue, separating those who "just do it" from those who *just don't.*

As John F. Kennedy observed in his Pulitzer Prize-winning book *Profiles in Courage*, "The stories of past courage can define that ingredient—they can teach, they can offer hope, they can provide inspiration. But they cannot supply courage itself. For this each man must look into his own soul."

OBSERVATIONS

Unfortunately, words are cheap. If they cost as much as gasoline, I'm sure I would have used them more economically. But now I find myself with the need to review and condense what we've gleaned from Scripture.

Biblical emphasis: The Bible is not *The Iliad*. It does not bestow upon courage the status of uber virtue, though the Bible clearly assigns courage prominence, and in the arenas of crisis and conflict, we see that courage is indispensable. Because acts of great courage are also acts of great faith, faith tends to dominate our field of vision and eclipse our awareness of courage, leading us to value courage far less than the Scriptures do. Faith, love, hope, loyalty, and commitment each prime us and incline us to rise to the moment—but courage is a distinct virtue, an irreducible act of the will. We either seize the moment or live with remorse.

The paradox of courage: As Chesterton poetically observed, courage is "a strong desire to live taking the form of a readiness to die" and a willingness to walk within an inch of death in order to take hold of life.[8] Like the principle of resurrection, courage seeks to transform death into life.

Biblical motivation and encouragement: Recounting the heroics of Esther, Daniel, and a cloud of other witnesses, the Scriptures hold up the examples of courageous men and women. As negative role models have great pedagogical value, Scripture equally exposes us to the cowardice of those lacking courage when history called for their votes—Pilate, for example. Our ultimate example of courage is, of course, Jesus Christ.

> To this you were called, because Christ suffered for you, leaving you an example, that you should follow in his steps. 'He committed no sin, and no deceit was found in his mouth.' When they hurled their insults at him, he did not retaliate; when he suffered, he made no threats. Instead, he entrusted himself to him who judges justly. (1 Peter 2:21–23)

God's presence in the midst of our struggles is always a sustaining motivation, and this promise of "I will be with you" echoes throughout Scripture as God promises to escort the faithful as they walk the "green mile." But perhaps the most unexpected form of encouragement is the stern exhortations that state in no uncertain terms that retreat is unacceptable. To remove retreat as an option is to restore clarity and focus to a mind fractured with anxiety and fear. Lastly, the Scriptures provide encouragement through vision and hope. Dire circumstances create a stage and spotlight for courage to perform, but the act is done in the enclosure of darkness. Scripture sheds light on the significance of the moment, as well as the life and reward awaiting the completed performance. "He who overcomes will inherit all this" (Rev. 21:7).

When courage is imperative: Courage is most called on as the kingdom of God expands and conflicts with the kingdoms of this world. Why did Joshua need courage? He needed it to fight a war to expand God's kingdom on planet earth. Why did the disciples need courage? For the same reason. As Satan and the world stand opposed to the kingdom of God, courage is a necessity in any effort to expand God's kingdom. Put another way, expansion of God's kingdom will always meet with rabid, tenacious, even violent opposition, and it will take great courage to meet that opposition without running away.

If this were a class in leadership, we would now close our books, go home, and do our assigned reading in *The Life and Times of William Wallace*. But this is not a leadership class, and so what we must do instead is consider the implications of this for how we live.

CHAPTER SIXTEEN

ORDINARY HEROES

EVERYDAY COURAGE

So far we've been speaking about courage with a capital C—courage in the face of ultimate, epochal, life-and-death decisions in which the fate of the free world hangs in the balance. That's fine; we needed to enlarge the picture to study the pixels. But we need to take the discussion out of the clouds and see how courage plays out at street level, in the day-to-day functioning of ordinary mortals. Kennedy was right when he observed in *Profiles in Courage*,

> *Without belittling the courage with which men have died, we should not forget those acts of courage with which men ... have lived. The courage of life is often a less dramatic spectacle than the courage of a final moment; but it is no less a magnificent mixture of triumph and tragedy.*[9]

If courage is a necessary ingredient in the expansion of God's kingdom against hostile opposition, we should expect to need it daily and carry it with the regularity of bottled water—for what else is being a Christ follower about but the expansion of God's kingdom in us (against the opposition of the flesh) and in the world (against the opposition of Satan)?

Our witness in the world will inevitably meet with opposition, and without courage we will not succeed. Living out a godly lifestyle can and will at times scandalize and offend the ungodly, and without courage we will not succeed; spiritual growth will meet with fierce resistance from our own flesh, and without courage we will not succeed.

The Christian life is a battle, and I cannot think of many successful militias that have found courage to be superfluous. With this in mind, let's look at the role courage plays in our daily battles against the flesh, the world, Satan, and anything else that gets in our way.

COURAGE: SANCTIFICATION'S MISSING INGREDIENT

For spiritual growth to take place, repentance must take place. For repentance to take place, one must be confronted with the truth of his or her sin, and to hear that truth takes courage. To hide from that truth is to stunt spiritual growth. As spiritual health and medical health are not without parallels, let's consider an example.

Some years ago I began experiencing shortness of breath. Walking up a flight of stairs felt like walking up to the torch at the top of the Statue of Liberty. My sedentary lifestyle, augmented by a unique high-fat, high-carb, low-fiber diet, was certainly a potential catalyst, but I suspected the problem was far more dire. There's a history of lung disease in my family, and I couldn't help but think that something was seriously wrong—yet I still didn't want to go to the doctor. The reason was simple: I was scared to hear the truth. As irrational as it may be, I was happier not knowing. But murmurs and lies fill the vacancy of truth, and I began to imagine all manner of congenital defects. Eventually I came to believe that it would be better to know the truth and try to fix what was wrong than to live in the misery of worry, fear, and denial. So I made an appointment with the doctor and came to find out I have asthma. Asthma! Once I was willing to face the truth, then—and only then—could I get treatment, which in my case meant using a fluorescent purple inhaler.

I always hate to be taken for a dimwit as a reader, so I'll assume you see the spiritual parallels of my story without me making the correlations. Similar illustrations and parallels are everywhere. Harvard's leadership guru, Ronald Heifetz, observes the same principle in leadership: "The real heroism of leadership involves having the courage to face reality.... Mustering the courage to interrogate reality is a central function of a leader."[10]

As difficult as it is to hear the truth about our health or business, nothing requires more courage than to face a negative diagnosis of our soul, for this is the ultimate truth about us. While I can distance myself from my asthma and maybe even my leadership skills, *spiritual* truth is deeply personal. Hebrews 4:12 explains why truth can be so terrifying.

> *For the word of God is living and active. Sharper than any double-edged sword, it penetrates even to dividing soul and spirit, joints and marrow; it judges the thoughts and attitudes of the heart.*

This certainly explains it: Confronting spiritual truth is a knife fight. Spiritual truth threatens to mortally wound our pride, ego, and reputation; to kill our protective delusions and denials; to tear us from our medicating dreams and fantasies; to rip open our hidden motives, fears, and sins. It takes courage to face God's truth.

Of course, over the years we've all acquired thick layers of body armor: rationalizations, denials, and distractions that make us all but impervious to truth. In the end we hear only what we want to hear.

But the sting of truth is the very thing that can make us well, producing godly sorrow and true repentance. Experiencing the pain of our sin, not simply assenting to it, is what helps us to turn from sin and never go back. This experience also allows for a genuine encounter with grace. We experience grace as "relief" only when we have felt pain.

Some years ago I was with my wife at a Christian retreat. It was a safe environment in which to pray and process truth. As we sat talking, I asked my wife this question: "In the first years of our marriage, I wasn't a very good husband, was I?"

In essence I was giving her the knife of truth and asking her to stab me with it. Not because I wanted to die—quite the opposite. I didn't want the status quo in our relationship; I wanted more life out of our marriage. To use Chesterton's description, I was willing to walk an inch from death in order to get more life. When I handed her the knife, I didn't need to give instructions. Had they been necessary, they would have looked something like this: "I'm going to ask a question, and it will be hard for me to hear you answer. When I give you the knife, I want you to stab me in the chest with it; anywhere else won't penetrate all my layers of denial and justification. Emotionally, I'll probably thrash and roll around on the ground for a while. Just leave me be. And don't make excuses for me, as this will only hinder the process. Afterward I'll need to pray and ingest God's grace and forgiveness like a couple Tylenol. If we do this right, I should be better; we should be better; my relationship with God should be better."

Truth is our friend in much the same way as a red-hot poker in the eye is our friend. In reality, this conversation with my wife shouldn't have been traumatic. But it was. And I remember it because it was painful and also because it was the first time I made a connection between courage and my spiritual growth.

It has since become my habit to ask God in my quiet times specific and difficult questions, and I'll wait, wanting to hear the answer. Being charismatically challenged, I don't always hear an answer, so I've actually had greater success spring-boarding off the context of disagreements, personal criticism, or judgments of others.

I ask God things like: "Is this true about me?" "Am I trying to protect or defend myself?" "What do you want me to hear in these thoughts/comments/criticisms?" "What role did my own sin play in this?" Like global positioning, this courageous triangulation of God-me-criticism can be helpful in locating the truth.

And if you still haven't had your fill of truth, you can always interrogate others and ask them questions you don't really want to hear the answers to: "Do I talk too much? Do I talk about myself too much? Do I listen well? Does it seem like I think my opinions or ideas are better than yours? Do I gossip too much?"

I don't do this very often, partially because I know the answers and there's no point in humiliating myself—and partially because I lack the courage and can only, as T. S. Eliot said, "bear so much reality."

COURAGE TO LIVE THE TRUTH

Winston Churchill once said that "Without courage, all virtue is fragile: admired, sought after, professed, but held cheaply and surrendered without a fight."

C. S. Lewis rounds out the thought: "Courage is not simply one of the virtues, but the form of every virtue at the testing point."[11] Churchill and Lewis shared a similar observation that in moments of crisis, courage is the enforcing virtue that keeps all the other virtues intact and preserved from corruption or compromise. The moment a virtue is most needed is also the moment it is most difficult to perform. What good is a virtue like honesty if in dire circumstances you'd lie to save your own neck? Without courage, we'll shed any virtue like a raincoat at the moment we need it most.

If courageously embracing the painful truth about ourselves is the first way we can more closely resemble Christ, the second way is in the temerity to live out our faith under pressure, or at the "testing point" as Lewis puts it.

For example, it took no courage whatsoever for the Scottish missionary and Olympic runner Eric Liddell not to run on Sunday. However, it took a staggering amount of courage to hold to his convictions when an entire nation counted on him to do otherwise. It doesn't take courage to give your perspective on America's involvement in the Middle East unless you're General David Petraeus speaking to Congress and the fate of thousands of soldiers and the anger of millions of Americans hinges on what you say. Speaking your mind in such circumstances takes courage. (They should probably give him another medal because he doesn't have that many.)

These are extreme examples, but every day we experience this dynamic of having to live out our beliefs amid the tide of social pressures. In an interview about his book *The Mystery of Courage*, William Miller pays tribute to the more generic brands of courage and cowardice that occupy our daily interactions. Miller states:

> *I planned on writing about cowardice, the little, daily interactions that you walk away from feeling somehow diminished or demoralized because you didn't stand up, or somebody trod on you or 'dissed' you. You know for sure that you've been a coward when you engage in fantasies of revenge. You'll lie awake or spend the next two hours wishing misery on the person.*[12]

He's exactly right. I never struggle with gossip, exaggeration, or being critical or judgmental unless I'm with people. Nor do I struggle with materialism unless I'm exposed to advertisements for things I want. Lust isn't a problem as long as I never see a woman or go near a device that makes pornography a mouse click away. When we diligently seek to live a godly life in the context of a sinful world, we realize just how strong the winds are against us and how much courage we'll need to stand our ground. As C. S. Lewis said, "You only know the strength of the wind when you try to walk against it."

No environment or social context is without its pressures, but the nature of the secular workplace is one of the most challenging. I worked in the creative department of a New York City ad agency, so I'm not even sure where to begin here. But let me just say this: In the context of an important client meeting, it takes courage to stand up and say, "We can't lie and promote something that's untrue about your product." I know it takes courage; *if it didn't, I'm sure I would have done it.*

The last product briefing I attended before going into ministry was for an oil treatment you inject into your car's engine. What does oil treatment do? *Nothing.* Absolutely nothing. According to the product manager it was "like black magic: If you think it works, then it does."

Our assignment was to create ads making it seem like this product was valuable without making an actual claim that it did something (so our client wouldn't get sued). How do you live out your faith in this kind of environment, day in and day out, without leaving your Christianity at home?

How do you keep from bending to the incessant pressure to please, conform, fit in, get along, and get ahead, all while keeping the client happy? Is it me, or am I starting to sound like the Cowardly Lion? "What makes the elephant charge his tusk in the misty mist, or the dusky dusk? What makes the muskrat guard his musk? Courage!"

To stand up for one's convictions and live out biblical values in the public arena takes courage, for we do so only through risk of death: death to reputation, death to status, death to ego, death to acceptance and approval, death to popularity, death to relationships, death to upward mobility, et cetera, et cetera, et cetera. Yet as Chesterton said of courage, it is "a strong desire to live taking the form of a readiness to die."[13] We must be willing to walk within an inch of all this professional and personal carnage in order to pursue life. To be a coward would be to run from the conflict, to choose a lesser life, and to renounce greater life in the form of any and all spiritual blessings.

As I believe courage to be a missing vitamin in spiritual growth, I likewise wonder if our lack of emphasis on courage has been a major source of our less than compelling cultural witness. Such things are hard to prove of course, but one thing can be stated with surety: In countries where courage is valued or intrinsically a part of what it means to be a Christian, there's no shortage of zeal.

COURAGE TO TELL THE TRUTH

In affirming the sincerity of his commitment to the Thessalonians, Paul states, "We had previously suffered and been insulted in Philippi, as you know, but with the help of our God we dared to tell you his gospel in spite of strong opposition" (1 Thess. 2:2). It's a shame there weren't footnotes in the original manuscript, because a big fat one belongs next to the word *dared*. The footnote should read, "Acts 16:22–23," which says:

> *The crowd joined in the attack against Paul and Silas, and the magistrates ordered them to be stripped and beaten. After they had been severely flogged, they were thrown into prison.*

This passage describes what happened to the apostle Paul in the city of Philippi. After being beaten in Philippi, Paul heads to Thessalonica, but Thessalonica is only a couple days walk from there, so think about it: When Paul arrives in Thessalonica, his entire back is one raw, bleeding wound that's just beginning to scab over from his "severe" beating in Philippi. His head is probably throbbing with a fever of 105 degrees. So when it says that he "dared" to tell them the gospel, it means this: Not only had he just endured a "severe" beating—not only had he preached to them in considerable pain—but he did so knowing full well that the same thing was likely to happen again. Can you image this kind of courage?

It takes courage to hear the truth, it takes courage to live out the truth, and it also takes courage to *proclaim the truth* of the gospel. The apostle Paul "dared to tell [them the] gospel in spite of strong opposition." But note the context. He does not tell this to the Thessalonians to prove he was an apostle or that he had suffered for Christ. He shares the gospel with them to demonstrate his sincere love for them. Paul so wanted them to experience the life of the gospel that he was willing to face death to bring it to them.

I think when we encounter fear, an inability to communicate, or ignorance of what to say, we assume that there's something wrong with us, and that evangelism couldn't possibly be as difficult, as awkward, or as terrifying for others as we experience it to be. Actually, I think this is the norm. I think it's always been the norm. I don't think that people have ever just *shared the gospel*—I think they've always "dared" to share the gospel. As John McCain observed, "Courage is not the absence of fear, but the capacity of action despite our fears."[14]

We all stand at the end of a two thousand-year-old line of faithful witnesses, as the gospel has passed from person to person down through the ages. At every link of the chain there was an exercise of courage—someone "dared" to tell someone else the good news of Jesus Christ. The gospel has come to us by way of *courage,* and it will pass no further beyond us without *courage*. We are the lowest limbs on a spiritual family tree, branching back to the disciples, and our particular family line will cease to blossom when *courage* ceases to blossom.

> *And what more shall I say? For time would fail me to tell of Gideon, Barak, Samson, Jephthah, of David and Samuel and the prophets—who through faith conquered kingdoms, enforced justice, obtained promises, stopped the mouths of lions, quenched the power of fire, escaped the edge of the sword, were made strong out of weakness, became mighty in war, put foreign armies to flight. Women received back their dead by resurrection. Some were tortured, refusing to accept release, so that they might rise again to a better life. Others suffered mocking and flogging, and even chains and imprisonment. They were stoned, they were sawn in two, they were killed with the sword. They went about in skins of sheep and goats, destitute, afflicted, mistreated—of whom the world was not worthy—wandering about in deserts and mountains, and in dens and caves of the earth. (Heb. 11:32–38 ESV)*

LAST WORDS

In his book *The Things They Carried,* Tim O'Brien reflects on courage. He recalls a time in the fourth grade when a girl in his class was dying of cancer and some bully ripped the scarf off her head, revealing her absence of hair from the chemotherapy. O'Brien adored this girl, and as she burst into tears, he wanted to intervene, step in, and protect her. But he didn't. Years later he reflects in his book, "I should've stepped in; fourth grade is no excuse. Besides, it doesn't get easier with time, and twelve years later, when Vietnam presented much harder choices, some practice at being brave might've helped."[15]

Courage in the big choices is the extension of courageous choices we make—or don't make—every day. If we're dying every day, it won't be difficult to die *some day*. And so we embrace daily the death in courage.

CHAPTER SEVENTEEN

HUMILIATION

Terrell Owens is one of the NFL's leading receivers. T. O., as he's known, would insist that he is *the* NFL's leading receiver, and herein lies the problem with Terrell Owens. Owens is the wide receiver for the _____. (I've left this blank as to not date the book because wherever he's playing this year will probably not be where he's playing next year.) Terrell Owens has been passed from team to team like the flu, his attitude infecting whoever comes in contact with it.

As a rookie with the San Francisco 49ers he had the potential (and still does) to be as great as any receiver to ever play in the NFL. But it didn't take long for the T. O. hype to turn into grumbling and recrimination. He accused teammates of subpar performance, taunted opponents after touchdowns, and railed against management for refusing to run up the score when victory was in the bag. "We have no killer instinct, period," said Owens.[1]

Then there were the sideline tirades. After a touchdown catch on Monday Night Football, he reached into his uniform, pulled out a marker, autographed the football, and tossed it to Greg Eastman, his financial consultant.

The 49ers couldn't afford to keep Owens, and it had nothing to do with his salary, which was considerable. On his way out the door, Terrell did an interview with *Playboy* in which he accused his former quarterback, Jeff Garcia, of being gay. Owen's response to the media explosion he set off was to defend his claim: "Like my boy tells me: If it looks like a rat and smells like a rat, by golly, it is a rat."[2]

So off he went to the Philadelphia Eagles—a chance for a fresh start and an opportunity to make new enemies. In an interview he told ESPN that the Eagles would be better off with Brett Favre than Donovan McNabb as their quarterback and expressed outrage that his one hundredth career touchdown wasn't heralded by management with a celebration or parade of some kind.

The result of the media storm in Philadelphia was Owens wearing a Dallas Cowboy uniform when the 2006 season kicked off. Early on, T. O. accused Tony Romo of favoring Jason Witten with his passes. Owens told the *Dallas Morning News* why he insisted on voicing his discontent: "I'm not jealous of Witten. I'm not jealous of nobody. I can take the approach that I got paid, so screw everything, but that's not me."[3]

During later games Romo threw to T. O. whether he was open or not. The placating orders came from on high, causing dissension among the other Dallas players. There was a solution for all this controversy that had worked quite well for the 49ers and the Eagles, and in 2009 Owens was on his way to the Buffalo Bills.

In the world of professional football, the world of business, and perhaps most worlds, T. O. doesn't have a humility problem; he has an emotional intelligence deficit, a very low "EQ," as they call it. Fundamentally, T. O. doesn't view himself much differently from the way the rest of us view ourselves; he simply doesn't know enough (or care enough) to hide his true feelings. Most everyone constructs a mental narrative in their heads with themselves as hero but retains the good sense to keep it in their heads. T. O. simply lives out the fantasy.

We tend to write stories in our heads: editing, rehearsing, thinking up alternate endings, rearranging dialogue, dreaming up different plots and scenarios. While we experience life as a patchwork of people, places, and circumstances, our minds can give these things a broader context, organizing them into a narrative and making a story out of them. In writing our narratives, nobody sets out to write a fairy tale, but pride and ego inevitably elbow their way in—writing and rewriting the story, turning real events and real people into an extravagant work of fiction. Pride and ego have their own ideas on how the story should develop. Pride can turn our mental diary into an infomercial, shameless self-promotion and propaganda for the ego.

I was just taking a shower, and I always noodle on my story when I'm in the shower. I was editing a real-life conversation I had a few days ago. The conversation, as it actually went down, could have never made it into the final manuscript of my story. My mind had been dull and sluggish, and I just wasn't thinking well on my feet. So I was doing a little editing, trying to get the lines just right—sharpening the points I should have made, pondering the way I should have answered, and crafting the perfect comeback I should have thought of but didn't. I'm pretty happy with the dialogue now.

The voice of the narrator in any story can possess a Morgan Freeman-like omniscience. The narrator is the only one who sees things as they truly are, the one who "gets it." Everyone else in the story has a *perspective of truth,* but the narrator defines truth just as *you,* as the narrator, define your own story. You become the judge and moral compass within the story. Who else but the narrator is qualified to evaluate the rightness and wrongness of people's thoughts and actions? Who else could possibly speak with surety of another person's motives?

Not only are we the narrator, we're also the story's protagonist—the leading man or woman. What this means is that all the action of the story revolves around us. Other characters are defined by their relationship to the protagonist (to you or me), and when they're not in one of our scenes, we might safely assume that they continue to think and talk about us: things we said and did, classic sayings, and exploits.

This is the way sin distorts our story. This is how egomaniacs, narcissists, and arrogant dictators come to be—through the perversion of their mental narrative. Nobody wakes up in the morning and suddenly believes that they are God. No, our mental diary of life becomes a story, and you become the story's narrator and the story's protagonist. Then pride corrupts the plot, the story turns into self-aggrandizing propaganda, and the propaganda deceives and converts us until we believe the propaganda. But other people know who we are: We're the self-centered S.O.B. who thinks the world revolves around us.

Pride is this journey from humanity to deity, and our mental narrative is the corruptible vehicle that transports us. Humility is the voyage back to the truth about who and what we really are.

Humility's journey is about backtracking, retracing our footsteps back from the ledge over which pride fell. And that journey begins with the simple admission that we've been secretly writing such fiction about ourselves.

Stepping back further, we acknowledge just how self-serving and distorted our version of reality was; we recant of having written it, thought it, and believed it. Retreating further, we repent of the pride that authored such a subversive little tome. Arriving back at the beginning, we confess and apologize to God for writing such lies and believing them. Then we toss the book in the fire and let the flames turn it into a lamentation, a sacrifice of repentance.

FALSE HUMILITIES

There are other fictional accounts, internal dialogues of an even darker nature. While pride pulls and stretches our thoughts upward toward hubris, shame and self-loathing magnetize them to point down toward false humility. The narrative is just as twisted, just as bent, only it is self-destruction masquerading as humility. As Dag Hammarskjöld stated it, "Humility is just as much the opposite of self-abasement as it is of self-exaltation."

Depending on any number of factors, we vacillate between arrogant pride and servile self-loathing. Neither version is truly humble.

Many things, in fact, *appear* to be humility. But what we label humility may well end up being low self-esteem, a self-effacing manner, shyness, or even depression. Take the statement "I don't deserve you." This could be a very humble admission. It could. It could also be a way to manipulate you, a means to make me appear humble, a colloquial expression, a tactic to avert your anger, an attempt to stroke your ego, low self-esteem, or a combination of all these things.

Humility is difficult to define and nearly impossible to diagnose. Only *we* know when our humility is not an act, and even then we should pencil a question mark into the margin. As Paul observes, "Indeed, I do not even judge myself. My conscience is clear, but that does not make me innocent. It is the Lord who judges me" (1 Cor. 4:3–4).

Like the virtue of love, humility is elusive, and it's never purely attainable. And yet we can continually seek increasingly greater measures of it, and we can work so that we drift away from it to an increasingly lesser degree. Against the relentless undertow of pride, humility is always struggling to get back to that fixed point on the shoreline. That fixed point can be defined as follows:

> *A wholly accurate appraisal of ourselves (talents, failures, lackings, knowledge, limits, roles, and responsibilities); an accurate appraisal of God and our relationship to Him (He is the Creator, we are the creation; He is the King, we are His subjects); and an accurate appraisal of others (unbiased acknowledgment of the gifts and abilities of others, and unqualified respect for their thoughts, opinions, feelings, authority, and accomplishments).*

HUMBLING OURSELVES: A MAP OF THE JOURNEY

If humbling ourselves is returning to the truth about who we are, the best description of that journey can be found in Paul's letter to the Philippians. Before we focus on the death that lies in humility, let's look at the process as a whole.

> If anyone else thinks he has reasons to put confidence in the flesh, I have more: circumcised on the eighth day, of the people of Israel, of the tribe of Benjamin, a Hebrew of Hebrews; in regard to the law, a Pharisee; as for zeal, persecuting the church; as for legalistic righteousness, faultless. But whatever was to my profit I now consider loss for the sake of Christ. What is more, I consider everything a loss compared to the surpassing greatness of knowing Christ Jesus my Lord, for whose sake I have lost all things. I consider them rubbish, that I may gain Christ and be found in him, not having a righteousness of my own that comes from the law, but that which is through faith in Christ — the righteousness that comes from God and is by faith. I want to know Christ and the power of his resurrection and the fellowship of sharing in his sufferings, becoming like him in his death, and so, somehow, to attain to the resurrection from the dead. (Phil. 3:4–11)

Paul begins by stating that if salvation was something to be earned, he could muster an impressive résumé, more impressive in fact than any of the legalists who demanded strict observance of the laws and commandments as a prerequisite for salvation.

But when Paul came to Christ and received salvation, he reckoned his spiritual résumé—beautifully printed on sixty-pound ivory stock—to be nothing more than dung. It's an admittedly disturbing word, but *dung* is the actual word in the text, not "rubbish," as the translators have rendered it. I think the word *dung* was selected by God to shake us awake and shout at us. God chose *dung* here—and it is used elsewhere in Scripture—because dung is tied to our sense of shame. Dung evokes something that rubbish cannot.

And it is dung that depicts the outrageous nature of Paul's salvation and our own, the humiliation and shame of our unsanitary spiritual condition and the humbling absurdity of the transaction—*trading our dung for Christ's righteousness.* Coming to Christ is the ultimate humbling of ourselves—the prototype for all subsequent humbling.

Martin Luther, the German leader of the Reformation, was asked when it was that he realized salvation was by faith and not works. His response was "*in cloaca,*" which sounds rather spiritual until you translate it. The words mean sitting "on the toilet." Luther suffered from bouts of both crudeness and constipation, so it's quite possible that this *was* the actual location of his realization. But many scholars believe that Luther was actually using a common metaphor for "humbling oneself," which was popular in the Middle Ages, and a metaphor that's almost identical—and equally repugnant—to Paul's "dung" allusion.

And it is a pitch-perfect metaphor for humbling oneself, for if there is ever a time or a place when we are completely without pretense or posturing, it's on the toilet. Here we have no facades, no image management, no cover-ups, no masks, no masquerades—we are what we are. The outhouse knows no royalty, actors, or fashion models; it is no respecter of persons. The toilet is ground zero for humanity. The key to the kingdom is, in fact, the key to the restroom.

But here's the part of the passage that's easy to miss—again due to translation problems. Clearly Paul humbled himself when he came to Christ. We get that—couldn't be clearer. But the passage also states that in a manner similar to his salvation, Paul *continued* to humble himself. This was an ongoing practice in Paul's life. We also see Philippians 3:8 more accurately when translated, "What is more, I *continue to* consider everything a loss." Many translators fail to indicate the ongoing verb tense and omit the word *continue.*

Paul "continued" to humble himself; he made the trip back to truth over and over, as many times as he probably wandered from it and sought to define his sufficiency in anything other than Jesus Christ. Like a man with an aging prostate, Paul was always back and forth to the bathroom.

But Paul's objective was not going to the bathroom, considering his achievements to be dung, or denigrating himself in any fashion. Why did he strip himself of his accomplishments, reputation, and dignity? Paul says that he stripped himself naked that he might be clothed in Christ ("gain Christ") and that he might "know Christ and the power of his resurrection" (Phil 3:10). As we've seen throughout our study, death is just the path by which we get to resurrection—it is not our goal, but the way we get to our goal of new life. The death of humility is no different. We strip ourselves of all artifice that we might meet with Jesus face-to-face, that He might cover us, console us, and transform us.

It is from within this intimate encounter that we experience the other truth about ourselves: *what is true of us in Christ.* Though I am egregiously sinful, I am deeply, deeply loved. I have eternal life. I am forgiven. I have a future and a hope. I am a child of God and an heir of the kingdom. This, too, is the truth about me.

But let's not get too far ahead of ourselves, for the life that lies within humility grows out of the death that lies within humility. Humility is derived from the Latin word *humus.* Humus is basically compost; it's the product of decomposition—the dead, dying, and decaying life of plants and animals. The result of this decomposition is life. Humus becomes fertilizer for plants and allows the soil to pool and reserve water—yet again we see that death becomes life.

So hold your nose and let's dig our hands into the humus, the death in humility.

CHAPTER EIGHTEEN

STRIP SEARCH

By this point in the book, my hope is that your definition and perception of death has expanded (shrunk, rather, would be more to the point) as we see death in smaller increments, such as the death of a dream or a relationship or reputation or ego. These lesser deaths are no less a death; we experience the cessation of a kind of life, and we come to the very end of ourselves: "Indeed, in our hearts we [have] felt the sentence of death" (2 Cor. 1:9).

I hope you see this. I hope your field of vision has widened and that you now see the concept of death and resurrection with a broader perspective. If so, then seeing the death in humility should be obvious. When you humble yourself, in a manner of speaking, you are killing off your fictional self.

When I worked in the field of advertising, there was an expression used by creatives: "drowning your puppies." In the advertising world, puppies are pet ideas: the fiction you birthed or concepts you created for which you felt a special fondness. Typically they are clever lines or scenes that were particularly creative but completely superfluous or off strategy and therefore in need of rejection. Though they are just concepts and ideas, they are more than that; they are a personification of our creativity in some form. This is why it is so difficult to erase them—and why it felt like drowning puppies.

Our concept of the person we are, if left unchecked, will become ever inflating, distorting as it grows, becoming more and more powerful and omnipotent. We soon forget our proportions, as if we were looking at ourselves as from the front row of a movie theater. We become the image, actor, and projection. We are the great and mighty Oz, and humility is the barking dog that pulls back the curtain so that everyone can see the doddering imbecile pulling the levers.

To become small, we must cut ourselves down to size, or at the very least participate in the process as God does. But being cut down to size can be as painful as it sounds. We're like shrubs that start off as delightful complements to a landscape until we grow up and out like monstrous, green, man-eating Venus fly traps. To retain the shrub we need to be stripped back to the naked branches. This is the death in humility: to be stripped, to be found naked, to suffer humiliation.

We are all clothed and protected by many layers. Among the layers that insulate us are reputation, accomplishments, power, status, ego, and self-image. These are like our identity profiles on Facebook or eHarmony, as David Weinberger reflects in his book *Everything is Miscellaneous*:

> My list of interests isn't really a list of my interests. It's a complex artifact that results from my goals, self-image, and how others might interpret my list. I put "reading" on the list in part because it looks good. But that doesn't tell you much about me other than that I'm

the type of person who puts "reading" on a list of inter-
ests. A frank discussion of how a person constructed
her list would tell us more about that person than the
list does.[4]

Humility seeks the opportunity, whenever it's presented, to shed these illusory layers. Humility wants the truth. Why humility would desire this is complicated, but for the believer it's rather simple: While these layers buffer us from pain, they also hinder contact and intimacy with Christ. Jesus is truth and meets with us in truth. He meets with only the true us. Layers of artifice, falsehood, and fiction separate us from Him.

When we think of layers, we think of things extrinsic to us like clothing. Being publicly stripped as Jesus was at His crucifixion is indeed humbling. Yet Jesus was not just stripped of clothing, but layers of skin. Having no sinful veneers to be stripped of, Jesus' humbling was in being stripped of only those layers endemic to humanity: clothing and skin. We have many, many more layers that need stripping to get through the varnish and down to the bare wood. As our layers define us and are intrinsic to us, they feel much more like skin when they're peeled away.

This is the death in humility, the experience of being emotionally flayed.

NEGATIVE PRESS: STRIPPED OF REPUTATION

During the presidential race of 2008, vice-presidential nominee Sarah Palin emerged as an unknown figure, and the Republican Party guarded her exposure like a national secret. That was until

Katie Couric's damaging and severely slanted exposé, an interview resulting in a media black eye no amount of rouge could cover. Now the cat was out of the bag, and the Republican Party would need to grant a full exposure interview of Palin in hopes of setting the record straight. But who could be trusted to provide such balanced and unbiased reporting? Charlie Gibson, that's who. What an honor to be the one reporter entrusted to deliver to the American public the real Sarah Palin. (Not really.) In the world of news reporting, this was not a compliment, but an insult. It meant that the Republican overlords felt that Charlie, out of all the other potential interviewers, was most likely to throw Palin interrogative softballs. This is a great reputation to have for getting interviews, but not one that will get you a Peabody.

Charlie was not ignorant of this fact, and if you saw the interview you know that Charlie, known for his sincerity, was far more candid than he was sincere. He wanted America to get an authentic look at Palin, and not simply provide her with a PR opportunity. Charlie delivered. He reestablished himself as a man worthy of the ABC anchor desk. Whatever happened to Palin and her career was simply collateral damage in the crusade to preserve reputation.

Being the object of slander or gossip has always been a painful experience, but in his book *The Future of Reputation*, author Daniel Solove examines how the Internet has amplified shame to unimaginable levels.

Gossip, slander, and criticism now have broadband capacity, turning whispers and rumors into a quaint relic of twentieth-century living. Any life lived today in any semblance of community is guaranteed to generate negative press of some kind.

In fact, I just Googled me. Here's what someone thinks about a book I wrote:

> *I think I understand the approach being used here, but it strikes me as ... contrived. Forced. Glib. James [is] trying to reach people who have little or no knowledge of Scripture and Jesus. Fair enough. But it's rather ironic that he goes to great pains to disavow any adherence to creed or theological stance, yet assuredly takes up an exegetical method.*

They're probably right. But whether it's true or not—or whether any gossip, slander, or criticism is true or not—isn't all that relevant from humility's perspective. What is relevant is the opportunity it affords us to become small, to decrease in the eyes of the world and in our own eyes. We can seize the opportunity by embracing it, by allowing our reputations to suffer and resisting the urge to intervene and nurse them back to health. The opposite of humbly submitting to the loss of reputation is to fight to repair it, to try to somehow glue it back together. But this is to assert that we are better than what people have said about us, that our reputation should be greater than what it is, that we should be esteemed more than we are.

Humility doesn't want to say this stuff.

If humility is essentially the truth about us, how does humbling ourselves to the fabrications of gossip and slander equate to humility? How does it move us from fiction to reality?

For starters, humility is not agreeing with the falsehoods said about us; it is only agreeing not to adjudicate and fight for our reputation.

There are several reasons humility remains essentially a pacifist. First, humility recognizes this: Whatever we've been falsely accused of, we're probably guilty of having done, said, or thought far worse. Our public image, no matter how trashed and tarnished, is still better than the one we deserve. You may call me an idiot, but in ways immeasurably more than you ever dreamed, *I really am an idiot.* Humility recognizes that no matter how it's accomplished and by whom, being stripped of our reputation brings us closer to reality, and therefore it's a death not undeserved.

Second, humility—and this is important—also recognizes that we are not acquiescing to lies and slander, but to the Lord, who has allowed us to be humbled. It's a big difference. We humbly submit ourselves to God's dealings with us by resisting the urge to defend ourselves, manage our image, set the record straight, repair our reputation, or seek vindication. We entrust our reputations to the Lord. If He wants to save our stock, fine; if not, let it plummet. Vindication and revenge are on God's to-do list, not ours. We are not to seek the glory of our own name but the glory of God's name, entrusting our reputation to Him: "Humble yourselves before the Lord, and he will lift you up" (James 4:10).

However, there are times, for the sake of friends and family and even our witness, when we should seek to clarify our innocence. The motive in such instances is a concern for others and the reputation of Christ. As God humbles us, He will make it clear what should be said and what should be left unsaid.

INFIRMITY: STRIPPED OF VITALITY

It would seem quite natural that when we look up to the heavens and reflect that we are only seventy or so inches tall, live only seventy or so years, and can lift only seventy or so pounds, that we would carry an accurate appraisal of our limitations. This is totally not the case. Practically speaking, we live like immortals. It's only when we're sick or old that we perceive our frailty; the drastic loss of our capacity enables us to see the truth.

Confidence and strength are the illusions of vitality. Even so, such illusion may well have won the Cold War and averted a nuclear holocaust. At the Geneva Summit of 1985, President Ronald Reagan met with Mikhail Gorbachev for the first time in order to reduce tensions in the escalating arms race between the U.S. and Russia.

In a recent PBS special, Edmund Morris, Ronald Reagan's official biographer, observed how the summit was captured even before it began as Reagan, who was twenty years older than Gorbachev, walked out in the freezing cold to welcome him to the summit.

Down the stairs of the plane comes into the freezing air glided this great, blue-suited, unbelievably self-confident, calm president— without a coat on. Out of the big black Russian limousine stepped this awkward, short, heavily-coated, heavily scarved communist leader fumbling with his scarf and his coat as he approached this benign presence. As they met at the foot of the stairs, Reagan towered over Gorbachev and led him into the building.[5] The perception of Reagan's vitality created the illusion of strength, confidence, power, and invulnerability.

In reality, Reagan was already suffering from the onset of Alzheimer's. It was a carefully constructed facade. Vitality grants us a cloak of invincibility even when we're stripped of it—our health, youth, strength, wits, energy, and drive—even when we're humbled and brought low.

People sense weakness. In the eyes of the world, the weak, sick, elderly, and dying are almost seen as marginal people. In a weakened and humbled state, we are not viewed the same as others, but neither do we hold the same point of view as other people. We see through the other end of the telescope how small we are, how transient life is, and how desperately we need a savior. "For, 'All men are like grass, and all their glory is like the flowers of the field; the grass withers and the flowers fall'" (1 Peter 1:24). We are humbled.

Humility seizes the opportunity afforded by infirmity—an opportunity to feel week, impotent, reliant, and needy; an opportunity to feel the reality of our true condition. "That is why, for Christ's sake, I delight in weaknesses, in insults, in hardships, in persecutions, in difficulties. For when I am weak, then I am strong" (2 Cor. 12:10).

I hate public speaking. I simply don't have the constitution for it. Standing in front of people makes me nauseous, but worse than that, I get anxiety attacks while I'm speaking. Fortunately my nerves work for me—they actually help me to communicate better in the same way that drowning can help someone tread water faster. When I speak publicly, it's unfortunate that the energy I expend in my anxiety is, I think, what makes people want to hear me speak—desperation looks a lot like passion.

If it were up to me, I would never speak. But because of this I distrust my motives. So my habit is always to say *yes* if asked, then pray that I won't be asked again.

The degree of emotional suffering I endure is contingent on the size of the audience: a few hundred, not so bad; a few thousand, very, very bad. If it's very bad, my panic attacks can continue through the night before I speak, and when I don't sleep, I can spiral down fast.

At a conference I was speaking at a few years ago it got very, very bad. Outside of those close to me, I usually don't tell people about my issue because it's embarrassing and, like, why would I? But in this case I informed the conference team. One dear individual stayed up with me all night, walking with me up and down and back and forth in the hotel room, on the beach, and even in front of the pharmacy until it opened in the morning and my doctor could send sedatives to ease whatever imagined trauma was burning a hole in my psyche.

Well, word got around the conference, and by the time I spoke, everyone knew I was as mentally stable as Sweeney Todd. It was humiliating and humbling. As I spoke the next few nights I felt weak, vulnerable, and naked as I stood defenseless before a live audience.

The temporary loss of my mental health stripped me of my social immune system, my pretense, my defenses and facades. But the things that shield us from face-to-face contact with others also veil us from face-to-face contact with Christ, and this is the value of being humbled—of having our defenses swept away, to meet with Christ without the veils: "Declares the LORD, 'This is the one I esteem: he who is humble and contrite in spirit, and trembles at my word'" (Isa. 66:2).

While I didn't experience a rush of supernatural power or even a still, small voice reminding me that I wasn't alone as I stepped out on stage, God did lovingly confirm to me that He used the talk in the lives of those who heard it. More than one student came up to me afterward and said it was the most powerful message they had ever heard.

SUBMISSION: STRIPPED OF POWER

Let me begin with this disclaimer: I'm very glad that America is a nation and not a British seaport, that there's a McDonald's down the road and not a fish-and-chips stand, and that I don't have a picture of the Queen Mum on my wall. With that said, if you think back on the roots of the American Revolution, you have to admit that the Wesleyan Tories made a persuasive case. John Fletcher, a leading Methodist minister, wrote in 1776 that in light of the institution of slavery, colonial talk of liberty was—to say the least—hypocritical.

> *Do not the sighs of myriads of innocent [slaves] unjustly transported from their native country ... call night and day for vengeance upon us; whilst their groans upbraid the hypocritical friends of liberty, who buy, and sell, and whip their fellow men as if they were brutes; and absurdly complain that they are enslaved.*[6]

In light of this rather glaring inconsistency, Fletcher, John Wesley, and others suspected that the real issue for the colonists was not liberty but autonomy—individual power. Americans simply didn't want to bow their knee to anyone.

The colonists decried oppression, staged a revolution, threw off England's authority, and declared independence. Due in part to this history, submission to authority is not high on the list of American values. It's just slightly above our regard for imperial authority. Unfortunately the formula (assert oppression, stage a revolution, throw off authority, and declare independence) has been just a little abused.

There are, for example, thousands of denominations and independent churches in America that have their origins in this pseudo-revolutionary process: Claim oppression, stage a revolution, throw off authority, and open up a new branch farther down the road. I'm not questioning the need for, or wisdom of, denominations and their sometimes-necessary offshoots. But like the Wesleyan Tories, I think one has to wonder if, as a culture, we struggle with some significant authority issues.

My concern is not cultural criticism. It's just that when it comes to humility in the form of submission, I think we need to be aware of our cultural baggage.

Submission to leadership, especially poor leadership, provides an abundance of opportunities to humble oneself. The abundance is easy to chart; just think back to every time you've ever thought, *I can't believe I have to listen to this jerk.* Parents, bosses, professors, police, and government—we're always living under someone's thumb. Ideally, anyone occupying the role of "boss" in my life would be smarter, funnier, wiser, and more gifted than I am, as that would make the task of submitting to authority much easier. But it doesn't require humility to follow someone who's my better, just common sense. Logic dictates you submit to authority more knowledgeable than you. Humility dictates it when the order is reversed: "Slaves, submit yourselves to your masters with all respect, not only to those who are good and considerate, but also to those who are harsh" (1 Peter 2:18).

By definition, to be under someone's authority means we are not free to do anything we want, and any loss of freedom can be viewed as oppressive. All revolutions against leadership are, therefore, easily rationalized. But if the goal of the revolution is freedom, humility alone can provide that freedom. The real tyranny is that of our ambition, pride, ego, and need for control, humbling ourselves is the only route to independence. Humility perceives submission to leadership as an opportunity for spiritual freedom, to be out from under the yoke of pride's oppression, which is why Peter suggests, "Submit yourselves for the Lord's sake to every authority instituted among men" (1 Peter 2:13).

FAILURE: STRIPPED OF ACCOMPLISHMENTS

Though it's certainly possible to elaborate on other layers of pride that ought to be stripped from us and left at Goodwill, this will be the last we'll explore: *being stripped of our accomplishments.*

If you are even remotely familiar with baseball and its historic games, you know the name Bill Buckner.

In the fall of 1986, it had been exactly sixty-eight years since the Boston Red Sox had won a World Series—one of the greatest droughts in the history of sports. But they had made it to the World Series that year, and it was game six. Boston led the best-of-seven series three games to the New York Mets' two, and they had a two-run lead with two outs in the bottom of the tenth inning. Mookie Wilson of the Mets hit a routine ground ball to first base, and it went under Buckner's glove, through his legs, and out into right field. As a result, the Red Sox lost the game—and lost the World Series.

In that single instant Buckner's entire career of great accomplishments vanished. In Boston today, the Bunker Hill Bridge still goes by the name of "The Bill Buckner Bridge" because cars pass unimpeded through the bridge's Y-shaped legs.

Major failures, particularly public ones, have the power to wipe out years of personal accomplishments overnight. Woody Hayes was the legendary football coach of the Ohio State Buckeyes. The name Woody Hayes should be synonymous with winning. *It's not.*

In the Gator Bowl of 1978, Ohio versus Clemson, with one minute and fifty-eight seconds left to play, Woody's temper glowed from TV sets across the nation. Clemson's Charlie Bauman intercepted an Ohio pass and was forced out of bounds right in front of Coach Hayes. Woody hauled off and slugged Bauman in the throat, then beat on the face mask of his own player when he tried to restrain him. At 7:45 the next morning, Hayes' career came to a humiliating end.

It's hard to imagine how much of our esteem and significance is tied to our achievements until they're erased. Then it's really easy to imagine.

Though we see our accomplishments as extensions of ourselves, they're more like hair extensions or hair plugs or fake eyelashes. This is to say that they are not truly extensions of who we are, merely attachments. To be humbled, and at times stripped of accomplishment, is for us to recognize the difference: "For who makes you different from anyone else? What do you have that you did not receive? And if you did receive it, why do you boast as though you did not?" (1 Cor. 4:7).

The more you see yourself with the eyelashes of a fashion model or the mane of a rockstar, the more you view these things as attributes rather than adornments. We are not the source of our skills and abilities; our looks, our intelligence, and our accomplishments portray an exaggerated caricature of ourselves. We know this, but we don't *know* this—not until we're humbled.

I think this is the form of humbling we dread the most. It's probably because we fear that like Job or Bill Buckner, we'll be stripped of everything in a flash flood of humbling. I don't think this is typical of God's work in our lives. More typically we are stripped of accomplishment one sock at a time: failure to receive credit, passed over for praise or promotion, and so on.

Humility expects and understands the periodic need for someone else to get credit for something we did, to be ignored for an achievement, blamed for something we didn't do, or to fail in a public forum.

Sitting together, ego and accomplishment tend to act out, and humility understands why sometimes they need to be separated. I'm not saying humility is itching to see Marion Jones stripped of her gold medals, but it embraces the need, the means, and the results of being stripped of credit, accomplishment, and recognition.

As Thomas Aquinas put it,

> The spontaneous embracing of humiliations is a practice of humility not in any and every case but when it is done for a needful purpose: for humility being a virtue, does nothing indiscreetly. It is then not humility but folly to embrace any and every humiliation: but when virtue calls for a thing to be done it belongs to humility not to shrink from doing it.[7]

CHAPTER NINETEEN

BEING EVER SO HUMBLE

Each year Prison Fellowship ministers to hundreds of thousands of inmates in some 1,400 correctional facilities in 112 countries around the world. Here is where the ministry began—with the sentencing of its founder, Charles Colson, the first member of the Nixon administration to be indicted for Watergate.

"Morality is a higher force than expediency," he continued, glaring at notes before him. "The court does recognize," his tone softened slightly, " that Mr. Colson's public image has been somewhat distorted.... A thorough review of Mr. Colson's life ... shows instances of useful public service for others in trouble, qualities of the defendant which have rightly endeared him to his family, his close friends, and to clients he has effectively served."

I felt [my lawyer's] arm come around my back, squeezing me gently and holding on for what was coming. The kind words were to soften the blow. I was taking deep breaths now to control my emotions. I

*must show none, I thought, as my ears detected gentle
sobbing behind me....*

*[The judge] lifted the gavel in the air. "The court will
impose a sentence of one to three years and a fine of five
thousand dollars." Hardwood struck hardwood with an
ear-splitting whack. A half-muffled scream came from the
back of the room, a high-pitched voice crying, "Oh, no!"
Then absolute silence again. A tingling sensation swept
through my body like needles jabbing at my flesh. Then a
sharp feeling of nausea. [The lawyer] squeezed harder. I bit
my lower lip, praying that it was not Patty's voice that had
shouted. My mind blotted out the rest of the words [the
judge] now spoke—the penitentiary, date of surrender,
dismissal of other charges. The gavel fell again. Crack!*[8]

There is nothing more humbling than the public scourging of
one's reputation. On the day of Colson's sentencing, he joined the
ranks of the utterly humbled. In a sweep of the gavel he lost nearly
everything: his name, reputation, job, freedom, career—all gone.
The depths to which we are humbled is determined by the height
from which we've fallen. Unfortunately for Chuck Colson, 1600
Pennsylvania Avenue boasts the highest elevation on earth.

I picture Jesus right there with Colson, embodied by his lawyer,
arm around him, holding him, squeezing gently, and bracing for the
blow. It could have been different—Colson could have gotten off.
Watergate might have never happened, his sentence could have been
community service. *Thank God it wasn't.* If the outcome had been
different and Colson had been spared his humbling, thousands of

prison ministries all over the world would instantly evaporate, having never existed.

So here's the question: Do we simply wait for God to humble us and embrace it when He does, or do we choose to humble ourselves? *Yes.*

The closer we grow in intimacy with Christ, the more sensitive we become to impediments, distractions, and interruptions—*we'd like the booth in the corner, please.* Awareness of the encroachment of pride or performance alerts us to our need for humbling, and the humbling process may be initiated by either of the two parties in love—God or us.

Recognizing that humbling may originate with God keeps us spiritually alert, enabling us to see chastening circumstances as His handiwork. Thus identified, we seek to submit and participate in the process He's initiated, embracing whatever means of gravity God has employed to bring us back to earth.

On the other hand, if we feel distant from God, distant from ourselves, or are longing for a greater degree of intimacy, God invites us to initiate the process ourselves, humbling ourselves by faith as opposed to obedience. We seek some way to make ourselves small, trusting God's Spirit to engage and embrace us in our initiative.

When it comes to being humbled, God can and does work the process from His end. As I've just noted, we also have the prerogative to humble ourselves or to keep ourselves humble. How one attempts to engage in the process during a typical work week varies to some degree from person to person. I can only speak for me. So this is what I'll do.

I count three primary ways that I tend to the humbling of my soul on a routine basis. God, most assuredly, is also working the problem from His end. These are the paths I take to meet up with him: public confession, guarding the door, and incessant reliance upon Him.

PUBLIC CONFESSION

In the late 1990s on a small sampling of college campuses around the country, mostly Christian colleges, there were tremors of revival. The following is the account of the 1995 Wheaton College Revival.

> On Sunday evening, March 19, 1995, two students from Howard Payne University in Brownwood, Texas, spoke during a weekly student-led worship service at Wheaton.
>
> The two students "shared what God had done in their lives" during recent times of revival at their campus and at other schools, said Wheaton professor Tim Beougher. After they spoke, there was no exhortation or manipulation, the professor said. "There was no attempt to try and force a repeat experience of what had happened at Howard Payne University." But, "Immediately students began to come up to the microphone and confess sin," Beougher said. "The confession was deep. It was painful. God really did a work of breaking people."
>
> The service had begun at 7:30 p.m. Sunday. It did not end until 6 a.m. Monday.
>
> Normally, about 400 students attend the service. That Sunday, about 700 came. It was difficult to know

how many attended because many who were there left and went back to get their roommates and friends.

The "beautiful thing" was that when a person would confess sin, 20 to 50 students would gather around the person and pray for him. "There was a real spirit of love and acceptance," Beougher said. "You could not point a finger at anyone else," because "all of us there had been stripped bare before the throne of God."

When the students broke up at 6 a.m., they agreed to meet again Monday night, March 20. They started at 9:30 that night and attendance climbed to more than a thousand. The seats of Pierce Chapel were filled, and students stood two and three deep along the walls.

As on Sunday night, the service began with praise and worship. Then came more "deep confession."

Students were given an opportunity to throw away things "that were hindering your walk with God or that might trip you up in the future." Many went back to their rooms and returned with secular music discs, pornography, alcohol, credit cards and other items. One student even brought a rose, apparently symbolic of an unhealthy relationship. The meeting lasted until 2 a.m.

The next night, about 1,350 students gathered in the church's 1,500-seat sanctuary. After a time of praise and worship, confession of sin followed again....

On Thursday, it was time to celebrate. The students, 1,500 of them, held a "praise and worship service that

raised the roof," the professor said. "It was glorious....
It was a foretaste of what heaven is going to be like."⁹

I was fortunate enough to catch a glimpse of one of these outbreaks, which sounds like I'm one of those people who drive around chasing tornadoes—and maybe in a sense I was. From what I could see, it was certainly a powerful movement of the Spirit of God—Category 2 or 3 at least—but I couldn't say that what I witnessed was anything more than the power of public confession. That's not to say it wasn't "revival," but rather that when God's people humbly confess their sins to one another, people are revived.

For most of us, confession is a private affair. We tend to focus on the verse in 1 John 1:9: "If we confess our sins, he is faithful and just and will forgive us our sins and purify us from all unrighteousness." However, some of us tend to gloss over the directive of James 5:16: "Therefore confess your sins to each other and pray for each other so that you may be healed." In confessing our sins to God, notice that John emphasizes cleansing and forgiveness, while James says that confessing to one another makes us well—not just forgiven, *but healed.* Both passages and both truths are needed to bookend sin and keep it from sprawling.

Even non-Christians recognize the power of public confession. If you talk to just about anyone who has been through Alcoholics Anonymous (or any other twelve-step program for that matter), most will point to step five as the most pivotal. It states, "Admitted to God, to ourselves, and to another human being the exact nature of our wrongs." It is through publicly admitting to "another human being the exact nature of [their] wrongs" that people in these programs find freedom.

Why we've neglected the practice of public confession is the same reason we've neglected the practice of public stocks and pillories: It's unbearably humbling to publicly confess your most private sins.

My wife recently left town for a couple days to visit our daughter at college. Home alone, I was concerned that I might misuse my freedom while she was gone. I went to Taco Bell for dinner, which Katie would have never approved of, but that wasn't the unaccountable action I was concerned about. I had carefully planned, and have no remorse for, going to Taco Bell. What I didn't want to do was go somewhere on the Internet I shouldn't go. So I e-mailed my pastor and associate pastor to inform them of my situation and that I felt somewhat at risk with Katie gone.

> *Hey guys. Katie is away visiting Avery overnight. When I do so much writing I can feel a little detached. Anyway [for] whatever reason, today I feel a little susceptible to wandering on my computer to sites I shouldn't. So just wanted to bring you in, ease temptation, and not give Satan a foothold.*

While they are caring friends as well as pastors, I still felt embarrassed by my temptation to sin in this way and by my weakness and inability to handle it myself. I imagined respect for me would be lost (though of course it wasn't) the moment the e-mail was opened. While not a public confession of sin as much as a confession of sinfulness, it had the same hi-my-name-is-Rick-James-and-I'm-an-alcoholic kind of feel to it.

It is, however, an altogether different experience to meet with Christ and be in His presence in this condition, on these terms. Grace is palpable, not a concept but a breathable atmosphere. To be completely exposed and *then* forgiven is utterly transformational.

As long as we retain a shred of dignity, we are still clothed by something, still hidden in some way. We can still reason that what remains concealed could have been the deal breaker, the transaction that didn't go through because our grace limit was maxed out. When we come to Christ completely humbled, we experience—at least temporarily—the absence of insecurity and we perceive the unconditional nature of His love for us.

GUARDING THE DOOR

Keeping ourselves in truth, grounded in the reality of who we are requires a degree of vigilance in screening our thoughts. Once I begin writing in my head and the heroic ballad begins to take shape, it's very difficult to stop. It would have been wiser to have never picked up the pen than to try to rip up my copious self-adulating poem later by humbling myself.

While one can find amongst the founding fathers a host of humble examples, I think we need to do so soberly, realizing that much that looked like humility was not.

As Pulitzer Prize-winning historian Joseph Ellis explains, "Fame as they understood it was not just popular recognition during their lifetime; fame was forever.... The only election result that counted for them was posterity's judgment, and the only way to win that vote and achieve secular immortality was to conduct themselves according to a classical code that linked their personal ambitions, which were gargantuan, to the long term interest of the nation in the making."[10]

Living for posterity's applause, in the end, is no different than living for the applause of any audience. That said, I think the example of Washington is instructive. In 1775, John Adams shrewdly proposed George Washington to be the commander of the Continental Army. Adams rose and suggested to Congress, "A gentleman from Virginia who was among us and very well known to all of us," but before he could get to superlatives like "maverick" or "change we can believe in," Washington stood and left the room, not thinking it profitable to hear himself praised. Regardless of whether the gesture was for posterity or the health of his own soul, the example is a good one, as he guarded his heart, creating a wall of separation between himself and pride.

While not wildly successful at it, I try to continually filter out the helium in my head. One thing I try to do, or try not to do, is secretly congratulate myself on wise or intelligent things I've written or said. Otherwise I find myself basking in the glow of imagined worship and adulation, rewinding the good parts over and over again in my head.

In the movie *A Christmas Story*, the bespectacled adolescent hero Ralphie has repeated melodramatic fantasies: his teacher euphoric over his written report or his parents distraught by the tragic loss of his sight. Perhaps some people outgrow such solipsism, but honestly I never really did. I still have vain daydreams, which, as the saying goes, would be funny if it weren't so tragic. I therefore need to filter what I hear and rudely interrupt my own thoughts when they get out of line. I make such humble choices not because I'm humble, but because I'm terribly prideful.

Yet the discipline of our thoughts only goes so far—and not very—if our hearts are not redirected toward the Lord. As I've heard Larry Crabb say, "We are either self-obsessed or God-obsessed." In a state of self-obsession, it's rather impossible to think rightly about anything. However, a heart in continued praise, worship, and reliance carries along antibodies in its bloodstream, providing a degree of immunity to pride.

INCESSANT RELIANCE

In John 7:38, Jesus said, "Whoever believes in me, as the Scripture has said, streams of living water will flow from within him." As John goes on to tell us. Jesus was referring to the Holy Spirit.

I think people take "living water" to be something mystical like Perrier, allegedly discovered by Hannibal and his army of elephants. But "living water" was simply a term for fresh water, which one could drink or use to water crops or animals. The opposite of living water is not stagnant water but salt water, which cannot be used to water anything.

If there's a better metaphor for sin than salt water, I'm not sure what it could be. Think about it: The more you drink, the thirstier you get. You could die of thirst floating in the middle of the Atlantic Ocean. Salt water covers most of the planet. Ninety-seven percent of the planet's water is salt water.

Throughout each day we all sense the repetitive need for empowerment to meet life on its own terms. Our souls are profoundly thirsty. If you haven't noticed this thirst mechanism, watch a cigarette smoker. Every time they sense a need (or thirst) in their lives, they light up. If they feel lonely, they light up. If they feel scared or nervous, they light up. If they need confidence or motivation, they light up. If they're bored or dissatisfied, they light up. If they need wisdom, insight, or want to be reflective, they light up.

Of course we can find ourselves doing the same thing with coffee or bottled water or music or food or Red Bull or whatever. The point is that we all have the same thirsts, share the same trigger of reliance, and tend toward salt water rather than living water to meet our thirsts. Tasting salty, it does not quench our thirst; it exacerbates it. A few cigarettes become a few packs a day, a few songs an infinite playlist, a cup of coffee a quadruple espresso every morning. While we might not light up a Marlboro every few minutes, we light up something and are lit up by it. This is because we were created for worship; we were created with a need to be in constant and humble reliance upon the Lord. God made our souls a sieve, and we must drink constantly.

This life of humility and reliance is a redirecting of our thirst toward living water, drawing moment by moment upon the Spirit's empowerment to live out the Christian life: "Oh, Lord, please give me wisdom. Oh, Lord, please strengthen me. Oh, Lord, keep me from temptation. Oh, Lord, show me what to write next." (That last one was real, not hypothetical.)

Reflexively drawing upon the Lord throughout the day keeps us weak, needy, humble, and conversely, strong, comforted, and confident in and through Him. On a difficult day I may even draw upon the Lord every few minutes instead of every few hours. I think this is the essence of what Paul means when he says, "Do not get drunk on wine, which leads to debauchery. Instead, be filled with the Spirit" (Eph. 5:18). In some ways wine influences, empowers, and enables, and in that sense it tastes like living water. Yet it's a counterfeit, and to rely and draw upon it has the effect of salt water, making us thirstier. Paul tells us instead to humbly rely on the Lord for empowerment, drinking continually of living water to meet your needs.

A MUCH-NEEDED BATHROOM BREAK

There are exhaustive instructions on how to wash clothes under the lid of our washing machine. Putting the clothes in the washing machine is its own step, as is closing the lid of the washing machine. At the risk of over-explaining myself, it is a step-by-step process of how my humbling sessions with God tend to unfold.

I typically confess my sin whenever God makes me aware of it, and this means fairly often and usually in the midst of the hectic course of my busy day. But the problem is that simply pausing for confession, as important as it is, is not prolonged enough to stop my forward momentum. I never break stride, never slow down to repent, grieve over sin, ponder who or what I was trusting in, or what need I was wrongly trying to meet apart from God. I just keep going, repenting and adjusting my behavior like I would a tie.

In fact my momentary pause can amount to little more than a mental note, something like, "I gotta stop doing that." This turns into a consistent refrain: "I gotta stop doing that. I need to do better. Got to do better. Must stop doing that." This isn't even really confession any more, just course correction. All I'm hearing is the drumbeat of my conscience going faster and faster, "Dance, fat boy. Dance." My Christian life is reduced to sin-management, keeping up appearances, going through the motions, and swatting at sin with big, fat, slow hands.

At this point I'm dizzy and weary, and I have a choice: keep on performing, keep on dancing as fast as I can, or humble myself and admit that everything I'm attempting to do, all my course corrections and behavioral adjustments, is fruitless.

Should I wisely choose the latter, I wander off by myself somewhere to be alone with God. Then, as Luther so eloquently put it, I get naked before God. The first thing to be shed is my sin. Not a quick touch-up, but a thorough flossing of my thoughts, actions, and motivations. I get specific and detailed about all that I've done wrong. When I humble myself I get down into the thick shag of my heart and soul and embrace the very fiber of my bentness, acknowledging exactly what I've thought, exactly what I've said, exactly what I've believed, and exactly what's wrong with me.

After shooing away all the sin that's been buzzing around my decaying conscience, I get brutally honest about all the ways I've sinned. I acknowledge to God the times that I've thought too highly of myself and of my thoughts and opinions. I admit where I've pretended to know more than I know and acted like something I was not. I tell Him of the things I've done strictly for the praise and approval of others. I describe any occasions when I was emotionally fraudulent or manipulative—pretending to care instead of caring. I get it all: Under the couch, behind the seat cushions, I tear apart the house looking for dirt.

Last, I try to be brutally honest about all my vain thoughts and imagining. These I tend to begin with the formulaic "can you believe?" statements like "Can you believe I was actually thinking about how much people must like me?" or "Can you believe I was undressing that woman in my mind?" I'm sure God has no difficulty believing it, but I do, which is why I need to articulate it. It's even embarrassing for me to say these things in front of me.

At some point the process winds down and I feel like a jack-o-lantern, with everything on my inside scooped out and sitting on the table. I am completely naked.

INTERMISSION

This is not the end of my humbling session, just the intermission. The trip I've just taken to the restroom is only half the journey. In David's psalms of humility, you'll often find such an intermission. After pouring out the wretch of his soul comes the line, "But you O Lord...." This is the resting place, the pause signaling a shift of focus. What follows is David extolling the Lord, clothing himself in the grace and glory of God.

As disciples we value death, not for death's sake, but because we can't get to resurrection unless we go through it. What is the life that awaits us after the death in humility? What makes the humiliation and humbling of ourselves worth it? *Jesus*. We strip down to the bare truth of who we are because we want a deep encounter and a deeper experience of Christ.

Jesus is truth, and He relates to us in truth. We do not relate to Him with any intimacy in our mental story, the one that pits us as the hero and sees the world orbiting around us. The "us" of our vain imaginings is fictional, and Jesus does not relate to fictional people. It is only when we humble ourselves that we experience Him and taste His presence. Jesus relates to us as we are, not as we imagine ourselves to be. When we humble ourselves, we see ourselves clearly. But more important, and far more interesting, *we see Jesus*. We connect with Him at a very deep and intimate level.

Intellectually, I know that a coat keeps me warm, but I only experience its warmth when I've been chilled to the bone. Our nakedness puts us in a state to experience the presence, comfort, and unconditional love of Jesus Christ. Grace is tangibly felt, not simply discussed or thought about, and this is transformational.

Having embraced the truth of our dark side, an encounter with Christ brings us face-to-face with the brighter side of the moon. That is, the other truth about us: that we are forgiven, adopted, loved, protected, indwelt, purified, and redeemed in and through Jesus Christ. This, too, is what clothes our nakedness.

When Scripture speaks of the death that comes with humility, it cannot help but mention in the very same breath the promise of resurrection, that God "may lift you up."

> *Humble yourselves, therefore, under God's mighty hand, that he may lift you up in due time. (1 Peter 5:6)*

We experience that lifting up in our encounter with grace. But like Job's reversal of fortune, sometimes there are more practical tokens. Sometimes. Sometimes he blesses us with encouragement, recognition of accomplishment, restoration of our reputation, fruitfulness, and vindication. Death is always transformed into life, and life displays itself in many species. You can always count on being "lifted up," just never on the form it will take.

TIME TO WRAP THINGS UP

I find it necessary to complete this chapter today. As I've written each chapter, I've successively noticed God doing something in my life related to that given subject. When I wrote the chapter on evangelism, it seemed that everywhere I went, there were opportunities to talk about Christ (some of which I didn't take because I was very busy writing a chapter on evangelism). The chapters on trials were an unpleasant for obvious reasons, and I consider myself lucky to have survived writing them. When you sense this pattern, you really don't want to write a chapter on humility. The next thing you know the feds are removing your home computers to see what can be dredged up and reported on the six o'clock news. So far, so good, but that's why I'm getting edgy.

For me, death in humility is like the "Spirit of Christmas Yet to Come." I fear its specter more than the others. I'm generally unfazed by violence in movies, but I need to bite a pillow when a character makes a fool of himself. When I think of the sufferings of Christ, more than the pain, I think of the humiliation: everyone thinking He's a failure, laughing, mocking, and spitting on Him. There are a million ways to die, and I think I'd prefer the other nine hundred and ninety-nine thousand.

So I'm just going to run a quick spell check and hopefully get the first words on the page for a new book I'm calling, "God's Copious Blessings Upon His Children Despite Their Pride and Need for Humility."

CHAPTER TWENTY

———————————

WHAT IS LOVE, ANYWAY?

In 1956, when Shirley Polykoff was a junior copywriter at Foote, Cone & Belding, she was given the Clairol account. The product the company was launching was Miss Clairol, the first hair-color bath that made it possible to lighten, tint, condition, and shampoo at home, in a single step—to take, say, Topaz (for a champagne blond) or Moon Gold (for a medium ash), apply it in a peroxide solution directly to the hair, and get results in twenty minutes. When the Clairol sales team demonstrated their new product at the International Beauty Show, in the old Statler Hotel, across from Madison Square Garden, thousands of assembled beauticians jammed the hall and watched, openmouthed, demonstration after demonstration. Miss Clairol gave American women the ability, for the first time, to color their hair quickly and easily at home. But there was still the stigma—the prospect of the disapproving mother-in-law. Shirley Polykoff knew immediately what she wanted to say, because if she believed that a woman had a right to be a blonde she also believed that a woman ought to be able to exercise that right with discretion. "Does she or doesn't she?" she wrote.... "Only her hairdresser knows for sure." Clairol bought thirteen ad pages in Life *in the fall of 1956, and Miss Clairol took off like a bird. That was the beginning.[1]*

This, from a 1999 article Malcolm Gladwell wrote in the *New Yorker,* is as good an answer as any to the question, "When did media begin to change our perspective of sex in this country?" It's impossible to date such things, so let's just go with 1956.

And so here we are, over a half-century later, with notions of love, lust, sex, sexual identity, and infatuation as hopelessly jumbled in our heads as Julia Roberts in *Pretty Woman*: performing sex for money but afraid a kiss might be too personal. It's not an exaggeration to say that unless you know a person extremely well, you simply have no idea what they mean when they use the word *love.*

Amidst such confusion, sex becomes the lowest common denominator. As existential psychologist Rollo May observed in his masterwork *Love and Will,* "In such a contradictory situation, the sexual form of love understandably becomes our preoccupation, for sex, rooted in man's inescapable biology, seems always dependable to give us at least a facsimile of love."[2]

I suggest then that the place to begin our discussion of love is with a definition: what it is, how you measure it, and how to detect when it's simply not there. We want to know rather precisely what it means to truly love another person—and to truly love God.

Due to the immensity of the topic, thinkers, writers, and poets have always sought for handles, some way to lug around this weighty subject, some model or schematic that would help sort and simplify the data. In *The Four Loves*, C. S. Lewis proposes a four-fold model, dividing love into the following categories: friendship, affection, eros, and charity. By "charity" Lewis means "agape," but that's the downside of English authors, isn't it? Their English is all wrong (or, rather, *too right*).

The New Testament uses three distinct Greek words to differentiate between different kinds of love: *philos* (friendship/brotherly love), *agape* (grace/godly love), and *eros* (sensual love). This is helpful, and it certainly makes the language of breaking up much easier. ("Of course I love you … just in a *philos* kind of way.") But what we really need is a simple, easy-to-understand definition, something on the order of, "Love is never having to say you're sorry," except not that. That comes from the 1970 movie *Love Story*, and the seventies aren't a good place to find a definition of love.

To get to the truth about love, we must step away from the thoughts and images and philosophies of the world and search the words of Scripture for an answer. God only knows what love is.

As I surveyed the teachings of Jesus, one passage stood out as possibly the perfect candidate for a definition. The only problem is that the word *love* does not occur in it. But here, have a look.

As they were walking along the road, a man said to him, "I will follow you wherever you go." Jesus replied, "Foxes have holes and birds of the air have nests, but the Son of Man has no place to lay his head." He said to another man, "Follow me." But the man replied, "Lord, first let me go and bury my father." Jesus said to him, "Let the dead bury their own dead, but you go and proclaim the kingdom of God." Still another said, "I will follow you, Lord; but first let me go back and say good-by to my family." Jesus replied, "No one who puts his hand to the plow and looks back is fit for service in the kingdom of God." (Luke 9:57–62)

This discourse is typically viewed through the lens of the "call to discipleship." But why should the criteria for following Jesus be any different than the criteria for *loving Jesus?* Why would you measure one differently from the other? I believe what we find here is a very clear definition from Jesus of what constitutes a love commitment.

In the exchange in Luke 9, three would-be followers approach Jesus, and He gave a different response to each. Each of His answers added to the one before and filled out the definition of love. To the first pursuer, Jesus explained that the commitment to follow Him will entail personal sacrifice ("no place to lay one's head" serves as both example and shorthand for such commitment). To the second He declared that following requires a commitment to give Jesus ultimate priority. And to the third He said that following Him will require a commitment to persevere, following to the very end and not looking back. Love, then, according to Jesus, is a commitment given to another defined by personal sacrifice, prioritization, and perseverance. These are the dimensions of the commitment—the height, depth, and width of love.

Each facet of this commitment involves sacrificial choices, little deaths, and dying daily: choosing Jesus over everything, then choosing Him again and again and again. While these are clearly the metrics of discipleship, let's look at how this is also a measurement of love.

In 1985, I was working in New York, and my future wife, Katie, was a student at Syracuse University. On Fridays I would hop in my car, drive upstate to visit her, and be back in time for work on Monday. On one of those long weekends I asked her to marry me. Not in the sense of "Will you marry me?" but something more like, "Where do you find a justice of the peace in the Yellow Pages?" She said yes, and within the day we were signing a marriage license with the justice of the peace in Lafayette, New York. This, my friends, is the art of closing the deal: cutting down the time between proposal and wedding from about a year to roughly ninety minutes.

There in the living room of a retired judge and his wife (who served as our witness), we said our wedding vows. While we had foregone a traditional wedding (if traditional involves a church, family, friends, a cake, a tux, and a wedding dress), our wedding vows were quite traditional, containing the familiar phrases:

"Do you, Rick James, promise to take this woman … ?"

"In sickness and in health (sacrifice) …"

"Forsaking all others (priority) …"

"Till death do you part (perseverance) … ?"

Do you see it now? The clear parallel between the vows of marriage and the commitment of discipleship: They are one in the same. In essence, Jesus is asking His would-be disciples, "Will you marry me?" This act is staggering, *absolutely staggering*. And Jesus is stating with some precision what's involved in the commitment to love; He's articulating the vows. Like a marriage, the decision to follow will involve a million choices to sacrifice, prioritize, and persevere, a million choices to choose Jesus over and over and over against the onslaught of challenging circumstances, competing affections, and the erosion of time.

And though it will be the focus of the next chapter, we should observe up-front that love approaches sacrifice as an opportunity not a burden. Sacrifice, priority, and perseverance are the venues through which we demonstrate our affection for that which we love above all else. With that said, let's look briefly at each of the three commitments that define love.

SACRIFICE: FOXES WITHOUT HOLES

Economist.com subscription — U.S. $59.00
One-year subscription to Economist.com

Print subscription — U.S. $125.00
One-year subscription to the print edition of The Economist

Print and Web subscription — U.S. $125.00
One-year subscription to the print edition of The Economist and online access to Economist.com[3]

Perhaps you've seen this offer before (or one just like it). It's a question of value. What is something worth to you, and what are you willing to sacrifice (or pay) in order to get it? It's a question we are always asking ourselves and one we're not very good at answering. "We don't have an internal value meter that tells us how much things are worth," says Dan Ariely in his book *Predictably Irrational*, "rather we focus on the relative advantage of one thing over another, and estimate value accordingly." And this is how marketing is able to manipulate us: by providing us with several options. By establishing a price anchor on the very high side, the stage is set for us to choose option No. 2 and feel quite good about the cost associated with it. The highest priced item on a menu, says Ariely, is often there as a price anchor so you'll purchase the second most expensive item; the most expensive flatscreen TV is there to sell you the second most expensive, and on and on.

The problem, at least from a marketing perspective, is that when Jesus states that "the Son of Man has no place to lay his head," He doesn't provide a secondary level of commitment (Luke 9:58). He only provides the extreme price anchor of unqualified sacrifice. It's either all-in or all-out, and the same is true of the marriage commitment. This is what makes it different from all other commitments. You're only willing to pay an ultimate price for that which is ultimate in your affections. An ultimate price is a "deal breaker" if you don't love something ultimately. And because Jesus is up front about that commitment, it takes only minutes instead of years for a would-be disciple to turn and walk away: "At this the man's face fell. He went away sad, because he had great wealth" (Mark 10:22).

As Jesus illustrates in parables like The Pearl of Great Price, if you love something intensely, then any cost seems like a bargain. Like a

MasterCard commercial, "Sleeping out of doors without a pillow: $80.... Sleeping next to Jesus ... priceless."

My friend Will Walker includes in his book, *The Kingdom of Couches*, something that he did when he was dating his wife, Debbie. It illustrates well this sacrifice component in love.

> *The only dating relationship that ever ended well for me was the one that ended in marriage. That's a pretty romantic thing to say. Debbie says I used to be romantic. There was one particular day during the first summer after Debbie and I started dating that I really wanted to see her. We were both at our parent's house, she in Dallas and I in Fort Worth. That's about thirty-five miles between us, which is not a big deal if your car isn't in the shop getting fixed. Not to fear. I had an undersized mountain bike and a lot of time to kill.*
>
> *Turns out I needed about four and a half hours of time to kill, one way. Debbie didn't know I was coming, which was good because she has this strange sensitivity to breaking the law. Apparently it is illegal to ride your bike on the shoulder of the freeway, which is exactly what I did for about thirty of the thirty-five miles. The tricky part was the interchange from one freeway to another. Exit and entrance ramps were really not made for bicycles.*
>
> *My legs started cramping at the thirty-mile point, and by the time I reached Debbie's house, I was*

about dead. I did not know things, important things,
like you should drink water when you are riding a
bike for four hours, anywhere, but especially on the
freeway in Texas summer heat. Anyway, when I got to
Debbie's house, I was so exhausted that I asked her
to just put my bike in the back of her car and take me
home.[4]

Such stories are common to romance because somewhere during courtship there is both a need and a desire to demonstrate the cost you're willing to incur to show your affection. This is something that a diamond can never really do, because even a wretch can stop into Zales at the shopping mall. Sacrifice is the currency of love and provides an accurate rate of exchange while the willingness to sacrifice is equivalent to the value placed on the object.

Nearly three centuries ago, the Reverend Henry Scougal provided us with this reflection on love's sacrifice.

Love is the greatest and most excellent thing we are
masters of: it is indeed the only thing we can call our
own, other things can be taken from us by violence but
none can ravish love: if anything else be counted ours,
by giving our love we give all.... It is not possible to
refuse him any thing, to whom, by love, we have given
ourselves: nay, since it is the privilege of the gifts to
receive their value from the mind of the giver, he who
loveth, may, in some sense, be said not only to bestow
all that he hath, but all things else ... since he would

really give them, if they were in his power. The worth
and excellency of a soul is to be measured by the object
of its love: he who loveth mean and sordid things doth
thereby become base and vile.[5]

Translation: Our love is the one thing that's truly ours to give. Our heart and affection is all that we rightly own, and it cannot be forcibly taken, only willingly given. To give our heart is to give all that we have, for if we've given our heart, we would surely give anything else in our possession. That to which we give our heart is life's most determinative decision, for that choice reflects what we value most and to what we will conform. And thus the true value of any soul is directly proportional to the chief object of its affection. If you love beer above all else, your soul is worth roughly a buck-fifty; if you love God above all else, your soul is priceless. Love is measured by its willingness to sacrifice, and our hearts are measured by what they love. End of translation.

Scougal goes on to say that "perfect love is a kind … of voluntary death, wherein the lover dies to himself, and all his own interests, not thinking of them, nor caring for them any more, and minding nothing but how he may please and gratify the party whom he loves."

And I'm sure if Henry were here today, he would point out that each day is filled with dozens of opportunities to die. However, I fear we would lose him with modern examples such as washing the car, or cleaning out the microwave, or scouring the refrigerator, or mowing the lawn, or answering the phone, or picking up the dry cleaning, or driving to soccer practice, or any other of our modern ways to love and modern ways to die.

PRIORITY: GO FIRST AND PROCLAIM THE KINGDOM

If you had been born in the sixth century and found yourself a member of Saint Benedict's monastery, your daily calendar looked like this:

Matins, or vigilis nocturns (at 3 a.m.)

Lauds, or dawn prayer (at dawn)

Prime, or early morning prayer (at 6 a.m.)

Terce, or mid-morning prayer (at 9 a.m.)

Sext, or midday prayer (at noon)

None, or mid-afternoon prayer (at 3 p.m.)

Vespers, or evening prayer (at dusk)

Compline, or night prayer (before retiring)

The "hours," as they are known, comprise the daily prayer schedule observed in monastic communities around the world, a practice going back to the first centuries of Christendom. While he didn't invent this regimen, St. Benedict is most closely associated with it because he is the architect of monastic life as we've come to know it. The precepts of "Benedict's Rule" have served as the abbot's field guide for nearly fifteen hundred years. What most people don't realize is that he didn't write these "rules" for monks. He wrote them for laypeople as a guide for the average Christian who wanted to walk more intimately with Christ throughout the day.

But let me stop right here, as I am not advocating Vespers or Lauds, and you definitely didn't hear me advocate Sext. I mean, it would be wonderful if you observed the Hours, but that's not my point. (I often go to bed around the time Benedict was having breakfast.) What I want to highlight is this: The Benedictines wanted to keep Christ as the priority of their lives, so they made Him the priority of their schedules. The two are inextricably linked.

When the man replies to Jesus, "Lord, first let me go and bury my father," the emphasis falls on the word *first,* and that, as we know, is Jesus' parking spot. The commitment to love involves the daily choice and choices to prioritize and put *first* the object of our devotion, a commitment that's communicated by actions, actual adjustments to our schedules, versus words. And so Jesus says to the man, "Let the dead bury their own dead, but you go and proclaim the kingdom of God" (Luke 9:60).

Throughout our entire lives we are showered with assurances of priority and preference from our parents, significant others, spouses, teachers, and coworkers. But these assurances are only platitudes and remain so until demonstrated by actions. Until such point, desire has not moved from intent to commitment, and love is a commitment. Son, wife, friend, brother, or whoever: Until you make it into their day planner, you are not their highest priority—no matter what they say. The statements, "You are the most important thing in my life," and, "I just don't have time for you" cannot both be true.

This point was rather humorously made in the popular book and movie *He's Just Not That Into You.* The author, Greg Behrendt, attempts to disabuse the female population of the belief that it's possible to be the love of someone's life even if they never call, commit, communicate, or seem to care.

Here is some of Behrendt's wisdom (as taken from the movie).

> Don't let the "honeys" and the "babys" fool you. His sweet nothings are exactly that. They are much easier to say than "I'm just not that into you." Remember, actions speak louder than "There's no cell reception where I am right now." ... Calling when you say you're going to call is the very first brick in the house you are building of love and trust. If he can't lay this one stupid brick down, you ain't never gonna have a house, baby.... Every man you have ever dated who has said he doesn't want to get married or doesn't believe in marriage, or has "issues" with marriage, will, rest assured, someday be married. It just will never be with you. ... If you can find him, then he can find you. If he wants to find you, he will. If a guy doesn't call you, he doesn't want to call you.[6]

The book's enormous popularity speaks to the universality of the experience: our desire or willingness to live in denial by separating *the pledge of priority* from the *demonstration of priority*. Jesus defines love as "demonstrated priority" by the hundreds and thousands of decisions to give Him our time, attention, and affection, despite competing claimants.

For my wife, Katie, I think the final straw in our early years of campus ministry occurred when I came in at 3 a.m. from a four-hour counseling session with a college student. If it had been a serious issue like a parent's divorce, that would have been one thing. But this session was about girl problems. Students always have four hours worth of girl or boy problems.

And, as I said, this was the last straw. There had been a host of prior incidents: taking calls from students in the middle of the night, out playing with them on the weekends, students stopping by the house whenever. My personal boundaries in those first years were as secure as the border of Mexico. Katie loves the ministry and loves being in it. That wasn't the problem. The problem was that it had taken priority over her and everything else in my life. It was then, and only then, that she experienced frustration—or, to be more accurate, *jealousy*.

When we think of jealousy, we typically think of it in negative terms, but it's not intrinsically negative. God is jealous, right? Perhaps this definition of jealousy will exonerate it: Jealousy is the rightful desire for exclusivity in a relationship and the feelings associated with violations of that exclusivity. Jealousy is the form that passion takes to enforce priority in a love relationship. What's wrong with that? If priority is a measurement of love, jealousy is the warning alarm alerting of a potential breech.

This, I take it, is what it means for God to be jealous. It is His rightful desire for exclusivity in His relationship with us because demonstrated priority (forsaking all others) is a foundational tenet of the commitment to love.

Following through on our love commitment to God, as well as to others in our life, requires cutting out and cutting off certain activities, people, and events, and making such incisions can feel like lopping off pieces of ourselves. As our agenda equates quite closely with our lives, these decisions are experienced as little deaths—deaths gladly embraced for the object of our devotion.

PERSEVERANCE: DON'T LOOK BACK

The human heart is like those sticky red fruit roll-ups my kids are always eating, those things that look like cherry flypaper and taste like cherry flypaper. The human heart is only seen when rolled out over the course of a lifetime. There are certain deficiencies in love that only time will reveal. This is why love is not simply measured by intensity, but also by duration. You cannot know the heart fully until it's fully unfurled.

I came across this illustration of perseverance in a book that, as you'll see, is several decades old. It helps make an important point.

> In 1947, San Francisco's Potrero Hill was not only a poor South City neighborhood, it was a real ghetto. That year was the year Oren was born. Rickets, a poverty-related disease actually caused by malnutrition, was Oren's major problem. His vitamin- and mineral-deficient diet caused his bones to soften. His legs began to bow under the weight of his growing body.
>
> Even though the family was too poor to afford braces, Oren's mom refused to sit back, sigh, and resign herself to the inevitable.... She rigged up a home-made contraption in hopes of correcting her son's pigeon-toed, bowlegged condition. How? By reversing his shoes! Right shoe, left foot; left shoe, right foot;

plus an improvised metal bar across the shoe tops to keep his feet pointing straight. It didn't work perfectly, but it was good enough to keep the boy on his feet and ultimately able to play with his buddies.

By the time he was about six years of age, his bones had hardened, his legs were still slightly bowed, his calves were unusually thin, and his head was disproportionately large. Nicknames from other kids followed him around: "Pencil-legs," "Waterhead"; but he refused to let all that hold him back....

Those who don't know his background could easily think he got all the breaks. As they look at him today and see this fine and refined gentleman, they would assume he's always been wealthy. He lives in the exclusive Brentwood district of Los Angeles, drives a luxurious car, and has his elegant office in an elite bank building. He is now a busy executive with his own production company.

In today's terms, Oren has it made. That plush office with the name on the door belongs to Orenthal James Simpson. Yes, none other than "the Juice," O. J. Simpson.[7]

This is not a slight on the author, who is both a wonderful writer and teacher. At the time the book was written, O. J. was a media star, not a felon. But that's the point. He undoubtedly had a heart the size of a racehorse, but only time would show how defective it was.

You'll often hear lines in books or movies to the effect of, "We just fell out of love." Remember the words of that Righteous Brothers song? "You've lost that loving feeling.... Now it's gone, gone, gone, whoa-oh." What's that about? How does one just lose that loving feeling? To those who have *labored on* in love, both "in sickness and in health," the sentiment or idea of "falling out of love" is offensive. People don't fall out of love; they fail to persevere in loving. They *choose to stop* loving their spouse, or they *choose to start* loving something else.

Endurance is rendered in the King James Bible as "long suffering," which is the root meaning of the Greek word. There is accuracy in the label, especially when it comes to the "long suffering" in our relationships. But not in the sense that it's difficult to suffer someone's presence over the long haul like a houseguest who won't leave. Rather, it's the opposite: Keeping the relationship vital and alive over the long haul involves effort, *the suffering*. Allowing a relationship to stagnate and die requires no effort at all. Certainly this is true in our relationship with Christ. Nothing is so effortless as sitting back and allowing entropy to have its way, resigning to mediocrity and going through the motions.

In his final months on earth, Bill Bright, the founder of Campus Crusade for Christ, wrote this open letter in *Christianity Today,* which was titled "Benediction."

> Dear friends:
>
> As I write this, I am confined to my bed and am on supplemental oxygen 24 hours a day.
> In October, 2002, I celebrated my 81st birthday. Approximately three years ago, I was diagnosed with

pulmonary fibrosis, a progressive lung disease. The doctors told me there is no known cure for this condition.

I was told that the average remaining life of someone with pulmonary fibrosis is three years and at the most five years. That time has almost expired. Many people, aware of my physical condition, thought I would be gone from this world long before now.... In fact, the past two years have been among the most productive of my life....

Of course, if the Lord tarries, my day to enter glory will eventually come. What a wonderful day that will be! But it is a win-win situation for me. If I go, I will be with my wonderful Lord whom I have served for almost 60 years. If I stay, I will be able to joyously serve Him even more than I have in the past.

I am reminded of Psalm 150:6, "Let everything that has breath praise the Lord." As long as I am here, as long as I have breath, I will praise and serve the Lord.

That is also God's will for your life. If you trust in Him, it can also be a win-win situation for you. As long as you have breath, God's Word commands you to praise Him, and He also has something for you to do.

There are many possibilities. Perhaps you can be a prayer intercessor. There is not a more important job in the body of Christ than that of an intercessor. You can be a prayer intercessor while confined to a bed or a wheelchair. You pray literally anywhere. If you do not have the strength to pray aloud, you can whisper. If you *cannot whisper, you can move your lips. If you cannot move your lips, then pray silently, in your mind. God knows and reads your heart.*

Your humble prayers can actually help change your world! Are you still breathing? Then be encouraged, and get busy!

Yours for helping to fulfill the Great Commission each year until our Lord returns,

Bill Bright[8]

In his final weeks, Bill Bright called on those close to him to pray that in his pain and suffering he wouldn't say anything to dishonor Christ, that he might persevere to the very end in his commitment to love. Bright died July 19, 2003, and Chuck Colson provided this eulogy.

Bill Bright's death showed the world how Christians deal with suffering and death. And people will remember Bill not only as a great visionary leader who founded one of the great movements of our time, but as the man who finished well and overcame suffering by his indomitable faith in Christ.

I will remember Bill always for the profound influence he had on me, inspiring me not only to live well but, when the time comes, to die well.[9]

Love perseveres "'til death do us part." Love makes whatever sacrificial choices and dies whatever deaths are necessary to keep going, to be faithful to the very end.

THE HEART OF LOVE

I didn't give considered thought to my vows when I got married, as
I only had a few minutes to select them when I arrived at the justice
of the peace. Even if I would have had the time, I wouldn't have fully
realized—not even remotely—the content of that commitment.
Regularly I fall short, failing to sacrifice, prioritize, and persevere,
and yet here we are still married, an absolute miracle. All of which is
identically true of my relationship with Christ, also a miracle. And
yet somewhere in our hearts must be a willing submission to the
miracle, and a desire for that miracle.

Love is demonstrated, however imperfectly, in a willingness to
sacrifice, prioritize, and persevere in a commitment. And if the heart
of love is commitment, I think it would be true to say that the heart
of commitment is passion. As we'll see, passion fuels the death in love.

CHAPTER TWENTY-ONE

THE HEART OF LOVE

Over the last decade the twenty-four-seven prayer movement—inspired by the Moravians, an eighteenth century community of believers who managed to pray without stopping for an entire century—swept across the globe.

After visiting Herrnhut, the historic site of Count Zinzendorf's Moravian community, Peter Greig figured, "If the Moravians could do a century of twenty-four-seven prayer, we could at least try it for a month in our church back home." And he did.

In September 1999, Greig and a handful of friends began their thirty-day experiment and found that they couldn't stop praying when the month was up. They're still praying. Today there are roughly six thousand prayer rooms in ninety countries and counting. The movement has spread like a flame, and many would say it was Greig's impassioned vision statement, forwarded around the world, which sparked the movement.

Here is a condensed version of "The Vision."

> *So this guy comes up to me and says, "What's the vision? What's the big idea?" I open my mouth and words come out like this: "The vision?"*

The vision is JESUS—obsessively, dangerously, undeniably Jesus.

The vision is an army of young people. You see bones? I see an army. And they are FREE from materialism. They laugh at 9-5 little prisons. They could eat caviar on Monday and crusts on Tuesday. They wouldn't even notice. They know the meaning of the Matrix, the way the west was won. They are mobile like the wind, they belong to the nations. They need no passport. People write their addresses in pencil and wonder at their strange existence. They are free yet they are slaves of the hurting and dirty and dying. What is the vision? The vision is holiness that hurts the eyes. It makes children laugh and adults angry. It gave up the game of minimum integrity long ago to reach for the stars. It scorns the good and strains for the best. It is dangerously pure.

Light flickers from every secret motive, every private conversation. It loves people away from their suicide leaps, their Satan games. This is an army that will lay down its life for the cause. A million times a day its soldiers choose to lose that they might one day win the great "Well done" of faithful sons and daughters.

Such heroes are as radical on Monday morning as Sunday night. They don't need fame from names. Instead they grin quietly upward and hear the crowds chanting again and again: "COME ON!"

And this is the sound of the underground. The

whisper of history in the making. Foundations shaking. Revolutionaries dreaming once again. Mystery is scheming in whispers. Conspiracy is breathing.... This is the sound of the underground.

And the army is disciplined. Young people who beat their bodies into submission. Every soldier would take a bullet for his comrade at arms. The tattoo on their back boasts "For me to live is Christ and to die is gain." Sacrifice fuels the fire of victory in their upward eyes. Winners. Martyrs. Who can stop them? Can hormones hold them back? Can failure succeed? Can fear scare them or death kill them?

And the generation prays like a dying man with groans beyond talking, with warrior cries, euphoric tears and with great barrow loads of laughter! Waiting. Watching: 24—7—365.

Whatever it takes they will give: Breaking the rules. Shaking mediocrity from its cozy little hide. Laying down their rights and their precious little wrongs, laughing at labels, fasting essentials. The advertisers cannot mold them. Hollywood cannot hold them. Peer-pressure is powerless to shake their resolve at late night parties before the cockerel cries.

They are incredibly cool, dangerously attractive inside. On the outside? They hardly care. They wear clothes like costumes to communicate and celebrate but never to hide. Would they surrender their image or their popularity? They would lay down their very *lives—swap seats with the man on death row—guilty as hell. A throne for an electric chair ...*

And this vision will be. It will come to pass; it will come easily; it will come soon. How do I know? Because this is the longing of creation itself, the groaning of the Spirit, the very dream of God. My tomorrow is his today. My distant hope is his 3D. And my feeble, whispered, faithless prayer invokes a thunderous, resounding, bone-shaking great "Amen!" from countless angels, from heroes of the faith, from Christ himself. And he is the original dreamer, the ultimate winner.

Guaranteed.[10]

I apologize for having involved you in an experiment without your consent. But while reading Greig's passionate words and vision, you should have noticed a peculiar shift in your feelings. Before reading it, you would have no doubt been *willing* to sacrifice anything for Jesus, but after reading it, I'd venture that you *want* to suffer and *desire* to sacrifice. This is passion, and its clearest demonstration is the cross:

> *Let us fix our eyes on Jesus, the author and perfecter of our faith, who for the joy set before him endured the cross. (Heb. 12:2)*

Jesus was not simply willing to sacrifice and submit Himself to death, *He wanted to.* It was His ambition, His joy, and the desire of His heart. This is not just a nuanced point about the nature of love, but a very distinct experience flowing from the intensity of passion. The word *passion* has been so overused that its gears are stripped, and it no longer provides any conceptual bite. But passion bites; it kicks, screams, and claws; it will do anything to obtain the object of its affection.

Passion is another paradox—finding joy in pain, pleasure in sacrifice. Passion experientially ties love and death together. When we think of passion, we typically think of it as a burning romantic or sexual desire. While the flames of passion can certainly move in that direction, passion itself is innocent of any wrongdoing. It's misplaced passion that burns destructively, just like it's people who start forest fires, not fire itself.

Passion is a fire, enflaming the heart, mind, and will ... but to do what, exactly? That's the question we each decide. Passion longs to sacrifice in order to satiate its consuming intensity, and passion longs to sacrifice in order to express and demonstrate its devotion. But we determine passion's object, we decide who and what will have the highest place in our affections.

QUENCHING THE FIRE

In the late nineteenth century, as renowned mathematician Henri Poincaré was boarding a bus, insight into non-Euclidean geometry arrived unannounced in his brain.

"When I put my foot on the step," wrote Poincaré, "the idea came to me without anything in my former thoughts seeming to have paved the way for it." Life is filled with such "eureka" moments; that's how I discovered *passion*—a personal discovery, not like I established a new square on the periodic table of elements or anything.

It was close to midnight, and my wife and I were snuggled under the covers, reading our favorite anthologies. Katie, as always, was reading someone smart, someone dead, someone Russian. I, as always, was reading something *Conspiracy*, something *Bourne*, something *Ultimatum*.

Nearing lights out, Katie and I started talking, and I was swamped with a wave of love and awe for how much I loved this woman. At that moment, perhaps sensing my weakness and vulnerability, she leaned over and said, "I left my Bible downstairs. Can you go down and get it for me?" I was exhausted, the heat had gone off in the house hours ago, it was freezing outside the covers, we had hardwood floors, it was dark downstairs, and there were undoubtedly wooden trolls lying wait in the darkness.

But I did it. I got out of bed, went downstairs, located the Bible, and on my way up the stairs this thought flashed into my head: "I'm so glad that was hard." And I was—I was genuinely glad for the opportunity to demonstrate my love. We've all had such feelings, and this wasn't the first time I'd felt that way. It was just the first time I noted the strangeness of the impulse. It was like the moment of discovery in a superhero movie, the first time a spiderweb shoots from the wrist, or cutlery springs from the knuckles—the realization of some latent power.

The intense love and devotion that welled up within me felt like a flame. And passion, like all fires, seeks something to consume. One way to spend its energy and satiate its appetite is sacrifice. Granted, mine was a really small sacrifice (someday I will stand with the martyrs and boast of the day I got out of bed), but it was passion nonetheless. I wasn't just *willing* to retrieve her Bible, it was "for the joy set before me." I *wanted* to sacrifice because it provided a way to spend the intense feelings of love pent up inside me. It was like a static discharge.

The intensity of passion compels us to find the most extravagant vehicle of expression in order to satisfy and satiate our feelings. And, no, buying the object of your passion a stuffed mammal or Beanie Baby isn't going to cut it. *What about baked goods or candy?* Perfect for a house warming, but this is not a house warming. *What about jewelry, diamonds, precious metals?* Getting warmer. *How about a Hallmark card?* How about you cut your ear off like Van Gogh and send it to her in a Tiffany's box? Now you're talking! Now she'll know how you feel about her. Now you can finally get some rest.

Do you see how the fire of passion escalates? In a quest to satiate itself, passion moves to the extremes, and nothing is more extreme than self-sacrifice. Pain, death, and sacrifice are the crack cocaine of passion's fix, the only vehicles potent enough to spend passion's desire.

Like many of the early Christians, Saint Ignatius died a martyr's death. This ancient account allows us to see the passion that fueled such sacrifice. Ignatius was not just *willing* to die for Christ—it was his driving ambition.

> But [Ignatius] was grieved as to himself, that he had not yet attained to a true love to Christ.... For he inwardly reflected, that the confession which is made by martyrdom, would bring him into a yet more intimate relation to the Lord. Wherefore, continuing a few years longer with the Church ... he [at length] attained the object of his desire.

Then Trajan pronounced sentence as follows: "We command that Ignatius, who affirms that he carries about within him Him that was crucified, be bound by soldiers, and carried to the great [city] Rome, there to be devoured by the beasts, for the gratification of the people."

When the holy martyr heard this sentence, he cried out with joy, "I thank you, O Lord, that You have vouchsafed to honour me with a perfect love towards You, and hast made me to be bound with iron chains, like Your Apostle Paul." Having spoken thus, he then, with delight, clasped the chains about him; and when he had first prayed for the Church, and commended it with tears to the Lord, he was hurried away by the savage cruelty of the soldiers, like a distinguished ram the leader of a goodly flock, that he might be carried to Rome, there to furnish food to the bloodthirsty beasts.[11]

You can see this same ambition in the disciples when "the apostles left the Sanhedrin, rejoicing because they had been counted worthy of suffering disgrace for the Name" (Acts 5:41).

The death or dying of self is most ultimately seen in the most ultimate act, which is why Ignatius sought it so dearly. But it is this same motivation and impulse that fuels lesser degrees of suffering (little deaths and daily sacrifices). After all, physical death is just a different degree of physical torment, and physical torment a different degree of mental torment, and I suppose we could work our way back to a hand slap suffered out of love for Christ. All such sacrifice is a form or degree of death. Even the act of laying a dream, a future, a relationship, or wealth on the altar is driven by love and involves a death, a cessation of life, in some cruciform shape. To willfully give up and hand over all the moments of our future or all the lusts of our flesh can be as much of a sacrifice as the relinquishing of our body to a bloodthirsty beast—*with all due respect.*

You'll sometimes see the glimmer of passion in athletes. They're not just willing to endure sacrifice for their love of the game; they *want* to sacrifice. They want it to be difficult. They want to taste the iron of their own blood. They need a vehicle to spend that "Hooah! Thank you, sir. May I have another?" intensity, and the sacrifice intrinsic to athletics provides the means. Passion alone explains why an otherwise sane football player would gleefully smash his helmet against a locker, and why an otherwise sane football fan would sit with his shirt off … *in Green Bay … in January.* This athletic passion is what the makers of sports drinks and athletic shoes are always trying to tap into with their advertising. It would be impossible to fit another ounce of pathos into the three words "Just Do It." And Gatorade is literally marketed as passion in a bottle—"Is it in you?"

But when sports or anything else replaces God as the focus of our passion, it becomes idolatry. To perceive passion as a flame is cautionary as well as instructive; fire is dangerous and must be tended with care, which is why we don't let children play with matches. Our worship and devotional life is designed to stoke the fire of passion and direct it *toward God.* A failure to shepherd our affections toward God will always result in passion burning out of control and quenching its flames on lesser things. Passion is the incense of worship, a burnt offering presented to either God or mere idols.

Christians often observe that we are fortunate to live in a country where there isn't any persecution. In one sense I couldn't agree more, but in another sense I couldn't agree less. Without the fuel of suffering and sacrifice, passion smolders. With nothing to feed the flame, the flame flickers and goes out.

To misunderstand passion is to misinterpret the death in love. I just finished reading an article about a missionary titled, "Willing to Die, Ready to Live." The missionary seemed like a great soul, though I doubt he would have been happy with the tone of the article. Just listen to that title: "Willing to Die, Ready to Live." He sounds like a real can-do guy, someone with a vigorous constitution, able to sleep on bare earth.

If what could be said of me is that *I'm willing* to die for God, where else could your attention go but to *my* robust commitment? But if I *want* to die for God, *long* to die for God, that's a different matter. Passion points to the bride of our affection—who or what could be so great as to inspire such devotion?

Passionate players make you want to play that sport; superstars make you want to look up their statistics.

CARRYING THE TORCH

Passion is the drive to satiate the flame of intense affection, proclaim the intensity of that love and the grandeur of the object of that love. Passion is an evangelist. It's rather cliché to say that when you're in love you want to shout it from the rooftops. So let's just pretend I didn't say it but acknowledged that it's true. Of course if one had even the slightest question as to whether the feelings were mutual, they would be wise to keep off the rooftop. Not that passion is known for its prudence. It will shout its feelings from the rooftops, and if an echo is not returned … well, the rooftop is as good a place as any to hurl oneself from.

Perhaps the most memorable—certainly most visceral—scriptural account of passion is the story of David and Goliath. I won't retell it here, but there's a detail of the narrative often overlooked: God never told David to fight Goliath; God never told David to do anything.

David reacted out of passion, not obedience; there were no orders to be followed. When passion takes this "protect and defend" stance toward the glory of God, it's typically called zeal. Zeal propelled David to put his life on the line to declare and defend the glory of God: "You mocked God, therefore, I will serve your head to the vultures." Whether David won or lost, God's glory was worth the sacrifice, and David's sacrifice declared the intensity of his love and the worth of God's glory.

We just met a couple whose kids go to the same school as our kids. They were missionaries for many years in South Africa and recently moved to the U.S. As the wife told my wife about their children, she mentioned that one of them is named Stephen. My wife, Katie, said she'd always liked the name, and the woman responded, "We named him after Stephen in the Bible. We pray that someday God might allow him the honor of dying for his faith."

This says a great deal about what this couple values and how much they value it, doesn't it? When Katie told me this, I was so glad we hadn't named our children Brad and Angelina. The heart of a Christian witness is like that of a soldier: to declare, honor, and defend the name of Jesus Christ with one's life, and in so doing demonstrate the exceeding greatness of the Son of God.

Many summers ago I was asked to speak at a beach resort and provide morning devotions for the Christians vacationing there for the week. The organizers of the program also wanted me to stand at a podium on the boardwalk and speak evangelistically to anyone willing to listen.

It was a great idea … *for 1897.*

When I signed up for ministry, I signed up for many things. But the open-air proclamation of the gospel that was popular a century ago was not one of them. I'm a New Yorker, for heaven's sake. It would be impossible for me to imagine a more humiliating scenario (unless it was performed at my own high school reunion).

I didn't have to say yes; they graciously provided me a dignified "out" if I chose it. And from my experience with evangelism, I didn't hold out much hope that the endeavor would be fruitful. But I said yes, and I did so for this reason alone: It occurred to me that God was giving me the opportunity to honor Him. Somehow the sacrifice of my reputation would declare and uphold the value of His reputation. In fact, it was this particular passage that pushed me over the edge: "For it has been granted to you on behalf of Christ not only to believe on him, but also to suffer for him" (Phil. 1:29).

In the end, evangelism is as much about our heart, our passion, and our sacrifice as it is about people's response. I really believe this. A soldier's death is a precious sacrifice irrespective of the war's outcome.

Passion longs to sacrifice to demonstrate its intensity and declare the exceeding worth of the one it loves.

PASSION FOOLISHLY SPENT

As a missionary, he reached out to the most destitute in Europe, moving to the coal-mining district of Borinage in Belgium. He opted to live like those to whom he preached, sharing their hardships to the extent of sleeping on straw and living in squalor. His choice to live in the impoverished conditions of the coal miners he attempted to reach caused a scandal among the church authorities, and they dismissed him for "undermining the dignity of the priesthood."

After that, the object of Vincent Van Gogh's passion shifted from God to the love of his cousin, Kee. When his uncle forbade him to see her, he protested by sticking his left hand in the flame of a lamp, saying, "Let me see her for as long as I can keep my hand in the flame."[12]

And then Van Gogh's passion shifted again, this time to painting, Paris, and absinthe, where arguments with fellow artist Gaugin lead to the infamous severing of his left ear lobe. Then on July 27, 1890, at the tragically young age of 37, he walked out into a field and shot himself in the chest with a revolver.

Van Gogh is perhaps the most demonstrably passionate person in history, his affections so intense they could only be satiated and demonstrated through extreme acts. But his life serves more as a warning than an example: Here is the tragedy of misspent and misplaced passion. As absinthe, toxic paints, rage, and romantic obsession poisoned his mind, they also poisoned his passion.

A few months ago I played six degrees of separation on Facebook, tracing friends to friends of friends, to people I haven't seen or heard from in decades. I located a couple guys I knew from a decade past, two men I'd admired and considered extremely passionate in their commitment to Christ. If their Facebook profiles were any indicator of their interests and passions—and they typically are—Jesus was no longer one of them. This is something I've witnessed many times over the years: the loss or misdirection of passion.

There's my friend who left the ministry to pursue a homosexual relationship, a guy I ministered with who left his wife, another dear friend who removed himself from ministry due to a pornography addiction. There are others who have left their call to seek financial fortune. They're not dead, so their stories haven't stopped last time I checked. Maybe they're walking with Jesus again. I hope so. They were all passionate followers—and, as it turns out, they were all poor stewards of their passion.

As Paul lamented about a similar acquaintance, "Do your best to come to me quickly, for Demas, because he loved this world, has deserted me and has gone to Thessalonica" (2 Tim. 4:9–10).

Passion's flashing volatility, its white-hot intensity, its ability to permeate any barrier, suffer any sacrifice, and strike down any challenger makes it the most precious of commodities. I suspect this is why perfumers and sports-drink manufacturers always claim to have bottled the "unbottleable." But as surely as entrepreneurs and marketers send up their kites to capture lightening in a bottle, Satan seeks to drain our passion, deplete it like a perpetual torch burning in a Kuwaiti oil field.

Temptations abound, and passion can be bent toward greed or power, twisted into rage, diverted toward lust. It's just a slight pull on the reigns to send passion panting after the wrong scent. Sexual immorality steals our joy and spills our passion. It leaves us weakened, spent, and turns us into cowards. Having spent our passion on the flesh, we are left impotent in spirit. Once passion is drained or diminished, we are easily tamed and easily enslaved: Samson with a crew cut.

Even if it's not misspent on immorality, passion can be squandered trivially. One can sense the spiritual deformity in people who are passionate about the trivial and passive on matters of consequence. To misplace priorities is to misplace passion, spending it on ambition or fame or wealth or status or power or some other magic beans, returning home with empty pockets for family, God, and church.

Passion can also be unleashed in the direction of futility: something that is without direction, point, or purpose, a twitching chicken of activity without a head. I feel most passionate when I'm listening to music, but certain songs and rhythms easily stoke bonfires of vanity. I arrive home, click off the radio, turn off the ignition, and step out of my car completely *pumped … jacked … stoked … amped …* and for what? Dinner? I follow the fife and drum in a circle, passion for the sake of passion.

As passion aimed toward sex bears the scarlet *l* of lust, passion turned toward God is zeal. Romans 12:11 exhorts us to "never be lacking in zeal, but keep your spiritual fervor, serving the Lord." We are to keep our passion directed toward God, and "above all else, guard [our] heart, for it is the wellspring of life" (Prov. 4:23).

ONCE IN A LIFETIME

As we look forward to heaven, it's comforting to know that God will wipe away every tear, and suffering will be no more. But this also raises a question: Can passion be expressed without the endurance of some kind of suffering or sacrifice?

C. S. Lewis makes this suggestion:

> *Perhaps self-conquest will never end; eternal life may*
> *mean an eternal dying. It is in this sense that, as there*
> *may be pleasures in hell (God shield us from them),*
> *there may be something not at all unlike pains in heaven*
> *(God grant us soon to taste them).*[13]

C. S. Lewis projects that passion may always need a means of sacrifice to express itself. Yet Lewis knows from Scripture that suffering and death will not continue in heaven, and so he has inserted this qualifier: "something not at all unlike pains" and sacrifice may accompany us. Whether Lewis is right, and passion in some sense will have to endure or sacrifice in heaven; or whether he's wrong and it will be transformed into a higher form of love altogether, we are still left with this important fact, and one that should revolutionize our perspective: While on this earth we have a unique and unprecedented opportunity to demonstrate our love for God through the vehicles of pain, sacrifice, suffering, and death.

I have no idea what it will be like to love and worship God in heaven. But whatever it's like, it will not involve the endurance of suffering and evil. We have an opportunity that comes around only once every eternity to express our love through sacrifice. Each day contains opportunities to die little deaths in order to demonstrate and declare our love for God and those we value most—a unique window of opportunity that only a fallen world can provide.

If the heart of love is commitment, and the heart of commitment is passion, then the heart of passion is worship. This will be the last stop in our causal regression, as it will take us back to love's source: *God our Father.*

CHAPTER TWENTY-TWO

THE HEAT OF PASSION

Passion is a drive to sacrifice, but what is it that drives passion to love and sacrifice for Christ? What makes Christian passion different from ordinary human passion? Jesus.

When we are brimming and saturated with the object of our devotion, Jesus Christ, our affections overflow, and we pour ourselves out in acts of devotion. And while we pour ourselves out, God pours back into us. That's a mouthful, and with all the pouring and brimming and saturation, it sounds a little like Rachel Ray wrote it. But the goal of this chapter will be to unpack this definition—or perhaps recipe—for worship.

REVIVAL

When Moses came out from the presence of God, he literally glowed like a firefly. In an attempt to cover his fleeting radiance, Scripture tells us that Moses put a veil over his face, and I'm truly sorry for the irreverence, but I cannot help picturing Donner trying to hide Rudolph's nose. The apostle Paul picks up on this Old Testament event and applies and amplifies the concept to new covenant believers:

And we, who with unveiled faces all reflect the Lord's
glory, are being transformed into his likeness with ever-
increasing glory, which comes from the Lord, who is
the Spirit. (2 Cor. 3:18)

Simply, but rather strangely put, we are phosphorescent; we glow in the dark. *Phosphorescent* literally means "charged by exposure to light" or to "glow after illumination." This description isn't literal, of course; God obviously doesn't turn us into a glow stick. But freshly charged from the presence of God, the indwelling Spirit radiates through us, witnessed in our love and passion for God. Passion's glow is a byproduct of being saturated in Christ, showered in the presence of God.

The clearest, most extreme example of God-saturated individuals is found in the accounts of history's great spiritual revivals, where multitudes experienced a deluge of God's presence. Let me give you several snapshots.

Korea

In the beginning of the twentieth century, a spiritual revival encircled the globe, affecting the U.S., Wales, England, Brazil, Canada, Chile, Scandinavia, India, Ethiopia, East Africa, Korea, Norway, and China. During this time the Korean church experienced explosive growth, starting with the revival at Pyeng Yang in 1908. This is from an eyewitness account of the outbreak of that revival:

The room was full of God's presence ... a feeling of
God's nearness impossible to describe. The whole

audience began to pray.... It was not many, but one, born of one Spirit, lifted to one Father above.... God came to us in Pyeng Yang that night.... Man after man would arise, confess his sin, break down and weep. Some threw themselves full length on the floor; hundreds stood with arms outstretched towards heaven. Every man forgot each other. Each was face to face with God.

Everywhere the story was told the same Spirit flowed forth and spread. All through the city men were going from house to house, confessing to individuals they had injured, returning stolen property and money. The whole city was stirred.[14]

Wales

The global revival that ultimately touched down in Pyeng Yang battered the shores of Wales four years earlier. One individual experienced the initial stirrings: a college student named Evan Roberts. Over a series of months, Roberts found himself caught up in the presence of God, as he describes here:

For a long time I was much troubled in my soul and my heart by thinking over the failure of Christianity.... But one night after I had been in great distress about this, I went to sleep, and at one o'clock suddenly I was awakened up out of my sleep, and I found myself with unspeakable joy and awe in the very presence of the Almighty God. And for the space of four hours

> *I was privileged to speak face to face with him as a*
> *man speaks face to face with a friend. At five o'clock*
> *it seemed to me as if I again returned to earth.... And*
> *it was not only that morning but every morning for*
> *three to four months ... and I knew that God was*
> *going to work in the land and not this land only, but*
> *the world.*[15]

Following this personal awakening, Roberts dropped out of school and began preaching. Wherever he spoke, listeners experienced what Roberts experienced in the previous months:

> *Welsh newspapers printed the names of those being*
> *born into the kingdom. Roads to the Chapels were*
> *lined with people. Colleges closed down and students*
> *marched singing and praising God on their way to*
> *prayer meetings. Prayer brigades formed: one town*
> *boasted a get-out-of-bed prayer brigade where they*
> *would pray all night for God to rouse others out of*
> *their sleep, convict them of sin and save their souls.*
> *And indeed there were reports of people climbing out*
> *of their beds in the middle of the night, searching out*
> *a prayer meeting and crying out for the Lord Jesus to*
> *save them.*[16]

Church historian J. Edwin Orr reported that within three months, one hundred thousand converts had been added to the churches of Wales. Alcoholism dropped by 50 percent, crime was virtually nonexistent, and profanity all but disappeared from the Welsh language, which actually led to a reported slowing in the coal mines: "The horses are terribly puzzled. The haulers are some of the very lowest. They have driven the horses by obscenity and kicks. Now they can hardly persuade the horses to start working because there is no obscenity and no kicks."[17]

India

In 1891, the brilliant Hindu social reformer Pandita Ramabai experienced a profound conversion to Christianity. Following her conversion, Pandita built a shelter and school in Pune, India (south of Mumbai) for orphans, widows, and famine victims. She named her shelter "Mukti," meaning "salvation." For years she prayed and fasted for the salvation of the women who came to live there.

In September 1901, during a special prayer meeting held for an outpouring of God's Spirit, God's presence powerfully visited Mukti, and twelve hundred women were baptized in the course of two months. But Pandita's spiritual burden went beyond Mukti to the whole country of India itself. She organized her newly converted women into prayer circles (ten women in each circle) to pray daily for a miraculous movement of God across India. Seeing the need for evangelism as well as prayer, Pandita asked thirty of her women to give up their studies at the center to evangelize the local towns and villages.

As those thirty women prayed for God to empower them on their evangelistic mission, His presence manifested among them. "One of the thirty was so set aflame spiritually that the other girls saw a vision of fire engulfing her. One of the girls grabbed a pail of water to throw on her, only to discover that the fire, though visible, was not literal. It was the fire of the Spirit seen ... at Pentecost."[18]

As one witness described the scene, "One little girl of twelve is constantly laughing—her face, plain, even ugly, is beautiful and radiant. She does not know it. She is occupied with Jesus. You think you have looked on an angel face. Some claim to have seen the Lord—one, a blind girl. All speak of His coming again. One sang hymns composing them as she sang."[19]

The thirty women who had committed to witnessing in neighboring villages turned into seven hundred. Every day a group of sixty would go out, taking turns while the others remained and prayed. Of the churches that tended the fruit of this revival, the Methodists reported thirty-six thousand new members; the Presbyterians baptized eleven thousand; the Lutherans, twenty-one thousand ... and the list goes on.

THE SOURCE OF LOVE

Revivals and awakenings are special moments when God's presence moves palpably close to humanity. By definition, revivals are excessive. It's like Christmas. And while the idea is appealing, Christmas doesn't happen every day. In fact life would be quite bizarre and unbalanced if it did. But the exaggerated nature of revivals allows us to see some principles that might be otherwise obscured. What we want to observe is how passion overflows after sitting in the sun-baked presence of God.

If you can believe it, I actually found this self-published account of the Shantung Revival of the 1930s on eBay. This book was the testimony of a Chinese pastor permeated by God's presence as the revival spread through this northern province of China:

> *I have been preaching for 30 years and have not been worth my salt. I was so lazy, I could not walk a mile and half to tell people about Jesus. Since the revival I go to prayer meeting at 5:00 in the mornings, go home and eat breakfast, take a little bread for lunch and walk 25 miles witnessing in villages, then come home and go to prayer meeting at night. The next morning I'm ready to go again. Dozens of villages surround us, and we have witnessed in all of them.*[20]

The problem—*our problem*—is not a lack of passion. It is the lack of intimacy with the Lord which yields such passion.

Our own love for Christ is not the driving force behind this kind of passion, and if it were, we wouldn't get very far. Nor is the example of Jesus the force behind this passion, as though we could emulate Him by sheer force of the will. Rather, it is Christ's presence in us, fanned to flame: Jesus empowering us to love Jesus. To soak in and be saturated by God's presence is the animating power of love, because its source is God, not ourselves.

Spiritual revivals are not normal Christian life, just as martyrdom is not the norm—at least not for us. But daily deaths *are* the norm, as is daily renewal in the presence of God. And it is precisely this daily renewal—this time under the tanning lamps of God's presence—that is the true source of our radiant heat.

There have been points in our life and ministry when Katie and I have found our bank account short on money. It's a great way to learn to trust God.

In one particular instance we had twenty dollars to our name, which included checking and savings accounts as well as whatever we could find in the dryer. We used budget envelopes, a system where you use an envelope for each category of expenditure: an envelope for gas, another for repairs, another for gifts, et cetera. All that remained in any of the envelopes was a single, crisp twenty-dollar bill in the "groceries" envelope. This was the money with which we would feed our family for the next week.

Worried, fearful, stressed, and hungry (just the thought of a food shortage makes me want to eat), Katie and I took the twenty dollars and went into the family room. Then we had the most amazing time of prayer and praise, overflowing in our hearts with thankfulness to God for His countless provision over the years. We came out of the celestial huddle completely changed—and *saturated*. It was winter, and we had a fire going in the family room. Without need to confer or discuss, we both moved over to the fireplace and threw the twenty-dollar bill into the flames.

I think this is a federal offense, so now that I think about it, *this never happened.*

But in this make-believe story, which I just made up, hypothetically Katie and I were loving God, saturated in His presence, and our joy in Him overflowed in an act of worship where we poured ourselves out in the form of a sacrifice (a financial one). My face did not look like an angel, and I didn't dump a bucket of water on Katie because I thought she was on fire, but we felt renewed in God's presence as we worshipped Him. Passion was the residual glow. Our anxieties quickly receded in the presence of God's love. Two days later a check arrived in the mail out of nowhere, quite *expected,* though not presumed.

THE PHYSICS OF WORSHIP

Worship is one of those words similar to *holy*—we kind of know what it means, but we'd be hard-pressed to define it. The problem with words we can't define is that their meaning can shift without anyone noticing. Such is the case with the word *worship*. Worship to some Christians is now synonymous with singing praise to God, even though this aspect of worship is simply a single slice of a fuller definition.

Saturation

Worship, first and foremost, is about saturating ourselves in the presence of God. God created us to worship and because of this, it is a part of our spiritual DNA. Everyone must worship like everyone must eat. Everyone lives to be saturated—believers and unbelievers alike.

Picture the lunar landscape of a sponge: all the empty pockets and craters, like the nooks and crannies of an English muffin. Though grossly inaccurate, it's a helpful way to envision the soul, which was created for the wringing and absorption of worship. The soul desperately craves to be saturated; every person, therefore, finds something to worship, something that will saturate their souls. The drunk saturates himself with alcohol, the greedy with money, the lustful with lust, the workaholic with work, the worrier with worry: always and everywhere saturating, worshiping.

I didn't know this, but apparently there are two kitchen sponges: one for the dishes, the other for, I don't know … grime? I never took home economics in high school, so maybe I missed the briefing. My wife, Katie, was horrified when she came into the kitchen and saw me using the same sponge to clean the dishes that's used to wipe the mayonnaise off the kitchen floor. To make her point, she asked me to wring out the sponge in the sink. As I did, out came this black, vile, putrid flow of what I can only guess was the bubonic plague. Point made.

The answer as to why anyone would baste themselves in such vile toxins as worry, greed, lust, and jealousy is that the only thing worse is to be an empty sponge. We were created for worship, and no one can long endure the pain of being hollow—*saturated by nothing*. So we soak our souls in something, *in anything*, and that which saturates us oozes back out of us, making room for more of the same. Tragically, whatever we choose to saturate ourselves with, if it's not God, will erode our souls like alchohol erodes the liver of an alcoholic.

When we become Christians, it's not that we begin to worship, it's that we restore worship to its original design—we begin absorbing God (so to speak) and wringing out His love so we can get more.

A Cycle

Worship is saturation; to use another metaphor, it's also a cycle. Worship is a cycle like rain is a cycle. When we are saturated with God, we overflow toward God and others, and He in turn pours back into us. That overflow may take the form of singing praise, but it may also take the form of any number of other acts: service, repentance, thanksgiving, witness, et cetera. The cycle is simple: poured into, poured out, poured into, poured out.

So picture this: Your soul is parched and the sponge is dry, but in faith you squeeze out a few drops of thanksgiving toward God. You thank Him for the things He's doing in your life. It's a little sandy at first, a little dry: "Thanks, God…. Thanks that I have a house … and a dog … and that it's nice out … and you are benevolen…."

But you stay with it, and all of sudden you begin to notice your sponge filling up. There's more meaning in your words, the sphere of your thanksgiving begins to widen, and the reason is that as you've been wringing out, God's been pouring back into you. And so the more you give thanks, the more you *want* to give thanks. Once the cycle starts to flow, it perpetuates. You may find yourself giving thanks for mosquitoes or plumbing or Ritz crackers and sincerely mean it.

> *All this is for your benefit, so that the grace that is reaching more and more people may cause thanksgiving to overflow to the glory of God. (2 Cor. 4:15)*

Or picture this: You desire to praise God, but as you begin, your heart feels hollow, your words feel hollow. "God, you are so sovereign and omnipotent, so omnipotent and sovereign, so…." But then you say something a little different, in a way you've never said it before: "God, you're really smart." And this causes your brain to double-pump and engages your mind: "Yeah, You *are* smart—a genius, in fact!" The pump starts flowing, and you find yourself praising God for everything, overflowing toward Him, while God is concurrently sending life back into you.

The worship cycle is like priming a pump: a few drops, a few drips, then spurts, then a continuous stream. This is the engine that fuels passion and love. It involves small, impotent steps of obedience that open the floodgates of God's presence and power.

This dynamic process is the cycle of life. It is the water cycle observed in nature, the dynamic of marriage, and perhaps the essence (though clearly not identical) of the eternal commune of Father, Son, and Holy Spirit: "On that day you will realize that I am in my Father, and you are in me, and I am in you" (John 14:20).

Sacrifice

If you have never thought of it as such, sacrifice, too, is a form of worship—a primary form actually. As we pour out our lives, souls, and hearts to God (and others) in sacrifice and service, God pours back into us, resaturating us. It's a cycle of perpetual dying fueled by God's life pouring back into us and through us.

Note how Paul expresses his sacrifice as worship and as "pouring himself out."

> For I am already being poured out like a drink offering, and the time has come for my departure. (2 Tim. 4:6)

> But even if I am being poured out like a drink offering on the sacrifice and service coming from your faith, I am glad and rejoice with all of you. (Phil. 2:17)

A drink offering in the Old Testament was a sacrifice offered to God, a component of worship. They poured the drink out like gravy, basted over a sacrificial meat offering, consumed by the heat, and transformed—metaphorically speaking—into the aroma of praise spindling upward. Paul sees his life as being poured out in the suffering of sacrificial service to the Lord, and in context, this clearly implies martyrdom. Paul, however, also sees his sacrifice as an *ongoing martyrdom*, a constant dying, a continual pouring out and spilling of his life.

The million little ways to die that make up the Christian life are fueled by a million mini revivals.

YOU FIRST—NO, YOU FIRST

Imagine you found yourself in some random building on lower Manhattan. You've just walked up seven flights of stairs, and you're really thirsty. So you head to the seventh-floor water fountain and get yourself a drink.

Question: Where did that water come from? Answer: The water came from one of two sources, depending on the height of the building.

One way a building gets water is directly from the water main that snakes its way through Manhattan, a pipe seven feet in diameter that gargles 1.5 billion gallons of water a day through its esophagus. The speed and force of the water determines the pressure, and should you stick a straw into the main (which is basically what plumbing does), the geyser might climb to as high as ten or twelve stories— which means the water you're drinking on the seventh floor might well have come directly from the Manhattan main.

If you were on the seventeenth floor, however, your water would come from a different source. This is why you see all those water towers in silhouettes of New York. Taller buildings use the water pressure provided by gravity, siphoning the water down from a water tower on the roof. So the flow of water in any given building is either being pumped up or siphoned down.

The point I'm making is that the worship cycle can also flow in one of two directions. Spiritually speaking, this siphon effect occurs when you pour out your life in some form of sacrifice, completely devoid of spiritual energy or empowerment. Here is where faith is so important in day-to-day Christian living. You pour yourself out, but you do so in faith, trusting that God will pour life back into you. Let's take an unlovable person as an example. Somehow you choose to initiate love toward this individual, feeling the warmth and kindness you might feel for a member of Al-Qaeda. In so doing, you create a spiritual vacuum—a siphon—and it is quickly filled by the flow of spiritual resources—or God's empowerment. Now you miraculously find yourself overflowing toward that person with the care, compassion, and empathy that could only come from God alone.

In this case you've started the overflow cycle by faith, trusting that God will saturate you as you pour yourself out, which, of course, He faithfully does. As A. W. Tozer once observed, "The problem is not to persuade God to fill us, but to want God sufficiently to permit Him to do so. The average Christian is so … contented with his … condition that there is no vacuum of desire into which the blessed Spirit can rush in satisfying fullness."[21]

The other dynamic is more like tapping directly into the water main, when the worship cycle begins with God, with saturating ourselves in His presence. Out from our worship gushes joy, flowing over and out of us in some passionate display.

Have you ever enjoyed an amazing meal with family or friends and kept absolutely silent? It's impossible. It's like trying to pat the top of your head while rubbing your belly. You simply have to say, "Mmm," or, "This is amazing." Even if it's just a territorial grunt to let others know to keep their hands and feet away from your mouth, it's virtually impossible to eat good food without expressing your utter satisfaction.

Notice how the apostle John is propelled by his joy in Christ: "We proclaim to you what we have seen and heard, so that you also may have fellowship with us. And our fellowship is with the Father and with his Son, Jesus Christ. We write this to make our joy complete" (1 John 1:3–4). John is so saturated with God that he's compelled to write to those he loves and tell them, "You have to try this; it's the best thing I've ever tasted."

Let me return one last time to the example of revivals. Consider this chronicler's observation of a small revival that took place in western Canada in the 1970s.

> During the revival God was, to use Augustine's phrase, "cutting loose the cords of the tongue," and Christians who had vowed that they would never open their mouths either publicly or privately for Christ found that they were speaking freely.... Believers witnessed to their neighbors for the first time.... Many believers never knew what God could do through them when their lives were free from sin.[22]

I'm willing to bet they didn't need to hold an evangelism seminar following the revival. But as they experienced the presence of the Lord, they needed to share it in order to complete their joy. Revivals exaggerate spiritual principles that are in motion every day, though they can seem excessive or unreal at times.

Again, the problem—*our* problem—is not a lack of passion. It is a lack of intimacy with the Lord that yields such passion. As Watchman Nee observed,

> How hard we often find it to drag ourselves into His presence! We shrink from the solitude, and even when we do detach ourselves physically, our thoughts still keep wandering outside.... Yet it is only as we draw near to Him that we can minister.... Unless we really know what it is to draw near to God, we cannot know what it is to serve him.[23]

This chapter originally ended with that quote from Watchmen Nee. Other than as illustrations, I use quotes sparingly—only if the quote is truly needed and profoundly stated. The thing is, Nee's quote is not profoundly stated. So I wondered why I thought to place it here. Upon reflection, the answer is this: I felt it needed to be said, but that I wasn't the person to say it. I have many failings and failures, but the only real regret of my Christian life is not having spent more time in Christ's presence—just being with Him.

I'm not dead yet, so this can be remedied—and it will be remedied. And if you're not dead, well then, the same is true for *you.* "God, bless us both."

EPILOGUE

REQUIEM

Monday, 10:25 pm: I was on the verge of vomiting all over the bed. The pain couldn't possibly get worse than this. During one of the ten second breaks I asked all the women in the room if it would get any worse than this. They all looked at each other silently. No one would answer me.

It was going to get worse? It could not possibly get worse. Worse than that was dead.[1]

Heather Armstrong blogged through her journeys (several of them) from pregnancy to birth with such graphic, eye-popping honesty that she's now one of Forbes "Top 25 Web Celebrities."

But no matter how graphic or crude, written descriptions can never convey what it must feel like to push a human being through an opening the size of a Froot Loop. Yet as far as metaphors are concerned, childbirth is perhaps the best example of the theme of this book and the theme of the Christian life. Childbirth says it all. It says everything we've been saying but says it better, clearer, and more viscerally. Nowhere else in this world are death and life so seamlessly integrated and simultaneously contrasted as they are in childbirth. It's *Friday the Thirteenth* and *The Sound of Music* spliced into a single movie.

In fact the only way you could possibly push the contrast between death and life any further would be to exaggerate the two extremes. For example, if you imagined the agony of labor taking place in some vile location, like say a stable, and if the newborn baby was, I don't know, laid in an animal's feeding trough, while at the same time, this newborn child happened to be royalty, so, like, people came and worshiped him in the stable, but that would be so over-the-top—the birth of royalty in a pigsty—it's just hard to imagine.

And so it's here, in the birth of life, that we witness the clearest demonstration of how life works.

EPIDURALS

> *Monday, 11:00 pm: The epidural had taken effect. It was the best thing I ever felt in my life.... I started to sing. My mother and sister started laughing. I asked Jon if we could name the baby Epidural Armstrong.*[2]

Somewhere back in Eden the stinger of death lodged itself into childbirth, and the only effective pain remedy is a bigger, longer needle inserted directly into the spinal column. It doesn't remove pain, simply blocks it: It numbs the pain receptors. It's a beautiful thing. And as every father knows, when a woman requests an epidural in the violent throws of labor, you get her one ... *immediately*. Without making eye contact, you back slowly toward the door, making no sudden movements, and then you run and get the doctor.

But there are no epidurals in life, no drug to take away the pain of a failed marriage, the death of a dream, the loss of a parent or a child. But that doesn't stop people from trying to get rid of the pain. People turn cough syrup into crystal meth and get high from cans of Reddi-wip. Our fallen nature has the ingenuity of MacGyver, and it can turn anything into an epidural.

I heard on the news this morning that someone just bid, won, and paid 3.7 million dollars for an oil painting. Three million, seven hundred thousand dollars for a painting? Sounds like the painting is doing double duty as a piece of art and as an epidural. New statistics show sixteen million people suffer from sexual addiction in this country, only sex isn't addicting unless it's being used as an epidural. At the same time I see that some celebrity has just left his current spouse for a young, sexy, twenty-six-year-old *epidural*. Success, career, alcohol, money, drugs, sex, fame—you can get all these over the counter. The sting of death hurts like hell itself, and the way of the world is to numb that pain, to run as fast and as far away from it as possible.

This is our natural response to things unnatural, things not native to this life and this world as God made it: pain and death. Death is the Burmese python ravaging the ecosystem of the Florida Everglades and consuming all forms of life because Burmese pythons do not belong in the Florida everglades.

But in the judgment of Eden lies the path to redemption:

> To the woman he said, "I will greatly increase your pains in childbearing; with pain you will give birth to children." (Gen. 3:16)

The sentence for sin handed down by God is death, and the birth of life will now be accompanied by, and through, inordinate pain and suffering. Yet the sentence is at the same time the plan of escape: Life will now emerge out of death—death will be the means to life. The Savior's resurrection will be arrived at only by the Savior's death, and the path to life and resurrection will be the same for all members of the kingdom of God.

> *Then he called the crowd to him along with his disciples and said: "If anyone would come after me, he must deny himself and take up his cross and follow me." (Mark 8:34)*

One of the great obstacles to our holiness and transformation is that we still live like we're in the jungle and not the kingdom. We reflexively run from pain and death. We treat trials and hardship as menacing threats out to devour us. When pain ensnares us, we would rather gnaw off our own limbs than submit to captivity. The world is fallen, and while we still inhabit this jungle, we are not subject to its rules (run, hide, avoid all pain, survive). The kingdom of God is at work in our lives, and for us, death is the path that leads to life. To avoid trials and hardships, to avoid the little deaths that occupy our days, is to avoid the very path to life and transformation.

Scripture speaks to us as though we are scared animals cautiously creeping out of the woods toward civilization in hopes of finding some leftovers. However, the Scriptures seek to tame us, to reorient us to a fundamental change in the dynamic of life, to teach us to embrace what we have always feared. We are coaxed to submit to

God's will, to respond to His hand in everything, and to embrace suffering and hardship. We are patiently shown how death is a trusted messenger of renewal, transformation, and rebirth—and no longer our hunter.

LITTLE DEATHS

> *It was going to get worse? It could not possibly get worse. Worse than that was dead.*[3]

Labor feels like death. To an adolescent, a romantic break-up feels like death. Divorce feels like death. From wherever the sensation of life flows, its cessation feels like death. The damming of life creates death's valley. And as the world is filled with a million sources of life, there are also as many ways to die.

It is this ongoing experience of death that occupies the focus of biblical discipleship. When Paul states, "I die daily," or, "Death is at work in us," or when Jesus says, "Take up your cross," it is the daily deaths that are in view, with martyrdom somewhere off in the periphery. When we flip it around, seeing background as foreground, all the crucial texts of Christian living only appear to relate to .00001 percent of kingdom inhabitants: those who may literally die for their faith.

Spiritual growth lies not in seeing the magnitude of Christian martyrdom, but in seeing how miniscule it can be. Nothing is random, and spiritual maturity sees the purpose, opportunity, and blessing behind the apparently arbitrary obstacles, annoyances, and setbacks that cloud our days.

Several apparent works of Jackson Pollock were recently discovered to be forgeries, which raises the obvious question: How do you detect a forgery of random paint splatters on a canvass? Well, under a microscope there is evidently a discernable pattern in Pollock's seemingly arbitrary paint drips. Creating "randomness" was among his objectives, so this pattern was clearly not the conscious design or intent of Pollock. As he created his paintings both unconsciously and randomly, art experts believe the identifiable pattern could have only come from the patterns in the very fabric—mind, muscles, soul—of the man himself, an unavoidable result of Pollock's having simply concentrated while holding the paint brush. This identifiable structure stops at the edge of the canvas, exactly where his concentration would have, meaning randomness is never found where there is creative intent.

As believers, our lives are the objects of God's creative intent. Everything in our lives is sifted through His hands, and you know there is a pattern and a purpose for every splatter of paint. There is no experience of death, no matter how small, that does not carry with it the potential for life.

If someone jumped out and said, "Renounce Jesus as your Savior and place this mark of the beast on your forehead or I'll kill you," undoubtedly we would recognize this as a death to embrace. The common, household opportunities to die are not so clearly labeled, and what are viewed as mere annoyances will always be ignored rather than seen as opportunities.

Yesterday I felt somewhat critical toward my wife, Katie. I prayed and confessed it and throughout the day. I tried to divert my mind to the many wonderful things that are Katie. All day long this went on. At ten o'clock that night I finally saw it, staring right in front of me the whole time: *an opportunity to die.* And so without context, in the middle of an episode of *House Hunters*, I looked over at her and said, "I'm sorry I have not loved you as I should have today."

It was an admission of failure and of my sinfulness. It was embarrassing, and I felt stupid saying it. But her face lit up, and God's love poured into me in an instant: a moment of death followed by God's resurrection power transforming my heart and mind.

There is a place in the Christian life for death in discipline. But more often than not, the death that's called for is more personal, truly the death of ourselves—the death of our ego or reputation or self-sufficiency or pride. Self-discipline draws from the strength of the will, which is strengthened by habit. Self-inflicted suffering, however, draws attention to our weakness, then to God's grace and power as it channels through that weakness. This is also a clear demonstration of our death and God's resurrection power. This is why Paul, well acquainted with the dynamics of death, stated, "If I must boast, I will boast of the things that show my weakness" (2 Cor. 11:30). That is truly a dying to self—not self-discipline—a dying of self and not a disciplining of self. It's important that we see the difference.

Submission to the sufferings of Christ flows from both willingness and awareness. By awareness I mean that you recognize these little deaths for what they are: small opportunities to die to self. To see them as anything different will trigger in our minds the reflex to recoil and run from them.

CONTRACTIONS

Monday, 10:06 pm: I returned to the hospital bed and told Jon that the pain was getting a lot worse. In the middle of my sentence another contraction hit, and I almost bit my tongue off.[4]

"Nation will rise against nation, and kingdom against kingdom. There will be earthquakes in various places, and famines. These are the beginning of birth pains" (Mark 13:8). The Scriptures use labor in this passage where Jesus likens the signs accompanying His return to the painful contractions of childbirth. As a metaphor, contractions bring to our thoughts three big ideas: the idea of something growing in intensity and frequency leading to a birth of some kind; the idea of suffering and pain giving way to life; and the idea of recurring circumstances—something will happen again and again.

We all have an ultimate death and a glorious resurrection awaiting us that makes the daily deaths and resurrections of the Christian life—the labor contractions—a foretaste of the final reality. They recur daily, some with such mildness we barely feel a tremor, and some with such intensity it seems like the real thing—as if we are really dying.

The interplay between death and resurrection charted over the timeline of our lives is like a musical score. A symphony traditionally begins with the introduction of the chord of three notes (the tonic triad).[5] This triad lies at the core of the piece and functions like the plot of a story. The composer then wanders away from the triad, but never too far. He always brings back one or two of the notes, flirting with our ears, making us desire the harmonic consummation that is the triad coming back together. In the final movement, the acoustic courtship is ecstatically subsumed as the composer unveils the triad, leaving our ears enraptured in the harmony it waited and longed for. This is the sound of glory, the musical version of contractions leading up to birth.

The recurring chords of death and resurrection will someday crescendo. Somewhere there is a little plot of land with your name on it. We will die and be resurrected with our Christ. *End of symphony.* In the meantime, we are in the midst of a dress rehearsal: many, many dress rehearsals. This is how Scripture wants us to view our trials, and it's certainly how Paul viewed them:

> *I want to know Christ and the power of his resurrection and the fellowship of sharing in his sufferings, becoming like him in his death, and so, somehow, to attain to the resurrection from the dead. (Phil. 3:10–11)*

As we come to the end of our study, I hope that enigmatic passages such as this one are no longer enigmatic and that you understand the principles of death and resurrection that they convey. Dying for one's faith, should we be fortunate enough to physically do so, would only be the fitting—perhaps ironic—end of a life continuously reverberating with the chords of death and resurrection. In some way we are always dying for our faith, and in some sense we will all ultimately die for it.

> *For none of us lives to himself alone and none of us dies to himself alone. If we live, we live to the Lord; and if we*

die, we die to the LORD. So, whether we live or die, we
belong to the LORD. (Rom. 14:7–8)

FOR LIFE

Thankfully the birth of her baby is not where Heather Armstrong ends her blogging. She faithfully journals her way through the wonder of the first months of parenthood, writing letters to her newborn daughter, Leta.

> *Dear Leta, today you turn five months old.... You are*
> *becoming such a little person and every day I have to*
> *resist the urge to put you between two slices of wheat*
> *bread and lather mayonnaise on your head, gobbling*
> *you up in one bite.*[6]

Why would anyone in his or her right mind endure the pain of childbirth? The answer: for the birth of a child of course, for the sake of life.

One of the greatest moments in sports movie history was filmed on a stage in Burbank, California. It was Al Pacino's halftime speech as coach Tony D'Amato, the fictional coach of the fictional Miami Sharks in the Oliver Stone film *Any Given Sunday*. The words are powerful, but it's the course sandpaper grit in Pacino's voice that gives it its ethos. If you hear Pacino give it once, you'll forever believe that football is the reason we were all put on this earth. The context is a critical playoff game, and naturally Pacino's team is losing at halftime. To motivate the team to go out, spill their blood, and sacrifice everything, he injects them with the testosterone of these words:

Life is just a game of inches. So is football. Because in either game, life or football, the margin for error is so small. I mean one half step too late or too early, you don't quite make it. One half second too slow or too fast and you don't quite catch it. The inches we need are everywhere around us; they are in every break of the game, every minute, every second. On this team, we fight for that inch. On this team, we tear ourselves, and every- one around us, to pieces for that inch. We claw with our fingernails for that inch. 'Cause we know when we add up all those inches that it's going to make the difference between winning and losing, between living and dying. I'll tell you this: In any fight it is the guy who is willing to die who is going to win that inch. And I know if I am going to have any life any more, it is because I am still willing to fight and die for that inch, because that is what living is.

Obviously the goal of this book is a motivational one: to encourage us to pick up our cross and embrace the death implicit in following Jesus Christ. As I reflect on Pacino's speech and the power of its persuasion, I don't think any words could better articulate what I hope I have *not* done in these pages: play Vince Lombardi to sinful pride and anemic willpower.

The reason we die is for the sake of greater life, and that life is found in Christ. As has been repeated throughout these chapters, there's nothing warm or wonderful about death or dying, pain or suffering. We embrace them only as the vehicle to resurrection, only as the means to greater life, only as the way to deeper intimacy with Jesus. Christ dwells in us, is manifested through us, and experienced in us primarily through our deaths and dying.

When we die to self and embrace our trials, unjust suffering, and pain, we do so with the anticipation of how God will resurrect and transform those things into life. We cannot submit to death without the power of resurrection in us and the promise of resurrection before us.

But Pacino's speech from *Any Given Sunday* is absolutely correct about one thing: Life is a game of inches, not yards. We need to forget about the end zone and focus on the smaller units of death and resurrection. And those inches are everywhere.

> *The inches we need are everywhere around us. They are in every break of the game, every minute, every second. On this team, we fight for that inch. On this team, we tear ourselves, and everyone around us, to pieces for that inch. We claw with our fingernails for that inch. 'Cause we know when we add up all those inches that it's going to make the difference between winning and losing, between living and dying.*

AND MORE LIFE

> *Here at nine months, oh dear little Leta, we have hit the magical time when things are okay. This month I finally remembered why I wanted to procreate in*

the first place because you are just so cute that the
frightening thought of one day trying to have another
baby popped into my head.[7]

It would be quite disheartening if we ever noticed this trend: Having gone through the pains of childbirth, nine out of ten mothers refused to ever have another child. If that were true, it would be disturbing. It would, in effect, communicate that life is not worth the pain of death. *But this is not the trend.* Having experienced new life, most parents are willing to stand in whatever line is required to get seconds and thirds.

In these chapters we've seen that God can impart life through any number of venues: through encouragement and reassurance; through a reversal of circumstances; through rescue; by reward; through a re-energizing or rejuvenating of vitality; by resuscitation, renewal, or resurrection. Life can emerge from anywhere and everywhere. And these categories are just the phylum, not genus or species. There are 561 species of butterfly, and I wouldn't care to guess how many versions and variations of reward, rescue, or rejuvenation there may be. I'm sure a million of them.

Life is a positive feedback loop. The more you get, the more you want. Once you've had a child, a Barbie doll seems an absurdity. To experience true intimacy with Christ, real transformation, and God's resurrection power coursing in and through us, is to lose any desire we ever had for lifeless religiosity.

EPITAPH

In a book about death, I would imagine the closing words should be something of an epitaph. I've never written an epitaph. And for just such occasions we have Google. So I found these instructions from a website dedicated to helping one writing the perfect epitaph: A "good epitaph makes you think. It reflects the greatest achievements of the deceased, highlighting what they gave to the world."

If this is the case, then I think the most fitting epitaph is a word found on every tombstone: "Died." What more could be said of us than we were willing to take up our cross? What more could be said of us than our willingness to die allowed Christ to live out His life in and through us?

And so, dear friends, I leave you with this final word of encouragement: *Die.*

> Then Thomas (called Didymus) said to the rest of the disciples, "Let us also go, that we may die with him." (John 11:16)

ENDNOTES

Chapter One — Better Off Dead
1. Story from Joel Rosenberg, *Epicenter* (Carol Stream, IL: Tyndale, 2009), 205–207.
2. Virgina Woolf, *Collected Essays,* vol. 1 (London: Hogarth Press, 1967), 320.

Section One — Democracy of Death
1. Oliver Sacks, *The Man Who Mistook His Wife for a Hat* (London: Picador, 1985), 7.
2. Ibid., 10.
3. Jonah Lehrer, *Proust Was a Neuroscientist* (New York: Houghton Mifflin Harcourt, 2008), 96–119.
4. Rikki Watts, *Isaiah's New Exodus in Mark* (Grand Rapids, MI: Baker, 2000), 124–131.
5. As quoted in Tom Zoenller, *The Heartless Stone* (New York: Picador, 2006), 58.
6. C. S. Lewis, *The Weight of Glory and Other Addresses* (San Francisco: HarperCollins, 2001), 25.
7. Tom Zoellner, *The Heartless Stone* (New York: Picador, 2006), 40.

Section Two — The Wake of Faith
1. An overview of the documentary *Helvetica: The History of Type* can be found at http://www.pbs.org/independentlens/helvetica/makingof.html.

Section Three — The Life of Martyrs
1. William James, *The Principles of Psychology* (Cambridge, MA: Harvard University Press, 1981), 381–382.
2. Driving facts taken from Tom Vanderbilt, *Traffic* (New York: Knopf, 2008), 74–89.
3. Desiring God, "Ten Effects of Believing the Five Points of Calvinism," John Piper, http://www.desiringgod.org/ResourceLibrary/Articles/ByDate/2002/1519_Ten_Effects_of_Believing_in_the_Five_Points_of_Calvinism/ (accessed September 11, 2009).
4. Joseph Tson, Revival Forum (sermon), http://media.sermonindex.net/10/SID10929.mp3 (accessed May, 2008).
5. C. S. Lewis, *Letters to an American Lady* (Grand Rapids, MI: Wm. B. Eerdmans Publishing Co., 1967), 83–84.

Section Four — La Petite Mort (The Little Death of Trials)
1. Concept comes from Thomas Brooks, *The Mute Christian Under the Smarting Rod* (Sovereign Grace Treasures, 2006).
2. C. S. Lewis as quoted by Sheldon Vanauken, *A Severe Mercy* (New York: HarperOne, 1987), 188–189.
3. Ori and Rom Brafman, *Sway* (New York: Doubleday, 2008), 72.

4. Dietrich Bonhoeffer, *Voices in the Night* (Grand Rapids, MI: Zondervan, 1999), 59.
5. Fred Lucas, "Death-Row Syndrome Ignites Debate," *Stanford Advocate,* January 29, 2005.
6. Steven Levitt, Stephen Dubner, *Freakonomics: A Rogue Economist Explores the Hidden Side of Everything* (New York: William Morrow, 2005), 91.
7. Bill Bryson, *A Short History of Nearly Everything* (New York: Broadway Books, 2003), 97.
8. W. Hodding Carter, *Flushed* (New York: Atria, 2006), 118–131.
9. Edith Schaeffer, *Affliction* (Grand Rapids, MI: Baker, 1993), 27.

Section Five — Ode to Courage
1. "Bush Emotional at Medal Ceremony for Fallen Navy SEAL," ABC News' The Radar blog, April 8, 2008 (http://blogs.abcnews.com).
2. Ibid.
3. Ibid.
4. John McCain, "In Search of Courage," *Fast Company,* September 2004.
5. G. K. Chesterton, *Orthodoxy* (New York: Doubleday, 1990), 134.
6. Marcel Proust, *Swanns Way: In Search of Lost Time,* vol. 1 (New York: Modern Library, 1998), 60.
7. As quoted in William Ian Miller, *The Mystery of Courage* (Cambridge: Harvard University Press, 2000), 64.
8. Chesterton, ibid.
9. John F. Kennedy, *Profiles in Courage* (London: Black Dog, 1999), 246.
10. Ronald Heifetz, "The Leader of the Future," *Fast Company,* May 1999.
11. C. S. Lewis, *The Screwtape Letters* (New York: Harper Collins, 2001), 97–98.
12. Laura Miller, "The Mystery of Courage," Salon.com, October 25, 2000.
13. Chesterton, ibid.
14. McCain, ibid.
15. Tim O'Brien, *The Things They Carried* (New York: Broadway, 1998), 234.

Section Six — Humbled and Mortified
1. The Associated Press, "Tale of the Tantrums: A T. O. Timeline" NBC Sports (nbcsports.msnbc.com), November 23, 2005.
2. Ramon Alexander Jaime, "Owens's Rat Analogy Bites," *Los Angeles City News,* April 21, 2004.
3. Ed Werder, "Sources: T. O.'s Expressed Resentment Toward Romo," ESPN.com, December 12, 2008.
4. David Weinberger, *Everything is Miscellaneous* (New York: Holt, 2007), 155.
5. From "Ronald Reagan: The American Experience," aired on PBS. The transcript can be found at http://www.pbs.org/wgbh/amex/reagan/filmmore/index.html.
6. John Fletcher, *The Works of Reverend John Fletcher,* vol. 2 (Whitefish, MT: Kessinger, 2007), 325.
7. Thomas Aquinas, *Of God And His Creatures: An Annotated Translation Of The Summa Contra Gentiles Of Saint Thomas Aquinas* (Whitefish, MT: Kessinger, 2007), 303
8. Chuck Colson, *Born Again* (Old Tappan, NJ: Spire, 1977), 248–249.
9. Baptist Press article by Ferrell Foster. Reprinted by permission of Baptist Press,

www.bpnews.net.

10. Joseph J. Ellis, *American Creation* (New York: Vintage, 2007), 14.

Section Seven — The Passion of Love

1. Malcom Gladwell, "True Colors," *The New Yorker,* March 22, 1999.
2. Rollo May, *Love and Will* (New York: W.W. Norton, 1969), 14–15.
3. Dan Ariely, *Predictably Irrational* (New York: HarperCollins, 2008), 4–5.
4. Will Walker, *The Kingdom of Couches* (Orlando: CruPress, 2006), 60.
5. Henry Scougal, *The Life of God in the Soul of Man* (Harrisonburg, VA: Sprinkle, 1986), 64.
6. *He's Just Not That Into You,* DVD, directed by Ken Kwapis (Alliance [Universal]: 2009).
7. This book is by a wonderful teacher and author, and not wanting to reflect in any way negatively upon his work, I have opted not to cite.
8. Bill Bright, "Bill Bright's Benediction," *Christianity Today,* July 1, 2003.
9. Charles Colson, "Finishing Well," *Breakpoint,* July 2003.
10. Pete Greig, *The Vision & The Vow* (Relevant Books, 2004). Used by permission. To see an animated version of the poem go to 24-7prayer.com.
11. Alexander Roberts and James Donaldson, eds., *Early Church Fathers Ante-Nicene Fathers to A.D. 325,* vol. 1, http://www.ccel.org/ccel/schaff/anf01.toc.html.
12. A translation of Van Gogh's letter can be viewed online at http://www. webexhibits.org/vangogh/letter/11/193.htm?qp=feelings.apprehension.
13. C. S. Lewis, *The Problem of Pain* (London: Centenary Press, 1940), 139–140.
14. Robert Coleman, *The Coming World Revival* (Wheaton, IL: Crossway, 1995), 25.
15. As quoted in Richard M. Riss, *20th Century Revival Movements* (Peabody, MA: Hendrickson, 1988), 32.
16. Ibid., 36.
17. Ibid., 40.
18. As quoted in Wesley Duewel, *Revival Fire* (Grand Rapids, MI: Zondervan, 1995), 217.
19. Ibid.
20. Quoted in C. L. Culpepper, *The Shantung Revival* (Atlanta: Crescendo, 1971), 30.
21. A. W. Tozer, *Born After Midnight* (Camp Hill, PA: Christian Publications, 1983), 7.
22. Erwin Lutzer, *Flames of Freedom* (Chicago: Moody, 1976), 68.
23. Quote taken from S. J. Hill, *Enjoying God: Experiencing Intimacy With the Heavenly Father* (Orlando, FL: Relevant Books, 2001), 59.

Epilogue — Requiem

1. Heather Armstrong, *It Sucked and then I Cried* (New York: Simon Spotlight, 2009), 76.
2. Ibid., 77.
3. Ibid., 76.
4. Ibid., 75.
5. Alex Ross, "Whistling in the Dark," *The New Yorker,* February 2002.
6. Armstrong, 161–162.
7. Ibid., 238–239.

Talks, books, video, and other writings
by the author can be found at

RICKJAMESHOME.COM